THE MYSTERY OF GARABANDAL

Fantasy or Fraud? Ghost or God?

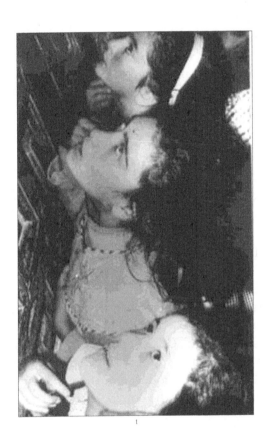

By LR Walker

ISBN-13: 978-0-692-29767-4
Library of Congress Control Number: 2014955495

Newtonia Publishing LLC
300 Lenora Street #153   Seattle WA 98121
newtoniapublishing@gmail.com

2021 Cover Design by *Green Bee Digital Solutions*

AUTHOR'S UPDATE

One day, a while ago, I received an unexpected phone call. To my surprise, Frank Lafleur, the son of Garabandal visionary Mari-Loli Mazon, was on the other end of the line. After reading my book, *The Mystery of Garabandal: Fantasy or Fraud? Ghost or God?,* he had felt compelled to reach out to me.

His mom *had* spoken of Garabandal before she died, he assured me, before she was on pain meds, when she was "fully lucid." Not only that, but some of what she said caused people to "nearly fall out of their chairs."

That intriguing conversation with Frank eventually led to a more in-depth interview with Mari-Loli's daughter, Maria Rosati. What she shared with me was an intensely personal and remarkable story that she generously agreed I could include in my book.

Even before I'd had these exchanges with two of Mari-Loli's grown children, the idea of an update of *The Mystery of Garabandal* had crossed my mind. It has been more than ten years since Mari-Loli passed away, but the changes that have swept the world, and the United States, during this time are astounding. In the midst of a plague year, with American cities burning in the midst of riots, the apocalyptic warnings of Garabandal no longer seemed quite so remote or unlikely.

Indeed, in the year of 2020, on the anniversary of Mari-Loli's death, Frank admitted, "I usually try not to put too much stock into date coincidences since I think there's a risk of running over into superstition. However, it was hard for us not to notice some parallels between her death in 2009 and the anniversary this year.

"My mother died April 20, 2009. That year April 20th was the day after Divine Mercy Sunday which is always the Sunday after Easter…Those dates are seared into my memory because they were some of the most difficult and painful of my life. The week leading up to Easter that year, Passion week, was for us deeply

3

sorrowful and painful to the point that we felt like we were living a version of the Passion ourselves.

"This year, Easter 2020 was again April 12 and thus this year the anniversary of her death was again the day after Divine Mercy Sunday. The dates coincided this year at a time when many people around the world were suffering the horrible effects of the disease which seems to grip the planet. People were dying of respiratory failure, slowly and painfully asphyxiating in a manner very similar to how my mother died (she died of fibrosis of the lungs). For many people, thousands of people, Holy Week 2020 must have felt like my family's Holy Week in 2009 except that many (most?) of these families did not have the privilege of gathering at their dying loved-one's bedside to pray and provide comfort during the final moments. Sadder still, since the Church was largely shut down in most places, few of those who died of Coronavirus would have had access to the sacraments.

"The dates won't coincide again in my lifetime. Out of curiosity, I looked at where Easter /Divine Mercy Sunday falls on the calendar going forward and it doesn't fall on those dates through at least 2085 (I gave up after that). What is the significance? Maybe nothing. But it was poignant for me personally."

Frank isn't the only one of Mari-Loli's children who has been deeply affected by reverberations from their mother's passing. The words Mari-Loli spoke about Garabandal before she died, and the question it opened up for her daughter, Maria Rosati, haunted her for nine years and led her to eventually share her story with others.

As a result of these conversations, I have included a new introduction written by Mari-Loli's son, Frank Lafleur. I also have added a final chapter to *The Mystery of Garabandal: Fantasy or Fraud? Ghost or God?* In this new chapter, Mari-Loli, and after her, Mari-Loli's children, answer a burning question for me which I reluctantly left unresolved at the end of the book: *What did she really believe about the Garabandal apparitions as she lay dying? Had she been tricked by the devil? Did the visionaries trick the rest of us? Had it all started as a joke, and ended up a nightmare?*

Or did Mari-Loli believe that the apparitions of Garabandal were true?

As I return to this question, and finally share a more definitive answer, I hope that readers will remember words of wisdom about the apparitions of Garabandal, and any other purported apparitions, prophecies and warnings which are making the rounds these days (and there are more than ever!) The "end times" do not mean the end of the world. They mean the end of *these times*, the end of a troubled era and the dawn of what the Virgin Mary in apparitions has described as "an era of peace," predicted in Catholic prophecies as the "triumph of the immaculate heart of Mary," when, according to the Book of Genesis, the woman and her offspring crush the serpent beneath their heel. This is also described in the book of Isaiah when swords are beaten into plowshares and the lion lays down with the lamb, and is described in the book of Revelation as the thousand-year-reign of Christ.

The purpose of any authentic apparition, warning or prophecy is never to incite despair, but to help lead us to God's true life and genuine peace. The message of Garabandal, and the message of the Bible in such books as Jonah, is that by turning back to God we can mitigate and even stop approaching disaster.

As many others have noted, the future is never set in stone because it passes through *us*. We are the wild card that can alter what lies ahead. May we navigate the storm with constant prayer and unfailing hope.

ACKNOWLEDGMENTS

I would like to thank Dr. Brian Miller, president of St. Joseph Foundation of Los Angeles Inc, for his permission and provision of materials regarding Garabandal, including the treasure trove of Garabandal materials placed in the public domain on the foundation's website, www.stjosephpublications.com

Additional thanks to Maria Saraco for her permission to use the invaluable materials from Saint Michael's Garabandal Center for Our Lady of Carmel at www.garabandal.org. I would also like to thank Maria Saraco for allowing herself to be interviewed about Garabandal, an interview included in this book.

I owe thanks to Harry Daley for his permission to excerpt from his book "Miracle at Garabandal." I also wish to thank Bishop William McNaughton for kindly allowing himself to be interviewed about Garabandal, an interview included in this book.

Finally, heartfelt thanks to Frank Lafleur and Maria Rosati for warmly and generously sharing their recollections and reflections about their mother, visionary Mari-Loli Mazon, for inclusion in this book.

Any views expressed by the author in this book are my own, and are not a reflection of views held by those who made materials available to me or allowed themselves to be interviewed.

Introduction by Frank Lafleur
(son of Garabandal visionary Mari-Loli Mazon)

Strange as it may seem, the book *The Mystery of Garabandal: Fantasy or Fraud? Ghost or God,* helped me personally to come to terms with Garabandal. Prior to my mother's death I didn't really give the apparitions a whole lot of thought. I saw my mother as we all see our mothers. She was the one who took care of me. As a child, she was the one standing in the kitchen in the morning making my sisters and I breakfast, even before she had a chance to comb her hair. She's the one who drove us to school. She was the one who scolded us for leaving our toys (and dirty footprints) scattered around the house. When I was in college living on my own for the first time, she was the one who worried ceaselessly when a day or three passed without me calling. Then finally when I was an adult she was the one patiently listening to me bloviate about my grand plans—and sometimes having to express her gentle but firm disapproval about the more ridiculous ones. She was my mother.

It was only after she died that I could finally start to consider the apparitions. The necessary first step was to answer a very basic question: What on earth happened there? I read a few other books before I read *The Mystery of Garabandal: Fantasy or Fraud? Ghost or God?* Those books for the most part approached the topic from the perspective, Of course it's true and it's wonderful! What I needed at the time was some cold analysis. I needed a book that at least recognized: Hey, the idea that the queen of the universe should see fit to appear to farm girls in a tiny, poor, muddy village in Spain ought to be met with a healthy dose of skepticism. This book was part of a broader process for me, but it was an important part.

For whatever it's worth, today I have absolutely no doubts about what occurred at Garabandal.

Sir Arthur Conan Doyle, speaking in persona of Sherlock Holmes, once said

When you have eliminated the impossible, whatever remains, however improbable, must be the truth.

Fraud? This hypothesis is for me the easiest one to reject. It is the question I think is answered with this book's newest

7

chapter. To believe the apparitions were a fraud is to believe that a humble God-fearing woman who has lived an otherwise holy and virtuous life, one that included decades of daily Mass and Holy Communion and daily 15 mysteries of the rosary, who was exemplary in fulfillment of her vocation as mother and spouse, would on her death-bed, in the full knowledge that she is about to undergo her final and irrevocable judgement, re-affirm to her family a grave lie that she saw the Virgin Mary.

Fantasy? Trying to explain Garabandal away as a case of over-active imagination requires us to believe that these four children, living in a remote village in 1960s Franco-ruled Spain where the Catholic Church was revered, would invent a message from the Virgin Mary which included the words,

Many Cardinals, Bishops and priests are following the road to perdition, and with them they are taking many more souls. Ever less importance is being given to the Holy Eucharist.

To say something like this today is sadly to merely state the obvious. At the time however it was so shocking that some contemporary observers came to see it as reason to condemn the apparitions. In Garabandal Spain, the idea of a Cardinal being on the road to perdition was unthinkable. So to believe it was a fantasy is to believe they invented a startlingly accurate prophecy when virtually nobody else saw it coming (outside of perhaps a few Vatican insiders).

The other answer to the Fantasy hypothesis is perhaps best expressed by one of the many witnesses of the apparitions phenomena. When the girls vocalized their doubts he retorted to the effect of,

Well if you made the whole thing up, let's just go up to the pines tonight so the four of you lock arms and run down the calleja backwards, like you did during the apparitions.

Of course they couldn't. Nobody can.

Ghost? As a Catholic, I understand otherworldly visits to have one of only two possible origins: Heaven, where God, the Virgin Mary, the Saints and Angels reside. And hell. Any apparition that is not from heaven is necessarily from hell and thus demonic. Despite what popular culture tries to tell us, we know from Catholic Tradition that there is no Casper the friendly ghost.

If the apparitions of Garabandal were demonic in origin, we must then account for all of the messages and emphasis being consistently orthodox: Prayer, Sacrifice, Penance, attention to the Eucharist, be good, repent, pray the rosary and so on. There is nothing heterodox in Garabandal. Garabandal is completely consistent with the constant teachings of the Catholic Church while the demonic is in opposition. Garabandal cannot be reconciled to the demonic.

And so having eliminated the impossible, I am faced with one final, breathtaking explanation: That the Holy Mother of God herself, the Gate of Heaven, The Morning Star, literally visited and spoke with four girls at Garabandal and one of the four girls happened to be my mother. Oh, and that for most of my life, I was too distracted to notice or care.

So what then?

I offer you a parting thought on one of the Garabandal prophecies which seems to be getting a lot more attention at the moment: The Warning. There is an error that I and many other people too easily fall into when we think about The Warning foretold at Garabandal. The error is a tendency to see The Warning as a solution and correction for the sins *other* people are committing. We may be tempted to look at the revolutionary violence in the streets, the terrible massacre that is abortion or the myriad evils that plague our governments and our Church and say, I can't wait for The Warning to happen - that will show them all!

But to look at The Warning this way is to miss the point entirely.

Assuredly, the day of The Warning will be a terrible day. Precious few of us will smile when we see our souls in the same light as God sees us. On the day of The Warning, as on the day of our final judgement, we will not be concerned with the actions of anarchists, the Bishop, the Governor or our neighbor but our own sins which we will probably realize to be much more grievous than we ever imagined.

One of my favorite Catholic bloggers, recently writing on the topic of whether Coronavirus was a (collective) punishment from God had this to say:

I would suggest that if we want to profit from this we should choose to view it as a chastisement not for the things that others have done that have scandalized us, but for our own sinfulness, which, if others knew its extent, would scandalize them.

He was not writing about Garabandal there but I think it applies to the Garabandal Warning perfectly.

If we believe in Garabandal then we need to change. I need to change. At the end of the day, the message of Garabandal is the message of the Church: Follow the commandments (be good), pray, sacrifice and do penance to correct our own sinfulness.

I wanted to share because the book meant a lot to me in answering one of the important questions of my life. And I am grateful.

Frank Lafleur
September 28, 2020

For Teresa Robins, faithful friend

THE MYSTERY OF GARABANDAL
Fantasy or Fraud? Ghost or God?

PART 1

The Ghosts of Garabandal—50 Years Later

2 *Mari-Loli, Jacinta, Mari Cruz, Conchita*

Your sons and daughters will prophesy,
your old men will dream dreams,
your young men will see visions.
Even upon your male and female servants,
in those days, I will pour out my spirit.

The Book of Joel Chapter 2 3

Chapter 1

What Four Girls Said They Saw

"Suddenly a very beautiful figure appeared to me, shining brilliantly without hurting my eyes."[4] **Conchita Gonzales, age 12**

Just log on to the internet. Type in "Garabandal." You'll see young girls marching backward over hills.[5] Falling intertwined in faints. Levitating, seemingly, inches above the ground.[6] And their faces—heads thrown sharply back, eyes fixed on some mysterious point in the air—are aglow. They are mesmerized by something which is invisible to everyone else. It's an impressive, disturbing performance, considering they are four 12-year-olds surrounded by a jostling throng of avid onlookers. It's even more impressive and disturbing when you consider that this same scene played out with these girls in the Spanish mountaintop village of Garabandal dozens of times from 1961 to 1965, with some estimates putting the number of visions at 2,000.

Each of those times, the girls claimed to be communing with Someone from another world—specifically, the Virgin Mary. Over the course of those years, the four girls spoke to the Virgin Mary frequently—and they listened. What they said they heard sent shock waves throughout the Catholic world, and beyond— shock waves that are still reverberating today. The messages the four girls claimed to receive gradually revealed a picture of a church in crisis and a world that faced an earth-shattering future that would unfold in their lifetime.

The girls' pronouncements about coming trouble in the church and world were met with fierce skepticism almost from
14

the first. In addition to those who charged the girls with being possessed by evil (based on the girls' strange physical poses, supposed levitation,⁷ and nights of screaming), and those who claimed the girls were putting on an act (revealing their true colors when they chose ordinary lives instead of the convent), there is a third body of critics: those who believe that a group of girls on the cusp of adolescence in a backward and insular society, in a fit of hysteria something like the Salem Witch Trials, may have together conjured up a psychodrama which, fueled by the spotlight and mounting frenzy, gained a frightening life of its own.

Those "girls" are now seventy years old. The future they predicted is here. The future they predicted is our own. For our planet, the Garabandal prophecies foretell a World-Wide Warning and a Global Miracle, whose purpose is to convince a world reeling from one catastrophe to the next that God exists. The Virgin Mary purportedly revealed the Year of the Warning to visionary Mari-Loli Mazon, and the Date of the Miracle to visionary Conchita Gonzales. But the Warning and Miracle, dramatic as they sound, are not even the most unsettling of the messages of Garabandal. One night, the young girls dissolved into screams. During this so-called "Night of the Screams," the girls say they were shown a tragic chastisement that would befall the entire world if the Warning and Miracle failed to trigger global change.

As disquieting as those messages were, the Virgin Mary's most shocking words at Garabandal were not for the world. They were for the hierarchy of the Roman Catholic Church, which was meeting at that time for Vatican II. Mary's messages at Garabandal for the world were not so different from her Church-sanctioned messages at Fatima or her on-going messages at the hugely popular but not-yet-approved Medjugorje. Yet in contrast to widespread knowledge about the apparitions at Fatima and Medjugorje, why were the messages of Garabandal so effectively suppressed? What was particularly threatening about the Virgin

Mary's words at Garabandal? Did it have to do with the fact that the Virgin Mary in 1965 presciently warned of coming scandal and turmoil in the Roman Catholic Church itself?

While some took the girls' disturbing words to be truth, others were scandalized and denounced them as frauds. So naturally the question arises: If the girls faked these visions for four years—how did they do it? More to the point—why would they do it? Were the girls manipulators or were they manipulated—were they pawns in the hands of forces bigger than themselves?

To answer these questions, we have to travel back fifty years, to the village of San Sebastian de Garabandal, Spain. At that time, the village consisted of fewer than 75 homes huddled together in the foothills of the Cantabrian mountains, in a remote part of northern Spain. Snowed in for months at a time during the winter, and hemmed in by mountains, this hard-to-reach village was isolated from the modern world. The 300 or so villagers lacked running water and electricity and used fireplaces and cook stoves for heat.

⁸ *Garabandal today*

Once spring arrived, a muddy mountain lane was their only connection with the outside world and was often traversed on foot or by donkey cart. In the summer of 1961, just before the apparitions commenced, cowbells chimed melodiously in the mountain pastures, and the wind sighed through a stand of pine trees overlooking the village—a pine grove which would eventually become the focal point of the unfolding drama.

In Rome, the Second Vatican Council had just been summoned and was about to shake the Catholic world to its core—but Garabandal was still a pre-Vatican II Catholic village in every sense of the term. Every day villagers stopped work to pray the rosary,[9] and each evening at dusk, a villager walked the lanes with a lantern and rang a bell as a summons to remember the dead and pray the day's last prayers.[10] And four twelve-year-old schoolgirls one evening claimed to have a supernatural encounter that would leave them and their village permanently altered.

[11] *The road to Garabandal in the past*

The most important event of my life was on June 18, 1961 in San Sebastián: it happened in the following way.

Thus begins the journal of Conchita Gonzales, the oldest of the girls, who was frequently described as the prettiest and the most intelligent, and who quickly emerged as the group's leader. She was the youngest child and only girl in a family whose father had passed away. She also recorded what began the day she and her friend Mari Cruz Gonzales, the youngest of the four girls, stole apples from a teacher's tree.

That evening, the two girls were followed and spied upon by two other village girls of the same age, Mari-Loli Mazon and Jacinta Gonzales (Jacinta also happened to be a second cousin of Conchita). Apparently, the girls had been feuding in recent days, and there was a split between them, with Conchita and Mari Cruz squaring off against Jacinta and Mari-Loli (the mayor's daughter).[12] Mari-Loli and Jacinta confronted the two apple thieves, who hid in a potato patch and fled into a field. But Mari-Loli and Jacinta called them out and threatened to tell on them, so Conchita and Mari Cruz emerged from hiding and the four joined forces, now as partners in crime, to pick apples together. They were about to become partners in something much bigger.

[13] *Jacinta, Mari-Loli, Conchita and Mari Cruz in 1961*

Once the girls had stuffed their pockets, they retreated to the now-famous *calleja*, a rocky, sunken lane at the edge of the village, to eat. Their actions seemed blissfully innocent, since these young girls lived in a small village seemingly lost in time. In 1961, the remote corners of the globe were rapidly nearing the end of any chance at isolation, but in Garabandal, the setting was still pastoral, the story almost fable-like. Unlike the coming-of-age experiences of so many today, there were no drugs, no alcohol, and no sex in this story. There were nearby sheep, an apple tree, and school girls making mischief. In fact, Mari Cruz would comment later that the bitter, unripe apples were plucked with the intent of hurling them at dancers on the square.[14] In any case, as the girls were munching on their stolen apples in the stony lane, the story took a fateful turn. The girls heard a clap of thunder.

And we all shouted out:
— It seems to be thundering!
This happened at 8:30 at night [15]

Those who have thoroughly researched the oddities surrounding Garabandal note that the children of Fatima also heard something like thunder before an angel appeared to them while they were tending sheep. Still others have remarked that the great Global Miracle of Garabandal is predicted to occur at 8:30 at night. A divine clap of thunder in literary history may signify the appearance of an angel or announce some other-worldly event, but at the time, the girls gave no particular notice to the thunderclap, and they kept eating. Once their appetites had been sated, they experienced a twinge of remorse over their behavior. It occurred to them that the devil would be laughing while their guardian angel would be wounded by what they'd done. Furious at the devil for leading them into temptation, they performed a childish ritual that was no doubt perfectly natural for that particular place and time, but which now seems eerily prescient in its summoning of Michael the Archangel and the Prince of Darkness to their little village.

Then we began to gather stones and threw them with all our strength to the left side, where the Devil is said to be.

...Suddenly a very beautiful figure appeared to me, shining brilliantly without hurting my eyes.[16]

And so it begins. In a matter of moments, all four girls are stunned by the sight of an angel. In fact, it appears that this was the girls' first "ecstasy."

A villager named Vincente Mazon happened upon them and was irritated that they were kneeling in the lane and not moving. Later, he looked back and saw them still kneeling, and although his wife told him to forget about it, he spent a sleepless night worrying about their strange behavior.[17] The girls in ecstasy see only the angel, and are completely unaware of the annoyed villager. The angel hovers, then disappears, and the girls, seemingly disoriented and in shock, run behind the village church and cry. They are uniformly upset and frightened after their encounter. Mari-Loli, years later in an interview, says that she was afraid of being reprimanded by the angel because they had been stealing apples.[18] The schoolmistress Serafina Gómez González finds them after the vision and responds to their tale by promptly praying.

[19] *St. Michael defeating the devil*

Yet soon afterward, both Mari-Loli and Mari Cruz's mothers threaten beatings over the tale, while Jacinta's mother says the tall tale went in one ear and out the other.[20] Conchita's mother reacts by skeptically chiding her daughter over her bizarre excuse for coming home late, although she also feels a strange chill at Conchita's words.[21] This is only the beginning of a very long, strange trip, but it's a good indication of the stark division between belief and non-belief that the girls' experience is going to instantly engender in others.

The very next night, June 19, the girls returned like moths to a flame to the same spot to see if they could conjure up the angel again. Conchita's brother warned her about village ridicule, and some villagers on the way met their claims with skepticism and laughter. The girls tried praying on their knees in the sunken lane, but boys threw stones at them. The angel did not show that night, and the girls went home, dejected. However, each of the four girls, in their separate homes, heard a voice in the night assuring them, "Don't worry. You will see me again."[22]

This development cheered them up considerably. The village pastor quickly got in on the act, interviewing the girls separately. Impressed with their consistency in details, the priest told Conchita to ask the angel who he was and what he wanted.[23]

[24] *Jacinta, Conchita, and Mari-Loli in ecstasy*

On the night of June 21, a group of villagers gathered around the girls as they prayed in the rocky lane, trying to summon the angel. The villagers laughed and talked, enjoying the entertainment, when the four girls suddenly snapped into ecstasy: the angel had appeared again. The villagers witnessed the abrupt change in the girls, and some of them then begged forgiveness for not believing.[25]

[26]*The Sunken Lane today*

Disturbingly for Jacinta's mother, in the next few days, Jacinta returned home with new, increasingly outlandish details of more angel sightings. She described the angel to her mother as having long hair and a complexion like chick peas.[27] Other bizarre angel details that emerged from the girls included pink wings, black eyes, trimmed nails and an age of about nine years old.[28] If the description of the angel sounds childish, perhaps it's because it was being described by children. Years later, Conchita would explain that they were "not exactly wings. They were not attached to his body. They were more like a halo would be, like a light gleaming from behind him."[29]

By June 22, only four days after the initial angel sighting, the crowds had already grown enough that Juan Alvarez Seco, the Chief Brigadier of the Civil Guard, was on the scene. Responsible for maintaining order, he placed two guards on duty in the village and began to investigate the various rumors that had begun circulating among the villagers. Already, speculation abounded that the girls were being hypnotized by a visiting professor, or that perhaps he was giving the girls drugs.[30]

[31] *The girls in ecstasy*

Others suggested that Conchita, the charismatic eldest, controlled the other girls. Finally, a doctor was called in to examine the girls and weigh in on the subject. His conclusion was they were epileptic.[32]

Jacinta's mother, increasingly disturbed by her daughter's tales and the village gossip, finally went to see her daughter in ecstasy for the first time. Upon seeing Jacinta in a trance and communing with the supernatural, her mother began screaming uncontrollably. "That was because I had never seen anything of the sort before and I was asking myself what could this be, although for the last eight days Jacinta had been describing to me what she was seeing at each ecstasy."[33] And no wonder. According to the eyewitness testimony of the villagers, the girls' expressions were noticeably transformed, becoming transparent, luminous, transfigured.[34]

³⁵ *Plaque marking St. Michael's first appearance in*
Garabandal on June 18, 1961

Matters took a significant turn on July 1, 1961. The angel once again appeared, and with the girls now familiar with and accepting of his blinding presence, he spoke. "I come to announce to you a visit by the Virgin under the title of Our Lady of Mount Carmel, who will appear to you tomorrow, Sunday." ³⁶

He had no name as of yet, but the girls would later be told the diminutive "nine-year-old" was Satan's chief nemesis: St. Michael the Archangel. St. Michael told the girls that the Virgin Mary would be coming on the Feast of the Visitation (the day when the pregnant Virgin Mary paid a visit to her expectant cousin Elizabeth who was carrying John the Baptist).

The girls then pressed St. Michael about a mysterious plaque or sign with strange writing that had been appearing at Michael's feet since June 24. They had not been able to make sense of the sign, and the Angel up to that point had only smiled but not spoken.

The sign bore the Roman numerals XVIII-MCM-LXI, and some words beginning with "One must..." The angel replied, "The Virgin will explain it to you." (In fact, the angel was carrying Roman numerals giving the date when the first message from the Virgin Mary to the world would be revealed—October

18, 1961—as well as a preview of the first message—something like a coming attraction. St. Michael had been revealing the reason for his coming almost from the beginning.)

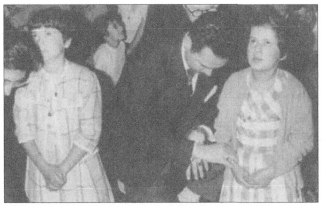

[37] *Girls being examined while in ecstasy*

Messenger from God though he was, St. Michael was not all business. On one occasion he complimented the girls' on their beautiful teeth, and showed them his own. He also kissed each girl on the forehead and both cheeks, concluding with a gallant, "Until tomorrow."[38]

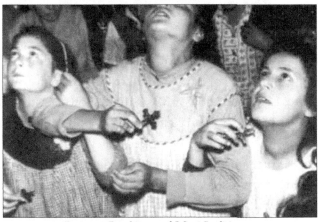

[39] *Jacinta, Conchita, and Mari-Loli in ecstasy*

On July 2, a large crowd, including eleven priests and numerous physicians, showed up for the first appearance of the

Virgin Mary. A fence or barrier, known as the *cuadro*, had been constructed to protect the girls from those gathered to watch. As the crowd milled about that day, and people prayed, all four girls suddenly cried, "The Virgin!" They would later report that a young Virgin Mary accompanied by St. Michael and a "twin angel" (later identified as St. Gabriel) appeared before them. At one point, Conchita exclaimed, "Oh! What an eye!"[40] The girls reported seeing a fiery frame or square surrounding a triangle with an eye (a traditional depiction of the Holy Trinity in paintings such as *Supper at Emmaus*, Jacopo Pontormo, 1525), along with indecipherable words they described as "oriental," which some have speculated was the Name of God in Hebrew. The girls believed they were seeing the Eye of God.

[41] *The four girls inside the cuadro*

The Virgin herself was not dressed as the children were used to seeing Our Lady of Mt. Carmel, in brown, but rather in blue and white. Like Our Lady of Mt. Carmel, however, the Virgin did carry a scapular[42] in her hands which bore the picture of a mountain on it.[43] The girls described the Virgin as having a "very unusual"[44] voice unlike any other and said that sometimes, as the apparitions progressed, she was carrying the infant Jesus, who never spoke but often smiled and laughed.

As the children spoke with the Virgin at this first meeting, Conchita opened her mouth to show a cavity, and the Virgin reportedly asked that the Civil Guard protect the children from the crowds. The girls begged Mary to let them touch her crown, and Mary presumably relented, as the girls then mimed passing something invisible around.[45] Years later, Mari-Loli would explain that the crown had twelve stars which she could not feel, but her hand was stopped by it when she tried to touch it.[46]

The Virgin concluded their first meeting by teaching the girls how to say the rosary slowly and well. (The rosary involves recounting the "mysteries" of Jesus' life from the Bible using a string of beads to keep track as one prays.) Jacinta admitted later that she did not know how to pray the mysteries of the rosary until she was taught by the Virgin.[47] Her father confirmed this, saying they never taught her anything; "the boys, yes, but the girls, nothing."[48] An observer said that hearing a tape recording of the girls as they prayed the rosary in ecstasy helped convince him of the apparitions. "They prayed with great cadence in their voices, unhurriedly, with tremendous feeling."[49] Fifty years later, it's possible to listen to an audio tape of the girls singing the same ancient greeting that the Angel Gabriel delivered to the Virgin Mary[50]—and it indeed leaves one with the eerie feeling that the girls were somehow caught between worlds.[51]

[52] *Conchita and Jacinta in ecstasy*

On July 4, the Virgin Mary reappeared and told the girls that the words on the mysterious plaque at St. Michael's feet were the first part of a very important message the girls had to make public on October 18, 1961. Conchita wrote in her diary that the Virgin had spoken of this message from her first appearance on July 2, but the girls, perhaps overwhelmed by all that was unfolding, hadn't really grasped what she was saying. So the Virgin began to explain and entrust the entire message to the girls for safekeeping several months ahead of time.

The apparitions would continue for the next four years, with the Virgin Mary apparently hovering in the air, invisible to the crowds of onlookers who swelled by the day, as the girls carried on lengthy—and often surprising—conversations with her. By 1965, some four years later, the onlookers had grown from a handful of villagers to thousands from all around the world. Many of them photographed and filmed the girls, who continued to perform under the blinding glare of cameras. And it was in 1965 that the appearances of the Virgin Mary in Garabandal, Spain stopped. The timing of the apparitions of Garabandal coincided precisely with Vatican II—a noteworthy point that will be examined. The surging crowds gradually dwindled, but, as the rest of this book will reveal, the village and the four girls' lives would never be the same.

For one thing, the girls would spend the rest of their lives either revered or reviled by followers and skeptics, an experience which may have driven three of the four to flee, not to the anonymity of a convent (which some Catholics insisted true visionaries would have done), but to the vast anonymity of a then mostly-Protestant, increasingly secular United States. These three young women, like the fourth who remained in Spain, essentially disappeared into lives of marriage and child-rearing. This unexceptional behavior and lack of overt holiness was evidence, claimed some skeptics, that the girls, far from being saintly, were deluded, or worse, that they deliberately deceived.

Were these girls, who lived in a different, perhaps clearer, moral universe than most of us do today, seized by guilt after eating stolen apples and hearing a thunder clap (which then led them to throw stones at "the devil")? Once they'd given into their impulses and satisfied their appetites, did they become increasingly worried about how their guardian angels (and possibly those in the flesh) would respond to their crimes? Mari-Loli did confess later that she had once been afraid of the Civil Guard. Apparently she and Jacinta had stolen a hammer some time before the apparitions, sold it for a few pennies, and bought a chocolate bar with it. For a while afterward, every time they saw the Guard in the village, the girls thought the Guard was coming for them.[53] If the visitation of an angel was a fantasy fabricated by guilt-ridden children who had stolen apples, did the swift arrival of the Civil Guard on the scene only pressure the girls to concoct an even more elaborate charade?

Having spent the first twelve years of their lives immersed in a pre-Vatican II Catholic village, is it possible they were about to unleash their own version of the sad story of the Garden of the Eden? Just as in the original story, the girls were about to hear sacred and profane voices—and chaos, confusion, and wonder would be followed by accusation, expulsion, and wandering. This story has not yet ended, but now that the "girls" at the center of this biblical drama are 60-plus-year-old women, should their claims be discredited or re-examined? Are the apparitions bogus or fast-approaching their fulfillment?

[54] *Garabandal today, with paved roads and electricity*

29

Critics point to the girls' own evolving doubts, contradictions and renunciations as proof that the apparitions were plainly not apparitions at all. In fact, self-doubt and vacillation began to plague the visionaries as time went on, and those episodes, which haunt this story, will be examined.

The least likely, and most disturbing, possibility is that the apparitions in San Sebastian de Garabandal actually did occur, and that the mother of Jesus appeared with an apocalyptic warning for both the Church and the modern world. This last explanation is obviously in a category all its own. If the events are false, the story of Garabandal is a fascinating and perhaps tragic human interest story with several possible explanations. If the events and warnings are true—then what do we do?

If the girls were telling the truth, exactly what in the message of Garabandal, more than fifty years later, is relevant today? Does Garabandal reveal a detailed map of the so-called End Times— not just how to survive them, but how to actually avoid a global disaster altogether? After all, fear of a world-wide apocalypse is no longer merely a religious obsession—it is also an increasing secular concern in the form of climate change, world-wide plague, global economic collapse, and a mushrooming variety of lethal weaponry and the madmen who possess them. By the end of this book, readers can judge whether the appearances of the Virgin Mary to four young seers on a mountaintop in Spain were historical fact, a devilish fraud, or the creative confusion of four burgeoning girls who would spend the rest of their lives trying to escape a human tragicomedy that they themselves had written, acted in, and produced. Then readers can answer for themselves the question, "What do we do now?"

Chapter 2

The Year of the Warning

"I know that it will be visible all over the world. I don't know if people will die. They could only die from the emotional shock of seeing it." **Conchita**[55]

[56] *Conchita and Mari-Loli in ecstasy*

As more people in the village began to believe in the apparitions, they would prod the girls to gather and pray the rosary so that the Virgin would visit again. But the girls would decline, saying, "We haven't been called yet."[57] In fact, each of the girls described three "inner calls" they would receive before the Virgin Mary appeared. The first call was the faintest, a joyful sensation, something like an early warning system. They were often not able to sit still after the second call, which was much stronger, and after the third call all the girls literally ran to the site of the apparition.[58] Separating them did no good—they would be placed in different houses and not allowed to communicate with each other, but still wound up at the same spot, at the same time, before falling into ecstasy.[59] The ecstasies took place in numerous locales—in the rocky lane where the angel first appeared, in the pine grove on top of the mountain, in practically every village home, and in the church, until the bishop forbade the girls to have ecstasies there. After that, the four girls would sometimes fall to their knees just outside the doors of the church and have their vision.

The ecstasies took place early in the morning, at noon, in the afternoon, and at night. Sometimes all four girls would be in ecstasy at the same time; at other times, two, three, or just one of them alone would fall into ecstasy. Sometimes the visions of the Virgin Mary lasted fifteen minutes, sometimes for hours. No matter the length of the ecstasy, it was never long enough for the girls. An ecstasy that lasted two hours, they said, felt like it lasted only two minutes. At the end of every ecstasy, the girls always recited the same litany: "Why are you going?" and "What a shame!"[60]

When the girls were touched during an apparition, they did not have warm flesh, but rather were described as rigid and trembling.[61] Mari Cruz's mother, when she first touched her stiff daughter and was unable to rouse her from her trance, was frightened that Mari Cruz was dying from an "attack" of some kind. Conchita once fell backward stiff as a board which caused those around her to cry, "Oh! my God! Conchita has killed herself!...Conchita has killed herself!" Villager Benjamin Gomez retorted, 'Here, stop that! If she killed herself, we will bury her tomorrow.'...But I knew very well that nothing would happen to her, having seen so much already..." Conchita actually rose up in one smooth, speedy movement without bending or supporting herself, just as she had fallen.[62]

The girls were impervious to pinpricks and burns which doctors actually administered during the visions and which at times led to scuffles when fed-up villagers intervened to stop the abuse.[63] One time, when Jacinta's father objected, the visiting doctor retorted, "Are you afraid that I'll destroy your daughter's little act?" At that point, "the young men jumped on him."[64]

The girls were captured on film completely oblivious to the blinding glare of spotlights, flashlights, and camera lights while in ecstasy;[65] however, as soon as the apparition ended, they immediately recoiled from the glare in their eyes. At the same time, upon coming out of an ecstasy, the girls would express surprise that it was dark out, since during the apparition, they said, it was bright as day.[66]

[67] *Girls being examined while Mari-Loli's mother looks on*

The four visionaries often remained in whatever position they were in when the vision appeared, as still as statues, even if the vision lasted for hours. This led to both comical and horrifying situations. Jacinta's mother recalled a doctor who came to prick the girls' legs and shine bright lights in their eyes while they were in ecstasy. He grabbed hold of Jacinta's leg as she fell to her knees in ecstasy, and she ended up landing on only one knee. The other leg, which the doctor had initially grabbed, now hung suspended in the air, folded beneath her and not touching the ground. Jacinta stayed that way for an hour, only one knee touching the ground, her hands in the air, much to her mother's chagrin, who confessed to wanting to beat the doctors that day. She also admitted that she frequently tried to mimic Jacinta's impossible pose, but was never able to.[68] (Conchita's Aunt Maximina also tried imitating Conchita's habit in ecstasy of running backward with her head tilted completely back and her neck stretched: "...well, I'll say this. It's not easy. It's hard to keep from suffocating.")[69]

There was also the mysterious matter of their weight. Sometimes bystanders would get their feet caught beneath the children's knees when they crashed to the ground in ecstasy, and the onlookers would be pinned that way for the duration since the girls took on a bizarre and seemingly impossible weight during the visions.[70] Grown men tried repeatedly to move the girls during ecstasies, but weren't able to.[71] The visionaries, however, could lift each other easily, "like a toy."

[72]*Mari-Loli lifts Jacinta during an apparition*

Sometimes, when they were all in ecstasy together, they lifted each other up to reach the Virgin Mary who was apparently elevated in the air.[73] At other times, the girls who weren't in ecstasy would rescue those in ecstasy from awkward or difficult situations. Villager Benjamin Gomez testified that although he could lift 200 pounds, he was unable to budge Mari-Loli during her ecstasy.

In fact, his struggle to lift her had raised her shoulders into an unnatural position, in which they remained for the duration of the episode.

"Look how you left her."

"I see, but what can I do now?"

Then one of the other visionaries, not in ecstasy, touched Mari-Loli's shoulders and they relaxed. As soon as the ecstasy was over, Mari-Loli's father allowed Benjamin to try again, and he lifted her easily.[74]

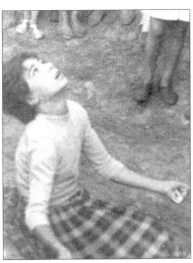

[75] *Conchita in ecstasy*

The "ecstatic marches" were also a sight to behold, according to eyewitnesses. Villager Pepe Diez testified, "I saw quite clearly that the rhythm of their legs was that of a normal running pace, but they were going forward at a tremendous speed. It was an extraordinary thing!"[76] Conchita's cousin recalled trying to keep up with Conchita during ecstatic marches and failing because she became "dead tired."[77] She also remembered that if she and Conchita were holding hands when the ecstasy occurred, she would not be able to free herself until the ecstasy was over. Conchita was once holding a sheep when the vision came, and no one could free the poor bleating sheep that Conchita was dragging around until someone had the presence of mind to use shearing scissors to snip the lamb's wool.[78]

On yet another occasion, a poor, robed *monk* was caught in the iron grip of Conchita at the moment of apparition, and was hauled around unceremoniously until he was released, sweat-soaked, at the end of the ecstatic march with the visionaries. "Oh! How it made us laugh! We were ashamed of ourselves, but we couldn't stop!" said one of the villagers who witnessed the event. She then remarked, "How come a man like that couldn't free himself from the grasp of such a small girl?"[79]

⁸⁰ *Jacinta and Mari-Loli on a high-speed ecstatic march over the rocky terrain at night, eyes turned upward*

In some of these filmed marches, the girls, necks craned, eyes fixed heavenward, linked their arms and sped swiftly up and down treacherous, rocky hills *backwards*, stepping delicately like dancers in the dark, leaving the rest of the village to scramble behind them in the dust.⁸¹ And sometimes, they went backward on their knees. "During the night, these runs were even more impressive...snowstorms and rainstorms...when the water would stream down over the faces of the children while they looked toward heaven with a smile as if it were angels falling...It was very difficult to understand, even when we were watching it."⁸²

Jacinta's brother Miguel was thirteen years old when the ecstasies began. One night he accompanied Jacinta and Mari-Loli to the cemetery gates, but abandoned them there out of fear. The girls went there frequently at night while in ecstasy, putting their arms through the bars of the iron gate and extending a crucifix they said had been kissed by the Virgin, moving their arms around as if a crowd on the other side had gathered to kiss it in return.[83]

On a snowy night, Mari-Loli headed out the door at 3 a.m., insisting that the Virgin was calling her to the *cuadro*. Mari-Loli's parents told her she was crazy and warned her of wolves, but they followed her anyway. They waited and froze for an hour in the bitter cold, while Mari-Loli, her face content, communed with the Virgin.[84]

[85] *Ecstatic walk backward on a stony path*

On another icy black night, Mari-Loli and her mother went to the church doors so Mari-Loli could receive communion from Michael the Archangel. Critics had begun to suggest that the apparitions were from the devil, and Mari-Loli's mother was frightened of who would show up. Mari-Loli, however, went into ecstasy and spent the time smiling and praying.

One morning at 5 a.m., Mari-Loli walked through the freezing, muddy, rocky village lanes on her knees, a sight which drove her mother, who was behind her, to tears. Then Mari-Loli said to the Virgin, "Ah! You say my mother is crying, oh, my mother is crying."[86] Villager Piedad Gonzales one night watched Conchita and her mother walking in snow and hail and thunder. Conchita walked with her face upturned and her arms outstretched, clutching a cross. The harrowing sight of the hailstones hitting Conchita's upturned face made Piedad cry, but she ventured out to join them out of sheer pity for Conchita's poor mother.[87] Conchita's cousin recalled following Conchita and Mari Cruz up the mountain to the Pines at 4 a.m. to witness an ecstasy, as well as watching an ecstasy in front of the church doors which lasted many hours. "I fell asleep against the door and when I realized everyone was leaving, the ecstasy was over."[88]

[89] *Conchita in ecstasy extending a crucifix to be kissed*

When one considers the lengthy statue-like poses, crushing body weight, and bizarre round-the-clock antics of the visionaries—high-speed "marches," synchronized oscillations, reported levitations,[90] midnight visits to the cemetery with crucifix in hand as if fending off vampires, backward slogs on knees in snow and hail—the natural question that arises is, *What was the point?* Was the Virgin—if it was the Virgin—emphasizing the presence of the supernatural, the unexplainable, indeed of the impossible? Was the sometimes bizarre nature of the apparitions intended as a humbling reminder that God's ways are not our ways?

Or did the collision of two separate realms lead naturally to mutual incomprehension? At times during the apparitions, the Virgin Mary seemed a bit put out by the reaction she was receiving.

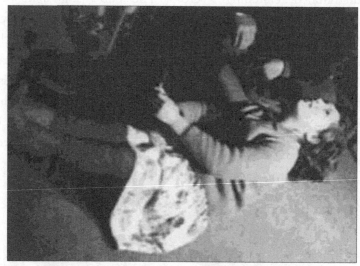

⁹¹ *Mari-Loli reportedly levitating*

Whatever the divine rationale at work (if the divine was involved), the appearances of the Virgin Mary became so frequent—sometimes practically around the clock—that no one was able to keep an exact count.

Messages and prophecies also began to tumble out at a dizzying rate. Among all these, the most sensational—although, according to the visionaries, not the most crucial—were surely the three great global events prophesied by the Virgin Mary. According to the children, the events would unfold as a series of chronological events, each one inextricably linked to the other.

First, the entire world would be warned by a cosmic cataclysm. Then, shocked and reeling, the world would experience an electrifying moment of truth, hope and consolation—a miraculous way out, so to speak. If the world embraced change, it would be transformed. If not, an almost unspeakable punishment would follow. The girls dutifully relayed this end-times scenario—Warning, Miracle, Possible Punishment—to the waiting throngs.

Of the three great global events, the Warning is by far the most peculiar. While the Miracle seems to follow fairly standard miracle lines by hinting at a great glowing sign in the sky, and the Punishment certainly appears to be one of the most horrific fates imaginable, the Warning begins with the mysterious collision of two stars in the sky—or does it? Reading the girls' descriptions of it requires a disorienting mental see-saw between the material and mystical worlds. Conchita has been repeatedly described as the "main visionary," and does indeed seem to be the one who saw and spoke with the Virgin Mary the most. She gamely tries to describe the Warning, giving the example of two stars colliding, creating a spectacular sight but not actually bringing harm. Yet Conchita, in her descriptions of the Warning, can't quite commit to *literal* stars colliding.

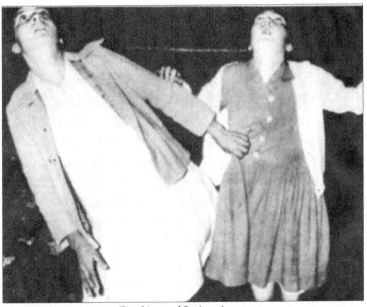

[92] *Conchita and Jacinta in ecstasy*

"It is a phenomenon which will be seen and felt in all the world and everywhere; I have always given as an example that of two stars that collide."[93]

Only one of the four girls was reportedly told the Year of the Warning: Mari-Loli. When one interviewer, in an attempt to ascertain the Year of the Warning, asked Mari-Loli if she herself would be alive for it, Mari-Loli laughed and replied, "I hope so." Clearly, Mari-Loli, who died a few days short of 60 in 2009, believed the Warning was within the scope of her own lifetime. (I spoke with Mari-Loli not long before she died, and our conversation is included in the book. A follow-up interview with two of Mari-Loli's children about her final words on Garabandal is included in the final chapter.) Mari-Loli's description of the Warning does not refer to cosmic collisions at all, but she does talk about airplanes suspended in mid-air. She says that when the Warning occurs, everything will come to a momentary standstill, including airplanes.

"She (the Virgin Mary) said that everything, everywhere, for a moment would stop and the people would just think and look inside themselves."[94]

Meanwhile, the youngest of the visionaries, Mari Cruz, was a few days short of eleven years old when the first apparition occurred and is the only one of the girls who remained in Spain rather than marrying an American. If Conchita is always described glowingly in Garabandal literature as the most intelligent and the prettiest of the girls, and privy to most of Mary's secrets, Mari Cruz was often painted as Conchita's opposite: she saw the Virgin Mary the fewest number of times, her parents disapproved the most, and her apparitions ended the soonest. She was subject to taunts by villagers for her unworthiness to see the Virgin Mary, and after the apparitions ended, she expressed deep and lingering doubts that they occurred at all. Yet Mari Cruz spoke about the Warning as recently as 2006, and in surprisingly soothing terms: "The warning (Aviso) has been misconstrued by some who see it as a threatening situation. I have a different idea about it. For me, I see it as a situation where a father scolds a son (in a gentle manner), but not a threat."[95]

Conchita also emphasized the "gentle" nature of the Warning in an interview about ten years after the apparitions: "Before the great Miracle, he will send a purification, a loving Warning…to prepare us."[96]

In a perplexing paradox, the girls seem at a loss to explain what exactly happens in the sky for all to see during the Warning. Noise and light in the sky, planes hanging in mid-air, if just for a moment. And the whole world watching. Is it a physical event that comes out of the clear blue sky, visible to all, like the shock of a plane crashing into a tower? Or is the Warning of a completely different nature altogether? Conchita claimed that the Warning would not hurt us, but on 9-11 many were killed. And although 9-11 certainly felt like a wake-up call to many in the USA, and its reverberations were global, it did not have the lasting spiritual impact that this Warning is predicted to have. Churches were packed in the U.S. after 9-11—but only for a few weeks. Everyone was shaken—but quickly began to disagree about what the correct response should be. 9-11 resulted in political polarization rather than spiritual purification. Hearts were mostly hardened as a result of 9-11, not changed. Yet some sort of spiritual purification is *certainly* what the Global Warning will bring, according to the girls of Garabandal. Jacinta's description, like Conchita's, starts quite dramatically in the sky, but suddenly leaps to a new dimension.

"The Warning is something that is first seen in the air everywhere in the world and immediately is transmitted into the interior of our souls…It will be for the good of our souls, in order to see in ourselves our conscience, the good and the bad that we've done."[97]

The physical event may be mysterious, but all the girls seem crystal clear about the spiritual one.

Conchita says, "No one will have doubts of it being from God, and of its not being human. I, who know what it is, am very much afraid of that day…You're going to see everything wrong that you're doing and the good you're not doing."[98]

Believers, non-believers, people of all religions and those of no religion will reach the same conclusion: The Warning is a direct sign from God. For this reason, Conchita said, "I believe it is impossible that the world could be so hardened as not to change."[99]

So based on the words of the visionaries, this will be an equal-opportunity Warning and will not discriminate on the basis of race, religion, nationality, gender, political or sexual preference, or disability. Everyone will be included, and our particular self-identification will be meaningless. We won't be in control—the Warning will light up our insides whether we want it to or not. The world will come to a shocked standstill for a moment, but it will feel like an eternity. What seems most striking about the Warning is not the potential cataclysm in the sky, but the certain tempest in our hearts. Father Gustave Morales, in an interview for *The Vigil* in 1988, recalled the girls describing the Warning like a fire that will not burn our flesh. "We will be filled with anxiety and would much prefer to be dead rather than to pass through this ordeal."[100]

Better off *dead*? Than enduring a few moments of conscience-pricking? It's easy to dismiss these statements as theatrical, but bombarded as we are with events 24-7, we may no longer be aware of—and cannot accurately assess—the state of the world we inhabit. All is not well, but we are thoroughly desensitized to most of it. Indeed, we experience most calamity as virtual calamity rather than actual calamity. How could we not? Who can say if a face-to-face encounter with God—and a sudden, blinding revelation of our own personal failure—might be, for many, a catastrophe more terrifying than a re-arrangement of the solar system, a fate worse than death?

In the 1960s, when these events unfolded, many believers in Garabandal—like Jesus' followers when he promised he would come again— thought the Warning and Miracle were imminent. Visitors to Garabandal from around the world even bought parcels of land around the village, to ensure they would have a prime spot from which to watch the Miracle. Some of those foreigners who bought up plots of land in hopes of being present for the Miracle have already passed away. On the other hand, the passage of time has afforded far greater opportunities to, as it were, "get the word out." Websites are already in place with post-Warning guidance, urging people who will presumably be reeling from the Warning to journey to Garabandal and wait for God's coming Miracle.[101]

The three great global events of Garabandal are supposed to unfold relatively quickly, one after the other, but the timing of the Warning was hinted at by Jacinta who said that the Warning would not come until conditions were at their worst. Although it seems impossible to guess what "the worst" might mean, or when it might be, there are actually some very specific events that are predicted to unfold before the Warning, which will be explored later. But according to Conchita, the Warning will be an unmistakable mile marker in human history:

"This Warning, like the Chastisement, is a very fearful thing...It will draw the good closer to God and it will warn the wicked that the end of times is coming and that these are the last warnings...No one can stop it from happening. It is certain..."[102]

[103] *The girls descending stairs at night, eyes turned upward*

Chapter 3

The Date of the Miracle

"I haven't the slightest doubt that this business of the children is true. Why can she have chosen us? Today is the happiest day of my life."
The last words of a Jesuit priest, just after he saw the Virgin Mary in Garabandal and moments before he died.

Thousands of on-lookers watched the radiant faces of the girls in ecstasy yet never caught a glimpse of the Virgin hovering in the air. Only one adult, in fact, ever "crossed over" and viewed the Virgin Mary in Garabandal along with the girls—a skeptical young Jesuit who died later that same night as he was departing from Garabandal. The conventional wisdom is that he "died of joy." Earlier that night, while seeing the Virgin alongside the girls, he had cried out, "Miracle! Miracle! Miracle! Miracle!"

The natural assumption would be that the Jesuit, Father Luis Andreu, cried out "Miracle!" in response to his wonder at suddenly seeing the Virgin Mary. But like everything else surrounding Garabandal, complications abound in this story, and unexpected twists and turns plague those looking for a straightforward narrative. In fact, the Virgin Mary told the girls that Father Luis Andreu had actually been graced with a preview of the coming Global Miracle. It was *this* Miracle that drove him to his knees in shouts of ecstasy. It was this Miracle, apparently— or the shock and joy of seeing it—that *killed* him.

But the story gets stranger. Despite being dead, Father Luis Andreu does not disappear from Garabandal—he makes additional appearances in the village as a friendly ghost. The girls relate their numerous conversations with him, passing on personal tidbits about him that they could never have otherwise known, stunning his surviving brother into belief, and leading his devout, widowed mother to enter a convent for the rest of her life.

Finally, Father Luis Andreu has a starring role in the last act of Garabandal. In addition to appearing alive and well to investigate the Garabandal apparitions (Act 1), then showing up as a dead (or rather undead) believer during further apparitions (Act 2), Fr. Luis Andreu's incorrupt body is also scheduled to make a reappearance on the date of the Miracle (Act 3).

What about this Miracle was so overwhelming that the mortal Father Luis Andreu couldn't even survive a preview of it? Before examining the Great Miracle of Garabandal and Father Luis Andreu's strange role in greater detail, it's worth mentioning some of the numerous, less spectacular "miracles" surrounding Garabandal. Like Jesus healing the sick and raising the dead, casting out demons and curing lepers, Divine Providence presumably chose to perform signs and wonders at the Garabandal apparitions in order to attract attention, encourage belief, and bring consolation. Some of the "minor miracles" occurred countless times throughout the apparitions, and are well-documented by videos, photographs and personal accounts.

The Minor Miracles of Garabandal

Those visiting Garabandal brought wedding rings, rosaries and religious medals by the dozens to the apparitions. They were often handed over to the visionaries in an unceremonious tangle, and the girls would then lift them up during the apparition to be kissed by the Virgin. Afterward, the girls unfailingly returned the newly kissed objects to their rightful owners without hesitation, even though the objects sometimes numbered in the hundreds, and the owners were complete strangers to the girls.[104] Some owners reported a lingering odor of incense on the rosaries and rings.[105]

In many of these cases, unexplainable exchanges took place between the visionaries and the strangers. One night, some in the crowd tsked-tsked disapprovingly when a brazen pilgrim threw in a *powder compact* to be blessed. However, the offending object was kissed first by the Virgin, who noted, "That belongs to my Son."

[106] *Mari-Loli offering rosaries to the Virgin*

Conchita later explained that it had served as a secret *pyx* during the Spanish Civil War, carrying the consecrated *host* (a piece of bread that Catholics believe has become the body of Christ), to prisoners who were about to be executed. There are many such recorded instances of the visionaries recounting stories they "could not possibly have known" about various rings, rosaries and medals, then returning the object unfailingly to the correct owner who confirmed the visionaries' account and, doubtless, became a true believer.

In contrast to apparition sites like Lourdes, Garabandal does not seem to be a place of numerous spectacular physical healings. It does, however, have some stories that fit this genre, including the reported cure of a young girl named Menchu Mendiolea of an "incurable illness" and a young boy named Alberto Gulierrez Orena who was left "deaf, dumb, and blind" after a car accident.[107]

Jesuit Father Ramon Andreu, who plays a significant role in the events of Garabandal, was seriously injured in a car accident on the way up the mountain in October 1961. Injuries that should have taken, according to visiting doctors, 20 days to heal, were healed in a few hours, about the time that one of the visionaries announced that the priest was cured.[108]

[109] *Mari-Loli holds up rosaries and other objects for the Virgin to kiss*

More common in Garabandal were the poignant stories of healings without cures, with which most people of faith are familiar. In the Gospels, Jesus frequently coupled his impossible-to-verify forgiveness of sin with the impossible-to-deny restoration of sight, limbs, even life itself. But spiritual rather than physical restoration is the more common experience of most believers today. One day a young couple showed up in Garabandal with a three-year-old girl who was "blind from birth," as the Bible likes to say. The parents tearfully begged Mary for a miracle, and the Garabandal visionaries joined in. In the deep silence of communal prayer, the little blind girl suddenly burst into a joyful song.[110] Her eyesight was not restored, but her distraught parents nonetheless left Garabandal with strengthened spirits. In a similar vein, an award-winning Spanish writer by the name of Mercedes Salisachs from Juncadella visited Garabandal after the death of her 18-year-old son, Miguel, in a car accident. "I changed into a different person, without any future except the past, without any hope except to die; but with the feeling that death ended everything, that hope was a great lie, and faith a childish device for holding us in line."[111]

After asking the Virgin one day for help (and receiving it), Mercedes decided to visit Garabandal. There the Virgin delivered a message to Mercedes through one of the visionaries that her son was not only in heaven but also by his earthly mother's side. Her faith and joy restored, Mercedes became a leading advocate for the apparitions there. Other such incidents could be labeled more accurately as conversions. A Jewish Parisian named Muriel Catherine,[112] a German Protestant named Maximo Foeschler.[113] The doubting priest whose vocation was confirmed and whose inner torment was relieved, the Catholic "party girl" who decided to become a nun.[114] There was also the story of the priest who came to Garabandal but kept avoiding the visionaries and breaking into sobs, because, the Virgin Mary told them, he no longer wanted to be a priest.[115]

The Medium-Sized Miracles of Garabandal

Between the daily, somewhat mundane miracles (if a true miracle can ever be called mundane), and the still-awaited Global Miracle, were a few "medium-sized" miracles at Garabandal that raised eyebrows.

From the standpoint of a non-believer, perhaps the most impressive is the true story of the Uruguayan rugby team that went down in an airplane in the Andes and was given up as lost. The story of the survivors has been well-documented in numerous books, including a book by Piers Paul Read, as well as memorialized in a gripping Hollywood movie starring Ethan

Hawke. Less well-known is the true story's connection to Garabandal.

Sisters Rosina and Sarah Strauch had sons, Fito and Eduardo, on the lost plane. The sisters had heard about Our Lady of Garabandal appearing to some children in Spain but, due to intense controversy, never being accepted by the Church. One of the Strauch sisters reportedly had been given a rosary that had been kissed by the Virgin at Garabandal. Rosina and Sarah decided to pray to Our Lady of Garabandal for the rescue of their sons. This not only would save their sons, they reasoned, but also provide an authenticating miracle for Garabandal— something the Virgin could not resist.[116]

Ten weeks later, when all hope was lost that there could be any survivors, sixteen of the forty-five plane passengers were found alive, including Rosina and Sarah's sons. Surely other mothers prayed for their sons, too, but their sons died. Yet anyone who has read this story understands how miraculous it is that *anyone* survived, much less sixteen people for ten weeks. The crash survivors, who also prayed the rosary nightly, came to an agreement to live off the frozen carcasses of their lost teammates. Then, when they realized they had been given up for dead, they used their only sustenance to hike out of the snow-bound Andes and save themselves.

Among Catholics and believers, however, the Garabandal miracle that garnered the most attention was the night a "host" (consecrated bread become Christ) appeared out of nowhere on Conchita's tongue. That dramatic night involved a breathless tale of how, amidst the shoving and chaos, a lone photographer, the Abraham Zapruder of Garabandal, managed to capture the exact moment a shining white wafer materialized on Conchita's tongue like a snowflake before vanishing.

Astonishingly, the four children themselves may have been the catalyst for this miracle, thanks to their own childish pleading to be vindicated. They reported on July 30, 1961 that the Virgin Mary looked grave when they requested a miracle to sway the crowds—obviously, it was not just when Jesus walked the earth that he had to endure an "evil generation that asks for a sign," as the Gospels describe.

But the girls had felt the sting of accusations of lying early on, and on August 4, they tried again. They begged the Virgin Mary to speak into a tape recorder as proof for those masses who couldn't see the Virgin and therefore wouldn't believe. Later, about 50 people listened as the tape was re-played. The girls were heard clearly asking the Virgin Mary to speak, and the Virgin could be heard refusing—*"No, no hablo."*[117] However, like an elusive mirage that one can never quite substantiate, no Virgin voice was heard on later re-plays. It was as if God teased and tormented with seemingly hard evidence, but then erased it— ultimately insisting that true faith take a blind leap. Nonetheless, many of the eyewitnesses subsequently signed their names confirming they had heard the original voice.[118] The story of the tape recording spread like wildfire from the original 50 eyewitnesses into the crowd, and into the permanent folklore surrounding Garabandal.

And so the girls continued to plead with the Virgin for a miracle that might prove they were not lying. The girls at times wept during apparitions because they weren't believed, crying, "My God, they don't believe us!" Mari Cruz's mother expressed great anguish for her daughter's suffering in the face of disbelief about the apparitions. "Oh, my child! My child! How she suffered."[119]

The visionaries even tried to guilt-trip the Virgin, reminding her of proof that was given at Lourdes and Fatima. It's easy to appreciate Mary's reluctance, since it's debatable how effective previous "proofs" were at Lourdes, Fatima, or even at an empty tomb in Jerusalem. For many, after some eye-popping miracle, the initial flurry of belief seems always to evaporate. Nonetheless, the girls persisted, asking the Virgin for a large miracle by turning the night into day, or even a small miracle by enabling them to fly.[120] Conchita wanted to know why the Virgin looked so serious when they asked for proof. Meanwhile, Mari-Loli demanded of Mary, "Give it right now, right away. You always say you will give it in time, in time..."[121]

Eventually, the Virgin consented, but she made the children wait almost a year. The Archangel Michael had already been distributing communion to the girls on days when the village pastor, a traveling priest, wasn't able to visit the remote village. St. Michael seemed to be giving lessons to the girls in how to receive communion, insisting that they fast and pray the "I Confess" beforehand, while offering thanksgiving and praying the "Soul of Christ" afterward.

Michael explained to the girls that the consecrated bread he distributed came from "tabernacles of the earth," which brings to mind enchanting images of Michael soaring low over continents looking for the perfect tabernacle to pluck from. (It is also a nod to the Catholic understanding that not even angels can consecrate hosts, only priests.) The exact tabernacles Michael was pilfering from were not revealed, and after the girls claimed they were receiving communion, the village pastor, Father Valentin, had started counting the communion wafers to see if the girls (or Michael) might be taking them from the tabernacle in the village church. Reportedly, some communion wafers had indeed gone missing.[122]

Yet Michael promised that on the upcoming night of the miracle, the village would see much more than Conchita miming communion and receiving an invisible host—everyone would actually *see* the consecrated host on Conchita's tongue. Conchita had not even realized that no one else could see the host when she received communion from Michael, and she immediately complained that this was only a "tiny miracle." Michael laughed, and the stage was set.

In the village, though, skepticism ran high. The village pastor, Father Valentin, was so doubtful that the miracle would occur that he told Conchita to stop writing letters announcing the upcoming miracle, which Conchita insisted she was doing at the

Angel's request.[123] Dr. Celestino Ortiz of Santander was one of the recipients of a letter from Conchita announcing the miracle. So concerned was he about Conchita predicting a particular miracle on a particular day that he went to see her and confessed, "I just don't believe that the miracle that you mention will happen."[124]

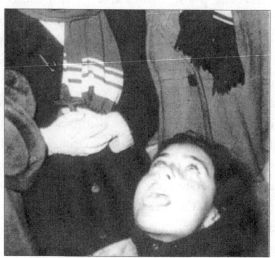

[125] *Conchita receiving invisible or "mystical" communion*

Nevertheless, on July 18, 1962, the day of the "little miracle," Garabandal filled with 2,000 to 3,000 pilgrims descending on the village. Villagers found themselves feeding visitors, some they knew and some they didn't, from near and far. They put in a long day of hard work and hospitality, cooking, serving, and washing up until late in the night. As the night dragged on without a miracle, many pilgrims departed, while others planned to stick it out for the night in villagers' homes or stables. Some people were afraid that the miracle would not take place because of holiday dancing in the village, while others feared that the presence of so many priests would thwart the miracle, since Michael usually gave communion only when no priests were present. Many worried that this so-called "miracle" would be an unfulfilled disaster. Conchita's own brother gave up finally and told Conchita she had deceived them all. But Conchita urged him to wait a little longer.[126]

Finally, at about 1:30 in the morning, at a time when most were now certain that no miracle would occur, a crowd began to shout and run: Conchita was on the move. She had received her call and was stepping out in ecstasy to make a miracle. By all accounts, the scene was complete chaos. Villager Pepe Diez was trying to accompany Conchita at her mother's request, but found himself being stripped of his clothing and his belt by the crushing mob trying to get closer to Conchita. "I began to be afraid, not so much for Conchita as for myself."[127] Conchita's own mother was convinced that the crowd would kill her.[128] When Conchita crashed to her knees to receive communion, Pepe Diez aimed his flashlight at her tongue—which was bare. "I had a terrible feeling of disaster."[129]

But then, about a minute later, Pepe Diez saw the communion wafer appear on Conchita's bare tongue. At first it appeared like any other communion host, but it began to expand in volume. "...I saw in that Host, a live force which reminded me of sea waves, sparkling and moving under the sun...a living thing, radiant from within."[130] Another villager described it as a snowflake lit by the sun's rays which did not hurt one's eyes.[131] A woman from Madrid named Maria Paloma was situated further away. She saw dozens of flashlight beams converge on Conchita's tongue, but strangely enough, an even brighter light shone from the girl's mouth.[132]

Interestingly, Conchita recorded in her diary that she received the miraculous host in her own home, since she was oblivious to the ecstatic marches and general running-around while in ecstasy and saw only what was in her "field of vision"—the Virgin, St. Michael, or the other visionaries. She recorded in her diary that Michael instructed her to recite the "I Confess" and "think about whom you are to receive." After the miraculous communion, an apparently exasperated Virgin Mary instantly appeared and remarked, "They still do not all believe."[133]

But some of them did. One Alejandro Damians of Barcelona was on hand with a camera and took "moving pictures" of the event. Damians reported that he had borrowed the camera from his cousin and was quite unfamiliar with it. In fact, Damians' cousin was originally slated to go but had to back out and asked Damians to go in his place. Damians did not want to go since he was at home enjoying the holiday, but finally succumbed under pressure from his wife and child. After a long drive and a tedious day in the village, the apparition began after 1:30 in the morning. Like many others, Damians was carried along by the surge of the mob which he described as a fantastic and terrifying sight.

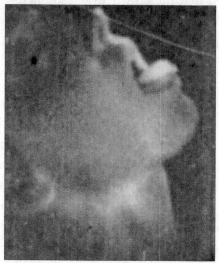

¹³⁴ *Miraculous visible communion wafer received by Conchita*

He was twenty or thirty feet behind Conchita when she crashed to her knees and the crowd swarmed past her, unable to stop. This brought Damians within eighteen inches of Conchita's face where he stood his ground. When she opened her mouth and extended her bare tongue, Damians says he watched the host materialize. Witnesses agree that Conchita held the host on her extended tongue for one to three minutes; Conchita says the Angel told her to wait until the Virgin appeared before swallowing. During this time, Damians pointed the camera and shot. However, he was quickly pushed to the ground, and did not believe he had captured the moment, since he didn't even know how to operate the camera. In actuality, he had recorded more than 70 frames of the miraculous communion which have been reprinted many times.[135] After he saw and had filmed the appearance of the host, Damians went into a corner and wept because he believed he had seen "the true God."[136]

Another photographer was also weeping that night. Dr. Jean Caux, a plastic surgeon from Paris, had come armed with expensive equipment and permission from Conchita to film the Miracle. According to Dr. Caux, nothing went right and he didn't capture a single frame. That, however, was not why he was weeping. Instead he wept because he, too, believed he had caught a fleeting glimpse of God before Conchita swallowed, and he was pierced with sudden sorrow for his sin when the brief shining moment ended and God "fled" from him. Dr. Caux believed he was in mortal sin and found peace by going to confession, but he was convinced that the "dagger" of sorrow which pierced his heart would not be removed until he saw the Great Miracle. He went "mad for God" because seeing the miraculous host made him feel "something so deep, unknown and terribly great..."[137] Other reports also circulated of witnesses who "couldn't stop crying" after seeing the Miraculous Host.[138]

¹³⁹ *Dr. Caux, who didn't capture the Miracle*

And so true believers tally up the list of miracles surrounding Garabandal, which skeptics just as confidently dismiss: from rosaries returned to rightful owners to lost whisperings on tape, from rescued rugby players to a magically appearing host. Yet all these supposed miracles pale in comparison to what is reportedly coming: the Great Global Miracle that will irrevocably confirm the truth of Garabandal and also, by the way, save the world.

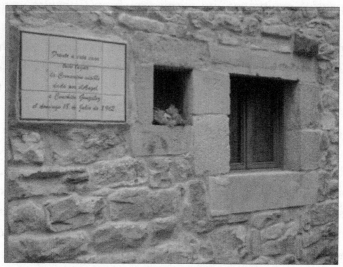

¹⁴⁰ *Plaque marking where Conchita received the visible communion wafer*

The Great Global Miracle of Garabandal

It was on August 8, 1961 that Father Luis Andreu arrived in Garabandal in a caravan of five cars. He and his brother, Jesuit Father Ramon Andreu, had visited Garabandal on July 29, with the express intent of investigating the phenomenon and reporting back to their superiors, and a photograph exists of Father Luis intently scrutinizing the girls while they are in ecstasy. Father Luis Andreu was disturbed by the apparitions, and openly wondered whether they might be satanic. He wasn't alone.

It wasn't just the wild strangeness of some of the apparition phenomena—the frozen poses as if the girls were carved from ice, the reported levitations, the synchronized speed walking up and down mountains in the dark that left even the fastest young men in the village gasping to keep up.[141] More worrisome incidents suggested evil might also be on the scene and at work. One time the girls recounted being afraid when a red cloud covered them.[142] Another time they were plunged into darkness and heard an unidentified voice calling them to follow, which frightened them.[143] No satisfactory explanation was ever given for these eerie episodes. If a portal really had opened between worlds in this Spanish mountain village, was it possible that not everything which crossed the threshold and called out to the girls was from God?

[144] *Father Luis observing an ecstasy in Garabandal*

Then something even more disturbing occurred. In ecstasy, the girls would "perform these extraordinary jumps,"[145] almost akin to flying, which even young girls trained in gymnastics were unable to copy. One day, numerous spectators observed Mari-Loli and Jacinta in the choir loft of the church during an apparition, gliding fearlessly along the balcony railing as if they were about to jump, which would likely have killed them. Jacinta's father, however, insisted that he and Mari-Loli's father were not concerned "since we had already seen so many things!" They heard the girls say, "Can we jump?...Oh, no? You don't want us to jump?" The girls didn't jump, but many visitors lacked the equanimity of the family members and were upset by the strange episode, and even Conchita questioned her friends' behavior.[146] Was this from God or from the devil? The incident has been mentioned as one of the reasons the bishop closed the church to the apparitions,[147] although in other sources it was the unruly onlookers crowding in to view the visionaries which caused the bishop to declare the church off-limits.

On Father Luis Andreu's return to Garabandal on August 8, he celebrated Mass in the village church where Conchita, Jacinta and Mari-Loli received communion. Afterward, the girls announced that an apparition would soon occur in the church. Just as promised, not long after Mass, around 2 o'clock, all four girls began chatting with the Virgin Mary.

One of the criticisms of the Garabandal apparitions concerned the girls' long, trivial conversations with the Virgin. On one occasion, the girls and Mary seemed to discuss fashion. The girls consistently said Mary appeared in a white robe and blue cloak, just as the Virgin first appeared as Our Lady of Mt. Carmel in 1251 to Simon Stock. But one day at Garabandal, Mary appeared in the brown habit of Carmel which the girls more readily recognized, and when the girls asked why the change, Mary replied that she was free to wear any color she wanted.[148] Mary also confided one day, in an apparent moment of "girl talk," that she had dabbed perfume on the sides of her sandals when she had lived on earth.[149] Sometimes the Infant Jesus appeared in Mary's arms and was duly passed around by the girls. On one occasion, Conchita asked where his father was.[150]

In her journal, Conchita explained the girls' sometimes trivial conversations with the Virgin like this: "(Mary) was like a mother who for a long time had not seen the daughter who was telling her everything that had happened. And much more in our case since we had never seen her. And she was our Mother from Heaven."

On the day that Father Luis died, the girls' afternoon

conversation with the Virgin included Conchita's new hair style, which had been shorn at the insistence of the villainous "Commission" which had come riding into town like gunslingers in black hats to investigate Garabandal on behalf of the Church. The Commission is portrayed in a fairly sinister light in some Garabandal literature, and it's noteworthy that much of that literature was written by extremely traditional Spanish and French priests in the 1960s. These priests were a far cry from rogue celebrity clergy of today who openly pit themselves against the Pope. Nonetheless, as we will see later, there were some very serious reasons for the Commission's skepticism and scrutiny, and in some ways the investigative Commission—which consisted of both clerics and laity, including doctors and psychiatrists—was given a bad rap.

Yet the Commission's ferrying of Conchita to a beauty operator in the city of Santander to get the girl's hair cut has to qualify as one of the oddest moments of Garabandal. The Commission had whisked Conchita away from Garabandal to Santander for what came across as an ominous, Inquisitorial-like "questioning." The assumption was that pretty, charismatic Conchita was influencing the other girls and it was time to stop the scandal. The Commission used a mix of threats and bribes with Conchita in Santander to pressure her into signing a denial of the apparitions—telling her she could end up in an asylum for the rest of her life while her parents went to prison; offering, on the other hand, to send her away to school to make a "senorita" out of her: "Do you want to be a senorita or a shepherdess for the rest of your life?"[151]

¹⁵² *Mari-Loli in ecstasy*

Some claim that the bishop thought Conchita's long, flowing tresses were too attractive (perhaps she wasn't considered nun-like enough to be receiving visits from the Virgin Mary.) Other sources say Conchita's ecstasies—which did not stop—were attracting far too much attention on the streets of Santander, and the Commission was simply trying to disguise her appearance from the crowds.

Conchita had an ecstasy in the streets of Santander at the exact time that the other girls were having one in Garabandal—an ecstasy that only ended when several men lifted Conchita from the street and carried her to a church. The men wrestled with Conchita due to her rigidity and weight while in a trance, until Conchita's mother cried out for them to leave her alone. "Shut up, Madam, nothing will happen to her," they replied.¹⁵³

The Commission had brought Conchita to Santander to stop the apparitions and instead she was creating a sensation there as well. To disguise Conchita from the growing crowds seems like the most likely explanation for the haircut, but it took a bizarre twist. As the beautician was sawing away at Conchita's thick braid, she noted that it was difficult to cut. From this, some members of the Commission allegedly concluded that "fluid" in

Conchita's braid was "controlling" the other girls. (Conchita confirmed in a 1973 filmed interview that some Commission members believed her braid was hypnotizing the other girls.)[154] So, in the spirit of Delilah robbing Samson of his mane and his power (with gender roles reversed), they whacked it off.[155]

Back in Garabandal, after mentioning Conchita's controversial haircut to the Virgin, Jacinta got Mary to admit her age (eighteen), and the girls remarked that one of the priests in town that day celebrated the Mass very slowly and extremely well.[156] The presider which the girls admired was Father Luis Andreu himself, and that Mass was his last. Twenty years later, in a filmed interview, Mari-Loli described Father Luis as intense and sweating during his last Mass, "as if he was living the Mass."[157]

During this vision, the girls walked backward to the altar of the Immaculate Conception (they always watched the Virgin as they walked, sometimes walking forward and sometimes backward). The "walking backward" detail has been suggested as somehow satanic, but in fact the girls always walked backwards *away* from the Blessed Sacrament, rather than turning their backs on it.[158] They then recited the rosary, and experienced an "ecstatic fall," a phenomenon in which they arched backward until their heads almost but did not quite touch the floor. They later gently rose up off the ground in unison without losing their balance, injuring themselves, or pushing themselves up. Family members had at times witnessed all four girls coming downstairs headfirst together in this inexplicable fashion.[159] Conchita herself, when not in ecstasy, was shocked to see the other visionaries do this, but had no recollection of doing it herself. "We were not aware of that. We were with the Virgin...without knowing if we were running or not, if we were on our knees, or lying on the ground."[160]

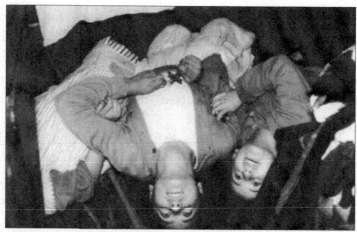

¹⁶¹ *Girls in an ecstatic fall*

After 9:30 on the night of August 8, the four girls were back in the church, mildly complaining that because they hadn't given any "proof," children threw stones at them and people said the girls were sick. "If you're pleased with us, then it's all the same to us."¹⁶² The girls proceeded to follow the Virgin Mary out of the church on an ecstatic march that included singing, and kissing something that hung invisibly in the air. Close behind was Father Luis Andreu, following them to "the Pines."

The Pines were a stand of nine trees on a hill overlooking the village. Conchita's own grandfather had planted the pines years earlier with a class of children receiving communion for the first time. Some people have noted that there are reportedly nine ranks of heavenly angels, and thus the Pines of Garabandal symbolize the heavenly host trumpeting the arrival of the Virgin Mary to the little town. This is where the girls finally stopped marching and settled into ecstasy, and this is when they expressed shock that Father Luis Andreu had entered their heretofore exclusive "field of vision." During their ecstasies, the girls were used to seeing only the Virgin Mary, Michael the Archangel, and each other. No one else was visible to them or existed for them while they experienced an apparition, including any of the four visionaries who were not participating in that particular apparition. Yet on that one strange night, the girls also saw

64

Father Luis Andreu. At that time, Mary informed the girls that the priest could also see the Virgin, and that he was watching the Great Miracle unfold before his eyes.[163]

Father Luis Andreu took notes that night, and his notes survived him. He jotted down the "impressive descent" of the girls as they practically flew down the mountainside from the Pines back to the church with "wings on their heels," as described by Fr. Royo Marin, O.P., another visiting priest.

Still in ecstasy, back in the church, Mari Cruz registered her anguish that her ecstasies seemed to be sputtering and dying, since the Virgin had not come to her in the previous few days. "Why do you wait so long to come to me and come more often for the others?"[164] Mari Cruz asked sorrowfully, at her inexplicable exclusion from the club. The Virgin, as if to make up for this, remained with Mari Cruz in ecstasy an extra-long amount of time that night, after the other girls' vision had ended.

Much was made of why Mari Cruz wasn't included in the apparitions with the same frequency as the other girls. Was it because Mari Cruz's parents were less faith-filled and more disapproving, which produced some sort of spiritual interference that prevented Mari Cruz from receiving the broadcast signal? (Mari Cruz's father reportedly did not attend Mass very often, although he had serious health problems.)[165] Or was it that the Virgin was simply respecting the wishes of her parents? Mari Cruz's parents reportedly had begun keeping her away from the other three girls, sending her out to the fields or shutting her up in the house. In fact, a few days earlier, Father Valentin recorded in his journal that Mari Cruz had spent the entire day in the garden with her parents, and the Virgin had later asked Mari Cruz why she hadn't gone to the Pines.[166] This suggests that it was not the Virgin who was avoiding Mari Cruz, but the other way around—or, rather, it was her parents who were erecting the barrier. Though this caused Mari Cruz much sorrow, it's hard not to feel some sympathy for the confounded parents sucked into the eye of this storm. A visiting aunt had confided that she believed the girls were sick, and Mari Cruz's parents were upset about what was taking place.

Mari Cruz, however, appeared to be benefiting spiritually from the apparitions, remarking that she had learned how to pray rather than just play, and asking a priest to pray that she become better every day.[167] The affection of the Virgin for Mari Cruz appeared constant—the other three girls in ecstasy were known to visit Mari Cruz's house and serenade her with songs from the Virgin: *Get up, Mari Cruz, since the good Virgin comes with a bouquet of flowers for her little girl. Receive the flowers that the Virgin brings so that you will be good, beautiful child, holy child, you are very dear, but you don't wake up.*[168]

One theory was that Mari Cruz's sad exclusion was to demonstrate that the ecstasies were not self-induced and the girls could not produce them at will—they were given by God, and God alone was in control. Whatever the explanation, there seems to be little doubt that some villagers taunted Mari Cruz about her seeming failure, and that Mari Cruz suffered both from the disgrace of the exclusion and, more significantly, from the heartbreak of being denied the Virgin Mary's presence.

While Mari Cruz would rapidly lose her luster as a visionary, Conchita would at the same time gain in favor and attention from both the Virgin Mary and the crowds. Conchita's apparitions would last the longest and would include some of the most striking revelations from the Virgin Mary. The girls had started out in the same boat, but cracks in their unity were starting to show.

Meanwhile, Mari-Loli realized that while streaking downhill from the Pines, she had dropped a "finger-rosary" belonging to Father Luis Andreu. She told Father Luis Andreu that the Virgin Mary had told her where the rosary was, but Mari-Loli's mother forbade her from climbing back up the hill so late at night to retrieve it. Father Luis Andreu told Mari-Loli if she did recover the rosary, to save it for his brother Ramon, assuring her that even if he himself did not return, his brother Ramon would.[169]

The next day, Mari-Loli recovered the finger-rosary, but Father Luis Andreu was by that time dead. Mari-Loli did indeed eventually pass the rosary on to Father Luis Andreu's brother, another Jesuit, Father Ramon.

That night, Father Luis Andreu's head must have been spinning from what had just happened to him on the mountaintop, but he was still playing it somewhat safe as he departed Garabandal. He confided in Father Valentin, the village pastor, that the children were telling the truth, but asked him not to tell anyone what he'd said because the Church could never be too prudent in such matters.[170] Father Valentin promptly recorded the conversation in a notebook he had been scrupulously keeping since the first reported angel sighting.

Apparently, though, Father Luis Andreu relaxed somewhat as the miles rolled past, and he began to talk freely and happily in the car about his experience. These are his reported last words: "I feel overwhelmed with joy. What a wonderful present the Virgin has given me! How lucky to have a mother like that in heaven! We shouldn't be afraid of the supernatural. The children have given us an example of the attitude we should take to the Blessed Virgin. I haven't the slightest doubt that this business of the children is true. Why can she have chosen us? Today is the happiest day of my life."[171]

After that, he remarked that he felt sleepy, lowered his head and coughed. He was dead. The young priest was physically fit and had no family history of heart trouble, so it became commonly accepted in Garabandal circles that he died of joy. It is curious to note, though, that Mari-Loli in 1984 described him during his last Mass as "intense and sweating." Was he ill? Did he have undiagnosed heart trouble? Was he "living the Mass"[172]—the sacrifice of Christ—in an intensely mystical way which took its toll? Or was that stunning vision of the Great Miracle too much for his mortal frame to bear? Whatever killed him, within two months of his death, his own widowed mother entered the convent of the Visitation of Saint Sebastian.

But this was not the end of Father Luis Andreu. The Virgin Mary told the girls they would speak with him on August 15, the Feast of the Assumption of the Virgin Mary into heaven. Unfortunately, Mary cancelled Father Luis' visit due to "scandalous carousing" that took place in the village that night.[173]

So Father Luis Andreu waited a day and showed up as a disembodied voice which was, according to Conchita's diary, "exactly like the one he had on earth." He asked the girls to deliver a message to his brother, and then proceeded to teach the girls some words, songs, and prayers in French, German, English, Greek, and Latin.

Presumably he had no need, after death, to show off his language-learning abilities, but was trying to demonstrate that the girls weren't faking it. Some said it was a sign that Mary had come for everyone.

When Father Ramon first heard that the girls had a message for him from his dead brother, he was "disconcerted." He believed the girls were merely upset about Father Luis' death, and he was disturbed about the spectacle of the girls "talking" to Father Luis—enough so that all Father Ramon wanted was to get out of Garabandal as quickly as possible.[174] But when Father Ramon received the message from his dead brother, he said he was "truly stupefied" at what the girls told him. They described Father Luis Andreu's funeral down to the smallest detail, including some deviations from tradition such as placing in his hands a crucifix instead of a chalice; they talked about how Father Luis had not made his profession of religious vows before he died, and they discussed the date, place and the fellow Jesuit with which Father Ramon had already made his vows.[175]

¹⁷⁶ *Father Luis Andreu's mother*

Conchita also wrote in detail to Father Ramon about what his brother said: "He (deceased Fr. Luis) asked me to tell you (living Fr. Ramon) that you yourself were acting very properly, that he desires very much that you come here (Garabandal), but you must continue to obey His Excellency, the Bishop."[177] (As the controversy gained steam, priests began to need the permission of the Bishop to visit Garabandal.)

All this brings us to the Miracle of Miracles: If what Father Luis Andreu saw his final night on earth caused him to die of joy, what exactly did he see? Maddeningly, he did not share what he saw before he died, and the girls themselves never saw the Miracle—they were only told about it by the Virgin.

Conchita has been designated as the key visionary in this prophecy. In an interview in the 1980s with Monsignor Francisco Garmendia, Auxiliary Bishop of New York, Conchita reported that, according to the Virgin, the Miracle will be on a Thursday. Conchita went on to say that the Virgin had given her the day, month and year.[178] What is clear is that it will be Conchita's responsibility to announce the Great Miracle exactly eight days before it occurs, and this she has not yet done.

Fathers Ramon and Luis Andreu[179]

When visionary Mari-Loli died in April 2009 just shy of 60 years old, websites and discussion boards were buzzing with rumors and misinformation about the event. Wasn't Mari-Loli the visionary who was supposed to announce the Miracle just before it occurred? If that's so, with her passing, doesn't that prove Garabandal is a false apparition? But it's Conchita upon whom the announcement of the Miracle rests. Conchita is about the same age as Mari-Loli, and if she dies before the Miracle, doesn't that mean Garabandal is false? It's an obvious assumption, but as of now, Conchita is still alive and well. Conchita has released tantalizing tidbits about the Miracle, like a trail of crumbs that devotees are following—or, more accurately, like pieces of a puzzle which believers are trying to piece together. Conchita has said the Miracle will coincide with an event in the Church and with the feast of a saint-martyr of the Eucharist, and that it will take place at 8:30 on a Thursday evening.[180]

During the Miracle, everyone in and around the village will actually see *something* in the sky, and the sick who are there will be cured. Conchita has assured us that it will be the greatest miracle Jesus has ever performed for the world, and that there will be no doubt that it comes from God.[181] Conchita also has said the miracle will last about fifteen minutes, and that it is completely different from the miracle of the sun at Fatima. Some speculate this Great Miracle is the same as that predicted in the New Testament as well as by various saints. According to the Book of Matthew, Chapter 24:

29 Immediately after the tribulation of those days, (when "things are at their worst", and after the Warning?)

the sun will be darkened,
and the moon will not give its light,
and the stars will fall from the sky,
and the powers of the heavens will be shaken.

30 And then the sign of the Son of Man will appear in heaven, and all the tribes of the earth will mourn, and they will see the Son of Man coming upon the clouds of heaven with power and great glory. [182]

Saint Faustina wrote in her diary that Jesus told her that after a great darkness, a great sign of the cross would appear in the sky and that *from the openings where the hands and the feet of the Savior were nailed will come forth great lights which will light up the earth for a period of time.* Will the earth be lit up for fifteen minutes, the "period of time" the Garabandal Miracle is predicted to last? Was this what Father Luis saw before he died? After the conscience-piercing of the Warning, and a terrifying darkness which covers the earth— will there be a great sign of Christ on the cross shedding light on the earth, proof that the world has not been abandoned by the mercy of God?

When one imagines a miraculous light in the sky, it's hard not to think of a hokey Hollywood movie scene. But if the earth truly had been plunged into darkness due to nuclear war, massive volcanic eruptions, or the collision with earth of a heavenly body, then lights pouring forth from the Savior's wounds which illuminate the *entire earth* would be unspeakably consoling and miraculous.

On the other hand, some speculate that the cross of Christ in the sky is what the whole world will see during the *Warning*— after all, the tribes of the earth will not rejoice, but mourn, upon realizing how tragically wrong they have been. For the Miracle, some point to another dazzling sign in the sky predicted in Revelation 12: *A great sign appeared in the sky, a woman clothed with the sun, with the moon under her feet, and on her head a crown of twelve stars.* [183] It would certainly make sense for the Virgin to appear, at long last, to confirm the truth of the apparitions at Garabandal (and perhaps at other apparition sites which echo this same prediction, such as Medjugorje.) Furthermore, Conchita's words about the Miracle recorded on September 5, 1962 allude to the Virgin: "You say there's going to be a miracle? And the miracle is going to be that?... And the Virgin will be seen?... And when?... So far off?... With me alone... No, I don't want that... Don't do that! Perform it with the four..."

And yet Conchita herself disputed in a conversation with a French visitor that the Great Miracle consisted of seeing the Virgin: "No, no it's not that!" She went on to explain that seeing the Virgin would be an apparition, not a miracle.[184]

Although we can speculate, we simply don't know the exact nature of either the Warning or the Miracle. Scriptures predict the sign of the Son of Man and a great sign of a Woman Clothed with the Sun *both* appearing in the sky (not to mention the sign of a seven-headed red dragon). Of course, it's quite possible that these signs won't literally appear, and the Great Miracle, if it's true, may be something else altogether.

Despite Conchita being given the exact date of the Miracle, we also don't know when it will occur. Based on various clues, it would appear, at first glance, a simple matter to solve the mystery of the date of the Great Miracle. How many "saint-martyrs of the Eucharist" can there be whose feast days are on a Thursday?

As it turns out, quite a lot, particularly since feast days can fall on different days of the week from year to year. Based on

Conchita's comments over time—including some in which she specified particular springtime months when the Miracle may occur (March, April, May or June)—many people have spent a great deal of time trying to pin down the exact saint-martyr, and websites and discussion boards offer competing theories.

The feast day of the saint-martyr appears to be a separate clue from the hopelessly vague "event in the Church" with which it coincides. Holy Thursday? A new pope? Vatican III? In some sources, Conchita is claimed to have described it as a great or important event which has occurred before in Church history, *but not during Conchita's own lifetime.* If this is the case, that would exclude a new pope and "Vatican III" as possibilities. At another time, Conchita went on to say: "Yes, I know what the event is. It is a singular event in the Church that happens very rarely, and has never happened in my lifetime. It is not new or stupendous, only rare, like a definition of a dogma—something like that in that it will affect the entire Church. It will happen on the same day as the Miracle, but not as a consequence of the Miracle, only coincidentally."[185]

This has led some to speculate that the event might be the declaration of Mary by the Catholic Church as *Coredemptrix, Mediatrix* and *Advocate.* A later chapter will examine what else this "event in the Church" could be.

Meanwhile, a couple of sensational predictions have been made about the day of the Miracle which either rest on wobbly legs or have collapsed altogether.

Conchita revealed that the day after the Miracle, Father Luis' body would be exhumed and found intact. Since Conchita made this prediction, the Jesuit graves where Father Luis Andreu was buried have been disinterred and relocated to another site. One story has it that Fr. Luis' body was found to be not at all "incorrupt"—but rather, as decayed as it should naturally have been.[186] However, another report has it that by order of the Jesuit provincial, Fr. Luis' casket was never opened up and the state of his remains is unknown.[187] Of course, if Father Luis' body is already dust, that will only make any miracle more spectacular.

A second prediction hinged on a blind man named Joey Lomangino. Joey Lomangino was a well-known Garabandal devotee who was blinded in an accident when he was sixteen years old. He was caught up in the Garabandal drama early on, becoming, in effect, one of the principal actors, when Conchita revealed to him that the Virgin Mary had promised that Joey's eyesight would be restored on the day of the Miracle. The actual note which Conchita wrote to Joey on March 19, 1964, said: "Today at the pines, in a locution, the Blessed Virgin Mary has asked me to tell you that you will receive "new eyes" on the day of the great Miracle."[188] (This has also been translated that you "shall see on the very day of the Miracle.")[189]

The Virgin's exact quote (according to Conchita) was this: "The first thing Joey shall see will be the Miracle which my Son will perform through my intercession, and from that time on he will see permanently."[190]

It was this promise about restoring young Joey Lomangino's eyesight which captured the collective imagination of Garabandal. Maybe it was due to Joey's poignant story of losing his eyesight and then, in an anguished spiritual search, going to confession with the famous stigmatic Padre Pio (now a saint). Padre Pio reportedly saw the anger in Joey's soul, recited Joey's sins to him before absolving him (rather than Joey doing the reciting), restored Joey's sense of smell (Joey's olfactory nerves had been severed in the accident), and affirmed, when questioned, that Joey should go to Garabandal where the Virgin Mary was appearing.[191]

In the early 1960s, many Garabandal devotees believed the Miracle might occur at any moment, and fully expected to see Joey's eyesight restored while he was still a young man. To Joey's credit, the long wait for healing did not seem to have weakened his own faith. Although he had withdrawn from the public eye in recent years as his health declined, he maintained an extensive website devoted to spreading the messages of Garabandal,[192] and, like the other major players in Garabandal, remained a devout practicing Catholic his entire life.

Still, as the years ticked by and Joey reached the ripe old age of *eighty*, believers began to hold their breath: Would Joey make it to the Great Miracle? And if he didn't, what then?

The date of June 18 marked both the beginning and the end of the Garabandal apparitions. June 18, 1961 was the date when Michael the Archangel first appeared in the sunken lane to the four girls. June 18, 1965 was the day of the Virgin Mary's final message to the world in Garabandal. This significant date in the history of Garabandal—June 18—is also the day when Joey Lomangino finally died in 2014, at the age of 83.

Joey's death would *certainly* seem to negate Conchita's prediction, unless one concedes that Joey has "new eyes" now that he's in heaven. Who is to say whether the first thing Joey saw on the threshold of eternity was the Great Miracle? Yet more likely, the Virgin's promise to Joey was simply misinterpreted by Conchita. Was the Virgin confirming that the blind and sick in Garabandal on that day will be cured (as Conchita has said) and Joey would have been included, on the condition that he was still around? Or was the Virgin making a spiritual rather than a literal promise? Conchita wrote Joey another note in 1965: "May your *new eyes* be for the greater glory of God and the good of many souls. God gives them to you because He loves you and wishes that you use them for His glory."[193] It's almost as if Conchita was speaking to Joey about the "new eyes" of faith he had received at Garabandal. Joey certainly spent the past fifty years working to spread the message of Garabandal, to help souls (particularly the blind and marginalized), and to give God glory.

Yet the most likely explanation for this unfulfilled prediction is that the promise of physical healing never occurred. Instead, Conchita made it up, because she was a young girl who wanted to console her new blind friend. Joey had confided in Conchita about his hope of being healed, and Conchita had promised to speak to the Virgin about him.[194] Maybe Conchita felt pressured to return with some good news. If Conchita concocted the entire Garabandal affair—a claim that will be examined later—then her guilt about suffering pilgrims like Joey Lomangino might very well have led her to promise more than she and the Virgin could ever deliver.

Of course, if the Garabandal prophecies are true and God is delaying their fulfillment to give the world more time to change, we should be grateful for the delay rather than disappointed— even if it means the Great Miracle was the first thing Joey Lomangino saw in heaven rather than on earth, and the rest of us missed his spectacular healing.

Whatever the truth, it's indisputable that the restoration of Joey's eyesight on the day of the Miracle had become one of the popular litmus tests for the authenticity of the apparitions. How will Joey's death affect those who still believe in the apparitions of Garabandal? To answer this, we may need to look toward yet *another* Garabandal prediction. The Virgin told Conchita on December 6, 1962 that something would happen a short time before the Great Miracle which would cause many people to stop believing in the Garabandal apparitions.[195] This failed promise about Joey Lomangino certainly fits the bill. Only the death of Conchita before she announces the Great Miracle would be more damaging to belief in the apparitions of Garabandal.

Promises or prophecies about Joey and Father Luis are minor compared with the heavyweight promise of the Miracle: The purpose of the Garabandal Miracle has been described as something intended to convert the whole world, and that Russia will be converted by it.[196] The prophecy about the coming conversion of Russia originated at Fatima, shortly after Russia's communist revolution, and the striking parallels between Fatima and Garabandal—as well as some significant differences—will be dealt with in a subsequent chapter.

In yet another twist to the Miracle, the fifteen-minute Miracle itself is separate from a *permanent sign* that will remain at the Pines of Garabandal, and which, strangely enough, will be possible to film or televise, but not touch. Like their description of the Warning and the Miracle, the girls describe the Permanent Sign as something that will obviously come from God. The idea of a permanent, visible *reminder* of the fifteen-minute Global Miracle is also very much a part of the prophecies associated with the Virgin Mary's ongoing contemporary appearances at Medjugorje. The undeniable link between the Virgin's words to three separate groups of children at Fatima, Garabandal and Medjugorje demands further exploration. If each of these apparitions turns out to be authentic, why did the Virgin Mary feel the need to appear in the early 20th, mid 20th and late 20th centuries with a very similar message? Why so repetitive? Was it because of the gravity of the message, or because of our own slowness? Or both?

One obvious answer is that human beings only last so long, and by appearing every few decades, the Virgin Mary is literally reaching a whole new crowd. From a marketing standpoint, it's a smart move, something like a re-make of a successful old movie. But is it possible that we also live in particularly dangerous times, and the Mother of Jesus is trying repeatedly to warn us? If her message began with Fatima in 1917 just before the Russian Revolution, picked up again in Garabandal in 1961 on the cusp of the construction of the Berlin Wall and the Cuban Missile Crisis, and continued in Medjugorje in the 1980s prior to the crumbling of the Iron Curtain and the outbreak of war in former Yugoslavia—how much of that message remains unfulfilled yet closer than ever? And what can we glean about the mysterious nature of the Warning, the Miracle, and the Chastisement, by examining Mary's words at all three sites—Fatima, Garabandal, and Medjugorje? The next section of the book looks at this aspect of the mystery of Garabandal. But first, we must look at the final global prophecy that emerged from Garabandal: the

Chastisement. The bad news is that it is truly terrifying. The good news is that it is described as definitely "conditional"—it all depends on us.

Chapter 4

The Night of the Screams

"Look, I don't want to brag, but I'm a man, it might be said, who doesn't know fear. I go out to all parts of the village, and over the distant trails in the night just like in the day. I have never been afraid. But on those nights of the screams, with everyone together in the darkness, in silence, hearing the girls' sobbing and screeching in the distance, I shook so that my knees knocked against each other so much I couldn't stop them. You can't imagine what that was. I have never experienced anything like it."[197] **Pepe Diez, stonemason in Garabandal**

The fourth angel poured out his bowl on the sun. It was given the power to burn people with fire. People were burned by the scorching heat and blasphemed the name of God who had power over these plagues, but they did not repent or give him glory.
[198] **Revelation Chapter 16**

...we saw an Angel with a flaming sword in his left hand; flashing, it gave out flames that looked as though they would set the world on fire...
The Third Secret of Fatima

¹⁹⁹ *Mari Cruz and Conchita in ecstasy*

On June 18, 1962—exactly one year since Michael the Archangel had made his first appearance to the girls in the rocky lane—he appeared again. He was by himself again, minus the Virgin, just as he'd been in the earliest days. After the Virgin herself had begun appearing, Michael had stepped aside, showing up only sporadically to deliver communion, and the girls had seen little of him. One of the girls remarked that Michael never seemed to grow or gain weight.

But now he was back, and giving instructions. The girls were to show up at 10:30 that night in the sunken lane at the edge of the village, in the exact spot where they'd first seen him one year ago. They had to come alone, and the villagers could come as far as the last house in the village, but no further. Accounts vary as to how this prohibition was enforced. Some say they didn't dare disobey, in light of what occurred. Others said when they tried to push closer, a mysterious force held them back.

This terrible tension of trying to push closer while being held back was triggered by something almost unspeakable: The terror-stricken screams and sobs of little girls alone in the dark. By the end of this event, the entire village of Garabandal was on its knees all night, confessing sin and receiving communion because they believed it was the end of the world.

The First Night

The Night of the Screams actually occurred on two nights. On that first night, villagers became frightened when they heard the screams from Mari-Loli and Jacinta, who were about 500 feet away. Then Mari-Loli and Jacinta came into view, trying desperately to push away something which was falling on them. The girls were crying out, "Don't tell us these things! Take us away...They should confess! They should get ready!"[200]

At the same time that this disturbing event was unfolding, Conchita, who was at home with an injured leg, was experiencing the event remotely, scribbling what she saw on a piece of paper that she held up in the air even as Mari-Loli and Jacinta were piercing the summer night—this one-year anniversary night—with their screams.[201]

After their screams had ceased, Mari-Loli and Jacinta also began writing: under the Angel's direction, they wrote down a rather odd message, which had an awkward, sing-song rhythm to it, like a rap song:

The Virgin told us:
That we do not expect the Chastisement;
That without expecting it, it will come;
Since the world has not changed.
And she has already told us twice; (some believe this refers to Lourdes and Fatima)
And we do not pay attention to her,
Since the world is getting worse.
And it should change very much.
And it has not changed at all.
Prepare yourself. Confess,
Because the Chastisement will come soon.

And the world continues the same . . .
I tell you this:
That the world continues the same.
How unfortunate that it does not change!
Soon will come a very great Chastisement,
If it does not change.[202]

After dutifully penning these "lyrics," Mari-Loli and Jacinta earnestly signed their names. The village was shaken, but hoped the worst was now behind them. It wasn't.

The Second Night

The next night, Conchita joined Mari-Loli and Jacinta in the dark. A Franciscan priest who was present that night tried to approach the wailing girls, but was thwarted, either by a villager or the hand of God, depending on whom you ask. As the screams grew more terrible, the priest became more agitated, shouting, "Ten Hail Mary's to the Virgin of Mount Carmel!"[203]

As the villagers began to pray, the screams subsided. When the prayers also subsided, the screams erupted again, louder than before. So the priest and the villagers picked up their prayers again, successfully extinguishing the screams.[204] Meanwhile, Jacinta's mother also tried to break through the cordon to reach her anguished daughter, but wasn't able to.[205] Villagers described themselves as feeling their legs trembling and giving way beneath them due to the feeling of menace in the air. One villager, Eloisa de la Roza, said, "The girls let out terrifying screams…And they said, Wait! Wait!…Everyone should confess! Oh! Oh!"[206]

Those words terrified the village. After the screams finally ceased, the tear-streaked girls returned to the trembling villagers and begged them to go to confession because something terrible was about to happen. The girls proceeded to stay up the rest of the night praying, and the traumatized villagers, unable to sleep, prayed with them, and began at dawn, one by one, to confess their sins to the Franciscan priest who was on the scene.[207]

Apparently, many of them believed it was the end of everything, and the entire village went to confession. And, for the few who were out in the fields and missed the drama, Mari- Loli and Jacinta penned a second verse, even more repetitive, awkward, and childish than the first—yet somehow, also more ominous.

> *The Virgin has told us:*
> *That the world continues the same, that it has*
> *not changed at all;*
> *That few will see God; so few they are, that it is*
> *causing the Virgin great sorrow.*
> *How unfortunate it is that the world does*
> *not change!*
> *The Virgin has told us that the Chastisement*
> *is coming.*
> *As the world is not changing, the cup is filling*
> *up.*
> *How sorrowful is the Virgin, although she does*
> *not allow us to see it.*
> *Since the Virgin loves us so much, she suffers*
> *alone, since she is so good.*
> *Everyone be good, so that the Virgin will be*
> *happy!*
> *She has told us that those who are good should*
> *pray for those who are evil.*
> *Yes, we should pray to God for the world, for*
> *those who do not know Him.*
> *Be good, be very good.*[208]

With those threatening words reverberating in everyone's ears—*few will see God*—the two Nights of the Screams drew to a disquieting close. Although Mari-Loli and Jacinta dashed off two pleading, distressed stanzas in response to what they experienced, none of them actually shared what they had seen. As details gradually trickled out of what the girls were shown on those two nights, an almost unbelievable, and truly terrifying, picture emerged.

The Great Tribulation

One surprising piece of the puzzle was that, technically speaking, the first Night of the Screams was not even about the Chastisement. Instead, the girls were shown precisely what event would precede the Warning, the Miracle, and the Chastisement. Something would happen which would set these three great apocalyptic events into motion. And what was it? The girls claimed that the sign of the end times was a "great tribulation" which would virtually destroy the Church. With the destruction of the Church and the abolishing of the great prayer that is the daily Sacrifice of the Mass,[209] the world would be thrown into chaos and terror.

In 1967, Mari-Loli told a Mexican priest, Father Gustavo Morelos, that on the first Night of the Screams, they saw masses of people screaming, suffering, and terrorized. The Virgin had told them that this great tribulation was in fact not the Chastisement, but would come "because a time would arrive when the Church would appear to be on the point of perishing...We asked the Virgin what this great trial was called and she told us it was communism."[210]

Communism? The communism that crumbled overnight with barely a whimper? Conchita's Aunt Antonia testified to having heard the visionaries say in ecstasy that if people didn't mend their ways, Russia would conquer the world.[211] The apparitions at Garabandal began in 1961, when the Berlin Wall was being constructed, and the "Night of the Screams" unfolded in the summer of 1962, just before the Cuban Missile Crisis, when the two superpowers engaged in a nuclear stand-off that almost ignited nuclear war. So the girls' terror of communism seemed, at that time, well-founded. Based on the intense persecution of Christianity behind the "Iron and Bamboo Curtains," (as well as the executions of thousands of Catholic clergy during the Spanish Civil War), it's easy to understand the girls' fear of a time when, as Mari-Loli described in an interview, priests would go into
84

hiding, and communism apparently would have covered the world.[212]

It seems that the girls' warning of communism overtaking the world—while perfectly understandable at the time—was a premonition of a future that never arrived.

Or was it?

In 1965, Conchita told German author Albrecht Weber that all the events would unfold when communism came again:

"What do you mean by comes again?"

"Yes, when it newly comes again," she replied.

"Does that mean that communism will go away before that?"

"I don't know," she said in reply, "the Blessed Virgin simply said 'when communism comes again'."[213]

Only recently, this idea might have seemed laughable. But capitalism, only a few years ago confidently seen as the clear ideological and economic winner on the world stage, currently has a soiled reputation as the global economy spins into chaos. Joint military exercises are a common occurrence between Russia and an emerging, powerful China. Meanwhile, the U.S., once the clear global counter-balance to communism, is deeply divided internally, as well as spiritually, morally, and economically weakened.

But what in the world does this have to do with the Virgin Mary? The peculiar fact is that based on her words about Russia both at Fatima and Garabandal, the Virgin appears clearly anti-communist. Today, the Cold War is often portrayed as the result of cartoonish, buffoonish paranoia on both sides. Communism is frequently depicted as a more equitable system than capitalism, which only the greedy seriously oppose. Aren't the Virgin Mary's politics out-of-touch and out-of-date? And doesn't this undermine the credibility of the Garabandal apparitions as coming from God, and make it much more likely that they spring from human beings formed by the politics of their times? The

Garabandal apparitions could arguably be viewed as a quaint Cold War artifact.

Yet the core conflict with communism, for Christians, lies not in sharing with one's neighbor, but in atheism. Communism denies the existence of God and, as a consequence, sets up the state as God instead: all-powerful, all-providing, and all-punishing. The United States originally declared its independence based on the belief that God has endowed all human beings with inalienable rights—but in communism, the highest authority is Government because there is no God. Government bestows and takes away all rights—it even bestows and takes away God. This is where the inevitable clash between communism and Christianity lies. And this is why some believe that Revelation 12—with its image of a heavenly battle between a pregnant woman giving birth to a male child and a red dragon bent on devouring him—is about the implacable enmity between true communism and the true church. One system is pro-God, and one is, quite simply, anti-God.

Pope John XXIII wrote in 1961 about the fundamental opposition between communism and Christianity, noting that previous popes had made it clear that no Catholic could subscribe even to moderate socialism. "The reason is that Socialism is founded on a doctrine of human society which is bounded by time and takes no account of any objective other than that of material well-being."[214] Of course, capitalism could also be described this way, and governments can be quite anti-God without wearing the communist label.

Eradicating God from society, and trying to eradicate God from human hearts, is the primary characteristic of the political system which the Virgin Mary opposes. The Catechism of the Catholic Church also addresses those who attempt to build a man-made utopia on earth while excluding God: "The Antichrist's deception already begins to take shape in the world every time the claim is made to realize within history that messianic hope which can only be realized beyond history through the eschatological judgment. The Church has rejected even modified forms of this falsification of the kingdom to come...especially the "intrinsically perverse" political form of a secular messianism."[215]

Although the messages from the Virgin Mary at both Fatima and Garabandal seem almost embarrassingly anti-communist to some modern ears, it's because the two belief systems are indeed incompatible.

Nevertheless, the predicted communist tribulation will involve something much more menacing than "moderate socialism." Based on the description of terror, it sounds like brutal totalitarianism. Mari-Loli told Christine Bocabeille that the Warning will come, "When Russia will unexpectedly and suddenly overrun and overwhelm a great part of the free world. God does not want this to happen so quickly."[216]

There's yet another clue about the "tribulation of communism" which may point, not to a past communist era, but to a future one.

In the same book by Albrecht Weber, Conchita reportedly stated that this communist tribulation wouldn't break out until the Pope returns from a trip to Moscow. It was a dream of Pope John Paul II to visit Moscow. Although he didn't achieve it, the dream certainly did not die under Pope Benedict, and Orthodox and Catholic theologians have been in ongoing discussions about greater church unity.

Pope Francis shows no sign of backing away from Christian unity. For the first time since the Great Schism one thousand years ago, the Patriarch of Constantinople attended the Pope's inauguration in Rome. The Patriarch, Bartholomew I, also met Pope Francis on a joint pilgrimage to Jerusalem—almost one thousand years after a Pope and Patriarch had excommunicated each other. Later, we'll look at how the fragmentation and reunification of Christianity may figure into the Garabandal messages and the End Times scenario.

As we've seen, the first Night of the Screams was a preview of the tribulation of totalitarian communism that is predicted to overrun the world and destroy the Church. Jacinta told Ramon Perez and Jacques Serre in an interview in 1979: "These difficult events will take place before the Warning because the Warning itself will occur when the situation will be at its worst."

In the midst of the resulting confusion, chaos and terror—when things are "at their worst"—will come the Warning, an electrifying awakening of each person's conscience, and then the Miracle, an irrefutable sign of God's love in the sky. These two signal events are meant to return the world to a God it no longer believes in, its own Creator.

And if the world doesn't then return to the God who created it? The answer to that question is what the girls saw on the second Night of the Screams.

Bowls of Wrath?

The End Times is a great and terrifying drama which unfolds throughout the Bible, but the timeline is difficult to piece together and understand.[217] There are various biblical references to a time of great distress or tribulation,[218] and it's debatable whether this refers to one time period only, or to multiple periods in history. What is clear is that in Matthew 24, Jesus describes a time of unparalleled distress, which has never occurred before, and *never will again*. In other words, it appears that life on earth will continue after this difficult period, and never again will there be such great tribulation. There is also disagreement about how close this "Great Tribulation" is to the physical return of Jesus Christ and the final judgment of all humankind.

The End Times or Last Days spoken of in the Scriptures may include the end of a particular age—an evil age filled with violence, war, and suffering—and the ushering in of a long-awaited era of genuine peace, of reconciliation with God and one another. The Book of Isaiah describes this time as a period when swords will be beaten into plowshares and all nations will stream to the holy mountain of God.[219] This passage specifically states that nations will not train for war anymore—a prophecy which has yet to be fulfilled. The Book of Zechariah also describes a time when the Lord will be king over all the earth, and Jerusalem will be completely secure.[220] The Book of Revelation speaks of a thousand-year reign of those who were martyred for Christ, and the Virgin Mary at Fatima also spoke of a period of peace that would be granted to the world. If there is an end of a time of unparalleled distress, followed by the granting of a period of peace to the world, it will not come about through any secular political system or earthly messiah—but only through God.

Still, human beings have a role to play in determining the outcome. A strong strain of Christian fatalism is embraced these days which insists that Christians can't change anything that's coming because it's set in scriptural stone. Yet there is another Christian view, which believes that it is not the will of God to bring about global change through death and destruction; it is God's will to bring about change through human repentance and divine mercy. It's sobering that the manner in which the kingdom of God arrives in its fullness ultimately depends on human response. Even if human beings choose to grow worse instead of better, the Bible in the last chapter of the Book of Malachi reveals a God who intends to eventually act decisively to end *all evil*:

> *For the day is coming, blazing like an oven,*
> *when all the arrogant and all evildoers will be stubble,*
> *And the day that is coming will set them on fire,*
> *leaving them neither root nor branch,*
> *says the LORD of hosts.*
> *20 But for you who fear my name, the sun of justice*
> *will arise with healing in its wings;*
> *And you will go out leaping like calves from the stall*
> *21 and tread down the wicked;*
> *They will become dust under the soles of your feet,*

on the day when I take action, says the LORD of hosts.[221]

This, after all, is what believers frequently plead for and non-believers frequently complain about: If God is good and all-powerful, how can he allow the continued suffering of children, and the ongoing triumph of evil? Apparently, God does not intend to allow it indefinitely.

But this raises another question: If the human race is in crisis and increasingly separated from its own Creator, why doesn't that Creator just show himself, answer the question about his existence once and for all, and end the discussion? That's precisely what the Warning and Miracle are all about: First, an irrefutable revelation of God to *each and every human conscience*; then a blinding Sign in the Sky to follow up. Short of dying and meeting one's Maker, what more could any human demand from God to prove His existence? Yet if the inner revelation and outer sign in the sky don't persuade, then, unfortunately, dying and meeting one's Maker is exactly what the Chastisement is all about.

The girls have described the Great Chastisement as something that will come directly from God. Mari-Loli gave a detailed description of it, and signed a copy of her description which she gave to her friend Maria Saraco in the early 1970s. I interviewed Maria Saraco in 2009, and she confirmed this story, and sent me a copy of the description that she has published in her newsletter, *The Vigil*, which is also available on-line.[222]

Here is how visionary Mari-Loli describes the Great Chastisement:

There will come a time when all motors and machines will stop; a terrible wave of heat will strike the earth and men will begin to feel a great thirst. In desperation they will seek water, but this will evaporate from the heat . . . Then almost everyone will despair and they will seek to kill one another . . . But they will lose their strength and fall to the earth. Then it will be understood that it is God alone Who has permitted this.[223]

In the 1960s, the description sounded so odd as to be unbelievable. All motors and machines will stop? But today, the description fits precisely with what we now know is an electromagnetic pulse, or EMP—something it's safe to say the girls of Garabandal knew nothing about. An EMP can be caused by nuclear blasts or solar storms. The U.S. Senate has held hearings on the possibility of EMPs being used in terrorist attacks, and NASA has funded the study of EMPs caused by "severe space weather." They agree that all electronic equipment would be "fried" during an EMP, and nothing electrical would work after that. In 1859, intense solar activity wreaked havoc on the telegraph system, knocking operators out of their chairs and setting fire to the telegraph paper rolls.

No solar event of that magnitude has occurred in our high-tech age, but some scientists are asking, "What if?" A recent American T.V. series opens with precisely this scenario: All electricity, all motors, all machines, all artificial power of any kind simply stop. The result, of course, is the disintegration of modern civilization. Although many assume we are going to destroy ourselves, the Garabandal description of an EMP sounds like it comes from the sun, and not from nuclear war.

… a terrible wave of heat will strike the earth…

Mari-Loli's description of the Great Chastisement also is frighteningly similar to the bowls of wrath emptied onto the earth in Revelation 16:

The fourth angel emptied his bowl over the sun and it was made to scorch people with its flames…the fifth angel emptied his bowl over the throne of the beast and its whole empire was plunged into darkness (no more electricity?)*…the sixth angel emptied his bowl over the great river Euphrates; all the water dried up…*

Horrifically, Mari-Loli's description of the Great Chastisement only gets worse:

Then we saw a crowd in the midst of flames. The people ran to hurl themselves into the lakes and seas. But the water seemed to boil and in place of putting out the flames, it seemed to enkindle them even more.

In a filmed 1984 interview, Mari-Loli said that what she remembered most from that night was people screaming and running to get into the water "but the fire was just all over the place."[224] What Mari-Loli saw was so terrible that she begged the Virgin Mary to take the young children away with her before it happened. Mary gave the unsettling answer that, "By the time this happens, all the children will be gone."

Some have said she meant that the children of 1962 Garabandal (for whom Mari-Loli was specifically pleading) would be grown and gone from Garabandal by the time this event occurs. But it remains a haunting reply, and a terrifying vision. It's impossible to find a silver lining in the horrific description of the Chastisement itself, and yet this very strange perspective on the Chastisement was given by the Virgin:

Jesus does not send the Chastisement to discourage you, but to help you and rebuke you for not paying attention to Him. He will send you the Warning to purify you and to prepare you for the Miracle. In this Miracle, He clearly proves the love He has for you as well as His desire for you to carry out the Message.[225]

To say that the human race would be discouraged by this particular Chastisement is an understatement. Was the Virgin saying that Jesus does not wish the *threat* of the Chastisement to discourage, but to help and rebuke? After all, she then reminds us of the purification process of the Warning as well as the emphatic love of the Miracle meant to return us to God without a Chastisement.

Another explanation for this strange statement is from Conchita, who herself used the word "chastisement" to describe the *Warning*: "It (the Warning) is like a chastisement. We shall see the consequences of the sins we have committed. I think that those who do not despair will experience great good from it for their sanctification."[226]

Maybe the Virgin Mary was referring to the Warning when she spoke of a chastisement that was meant to help rather than discourage. Whatever she meant, if the Warning and Miracle are enough to transform the human race, then the threat of the horrific Chastisement described here does not have to be fulfilled. Conchita in her diary described the Chastisement as completely conditional, and if the Warning and Miracle return the world to God, the Chastisement will never come.[227]

PART 2

Garabandal—The Missing Link?

[228] *Fatima, Portugal*

Chapter 5

Is Garabandal the Sequel to Fatima?

"...if we have not yet seen the complete fulfillment of the final part of this prophecy, we are going towards it little by little with great strides." **Sister Lucia, the sole surviving Fatima seer, in a letter about the Third Secret of Fatima to Pope John Paul II in 1982**

"With regard to this great vision of the suffering of the popes, beyond the circumstances of John Paul II, other realities are indicated which over time will develop and become clear." **Pope Benedict XVI commenting on the Third Secret of Fatima in 2010**

The Virgin's messages at Garabandal about a future communist tribulation and the subsequent conversion of Russia provide an undeniable link to the famous Church-approved apparitions in Fatima, Portugal. In fact, there are those who argue that Garabandal was merely a continuation and amplification of the Fatima message—the Fourth Secret of Fatima, so to speak. Is it possible that when the Catholic Church failed to release the Third Secret of Fatima in 1960, the Virgin Mary came along in 1961 and released it herself, at Garabandal? Or are the similarities merely evidence of apparition plagiarism?

Astonishingly, someone quite unexpected recently poured gasoline on the speculative fires surrounding the controversial Third Secret of Fatima. Pope Benedict himself hinted that the released Third Secret, however accurate and authentic it is, perhaps hasn't yet been *completely* fulfilled. Does Garabandal give us additional clues as to what that fulfillment might be?

At both Fatima, Portugal and Garabandal, Spain, the Virgin Mary came with warnings, and with ominous, apocalyptic predictions about what will befall humankind if the warnings go unheeded. Part of what Mary predicted at Fatima has indeed come tragically true; but then, so has part of what Mary predicted at Garabandal. Likewise, a final apocalyptic portion of the Fatima message may remain unfulfilled, just as it does at Garabandal.

The Fatima-Garabandal Link

At the time of the Virgin's reported appearances, both Fatima, Portugal and Garabandal, Spain were geographically remote, rocky, and rural. In both places, Mary supposedly appeared to children who were instantly caught up in controversy and subjected to severe skepticism, sometimes from the Church, and sometimes from others. (The children of Fatima were kidnapped, imprisoned, and threatened with being boiled in oil by Artur de Oliveira Santos, the district administrator, who was not a Catholic Church official but a communist and Freemason. Newspapers at the time spoke glowingly of Santos "who has been exemplary in the fulfillment of his duties," and witheringly of the similarities between Fatima visionary Lucia and "that ever-talkative parrot that was Bernadette of Lourdes.")[229]

At both Fatima and Garabandal, besides calling for prayers and penance from believers, the Virgin Mary delivered an apocalyptic warning if the world didn't repent. Yet the first clue to the connection between Garabandal and Fatima doesn't lie in any of these obvious parallels. Instead, the initial link between the two 20th century apparition sites lies in a seemingly inconsequential detail: what the Virgin Mary chose to wear. In the Virgin's last visit to Fatima, she appeared just as she appeared in her first visit to Garabandal: as Our Lady of Mt. Carmel.[230] For some reason, in the forty-year gap between apparitions, the Virgin Mary decided not to change her clothes.

Believe it or not, Mary's clothes matter. At different apparitions and in different devotional images, she has been granted an array of titles and has been clothed in an assortment of garb. Her clothing and appearance are usually loaded with symbolism befitting her message to a particular time and place. When she appeared in Mexico in 1531, her appearance and dress—including a black Aztec maternity sash tied round her waist—so moved the local populace that it resulted in mass conversions of millions of indigenous people, conversions that the Spanish colonialists had theretofore been unable to accomplish. Today, Our Lady of Guadalupe Shrine is the top religious destination in the entire world.

In Mary's last appearance in Fatima (and also Lourdes) and in her first in Garabandal, she appeared as "Our Lady of Mount Carmel" complete with scapular[231] in hand. (A scapular, based on a monk's garment, is a cloth religious medal worn under the clothes to signify special devotion to God.) Some assert that the Virgin's chosen apparel, along with other evidence, confirms that Garabandal is merely a continuation of her appearance and messages at Fatima. Of course, there is also the possibility that the girls of Garabandal were familiar with the Fatima apparitions. However, the Virgin Mary only appeared as Our Lady of Mount Carmel in her final appearance at Fatima, and she is generally known in connection with Fatima as Our Lady of the Rosary.

The Mount Carmel link between Fatima and Garabandal may also be significant because of Mount Carmel's connection to the End Times. The Hebrew prophet of Mount Carmel, Elijah, was a beleaguered voice of purity and righteousness in a cesspool of violence, corruption and idolatry, who had the power to stop rain and call fire down from the sky. Amazingly enough, Elijah is also supposed to put in an appearance in the Last Days. In the Book of Malachi, the Lord promises to send

Elijah the prophet,
Before the day of the LORD comes,
the great and terrible day;

He will turn the heart of fathers to their sons,
and the heart of sons to their fathers,
Lest I come and strike
the land with utter destruction.[232]

A famous and fiery scene involving Elijah takes place in the Book of Kings. All of the people of Israel, along with 450 prophets of the god Baal, gather with Elijah on Mount Carmel. Elijah proposes a duel: the 450 will call on Baal to send fire down upon the altar, while Elijah will call upon Yahweh. Whoever lights the fire wins, and the winner clearly has the pipeline to the true God. The prophets of Baal get to go first, and they spend hours leaping and cutting on themselves to summon the fire, which remains unlit.

Elijah steps up to the plate, and the rest is history: First, Elijah drenches the altar with water to make sure it's good and wet. Then he summons fire down which instantly turns the sacrificed meat and the altar to ash. The Israelites, who have been following Baal with wild abandon, fall to their faces in worship of Elijah's true God.

Mount Carmel is a symbol of turning away from false gods and back to the truth, and Mary's words at both Fatima and Garabandal, where she appeared as Our Lady of Mount Carmel, are certainly a call for repentance and return to God.

John the Baptist is traditionally viewed as being the return of Elijah when he appears on the scene dressed like the ancient Hebrew prophet, baptizing and preparing people for the imminent arrival of the Messiah. But the prophetic verse in the Book of Malachi says Elijah is going to come before **the great and terrible day of the Lord.**

The appearance of Jesus on earth 2,000 years ago is not typically viewed as the "great and terrible day of the Lord." Instead, Jesus came as the Lamb of God, brimming with mercy and desire to take away the sin of the world. However, some speculate the coming of Jesus did indeed kick off "the day of the

Lord" and the "End Times," which will continue until Jesus returns. Others believe the "great and terrible day of the Lord" is much more specific and finite. Whatever "the day of the Lord" means and whenever it's supposed to occur, the biblical descriptions are terrifying: a day of wrath, distress, anguish, ruin, devastation, gloom, clouds, thick darkness, trumpet blast and battle cry against the high towers; a day on which silver and gold will not save us, and the whole earth is consumed.[233]

The Book of Revelation also speaks of Elijah-like figures making an appearance in the End Times. In Chapter Eleven, there are two witnesses who come in the last days prophesying and "wearing sackcloth"—a sign of grief over sin. The two witnesses are described as two olive trees and two lamps *that stand before the Lord of the world*. Similar to Elijah, fire will be able to come from the mouths of the two witnesses and consume their enemies, and they also can keep the rain from falling while they are prophesying, as well as end the drought.

At the time the Book of Revelation was written, some identified the two witnesses as Peter and Paul. In our own times, speculation abounds about whether these "two witnesses" are two distinct individuals, or are merely symbols of the voice of "the law and the prophets" in the last days. If they are individuals, will these "two witnesses" actually be walking, talking human beings born and bred in our time, or will they be macabre, horror movie resurrections of long-dead personages like Elijah and Moses (the two witnesses at the transfiguration of Jesus), or Elijah and Enoch (two biblical figures who never died, but were "taken up into the sky.") Who the heck knows? But it's worth noting that the Virgin Mary was also assumed bodily into heaven according to Catholic belief, and appeared as Our Lady of Mount Carmel at both Fatima and Garabandal with words of warning and love for children whom she insisted were wandering dangerously far away from God.

Is it possible that the apparitions of the Virgin Mary in the 20th century offer an unexpected parallel to Elijah's ministry of miracles and warnings, as well as to John's spiritual preparation of the people for the coming of Jesus? Is it possible that the pure and righteous prophetic voice predicted to re-appear in the End Times to return the hearts of the children to their father looks nothing like we thought (he) would?

He will turn the heart of fathers to their sons,
and the heart of sons to their fathers,
Lest I come and strike
the land with utter destruction.[234]

If the Virgin Mary did appear at both Fatima and Garabandal, were there any similarities in her messages both times? Her messages at Fatima were limited to three famous secrets, now completely revealed, although the last one, in particular, remains steeped in controversy. At Fatima, Mary only appeared six times. At Garabandal, she hung around for much longer, and by all accounts, said a great many more things. Or did she?

Mary's official, on-the-record "messages to the world" at Garabandal were also strictly limited in both quantity and length; surprisingly, there were only two of them, which will be examined in a later chapter. Furthermore, the three children of Fatima, just like the four girls of Garabandal, were first visited several times by an angel, who gave the children communion and instructed them to pray before the Virgin appeared.

The Secrets of Fatima

What exactly did the Virgin Mary say to three shepherd children in Fatima, Portugal in 1917? The oldest of the children of Fatima was a ten-year-old named Lucia Santos, and she was also the sole survivor into adulthood; Francisco, nine, and Jacinta Marto, seven, both had perished by 1920, victims of Spanish influenza. Lucia later became a nun, and by 1941, at the age of 24, she was Sister Lucia and was writing down the first and second secrets of Fatima for the Bishop of Fatima.

According to Sister Lucia, the First "Secret" was a vision of hell.

Our Lady showed us a great sea of fire which seemed to be under the earth. Plunged in this fire were demons and souls in human form, like transparent burning embers, all blackened or burnished bronze, floating about in the conflagration, now raised into the air by the flames that issued from within themselves together with great clouds of smoke, now falling back on every side like sparks in a huge fire, without weight or equilibrium, amid shrieks and groans of pain and despair, which horrified us and made us tremble with fear. The demons could be distinguished by their terrifying and repulsive likeness to frightful and unknown animals, all black and transparent. This vision lasted but an instant. How can we ever be grateful enough to our kind heavenly Mother, who had already prepared us by promising, in the first Apparition, to take us to heaven. Otherwise, I think we would have died of fear and terror.[235]

What exactly was the purpose of this little horror show? Yes, there is a hell, and people can go there. Everyone knows that—well, maybe they did in 1917. Perhaps the Virgin Mary unveiled hell at the beginning of the 20th century because she knew that by the end of it, few would believe it even existed. Presumably it was not the intention of the Virgin Mary to simply terrify the children. Instead, she had a point: In her Second "Secret," she began to unveil a plan.

We then looked up at Our Lady, who said to us so kindly and so sadly: You have seen hell where the souls of poor sinners go. To save them, God wishes to establish in the world devotion to my Immaculate Heart. If what I say to you is done, many souls will be saved and there will be peace. The war is going to end: but if people do not cease offending God, a worse one will break out during the Pontificate of Pius XI. When you see a night illumined by an unknown light, know that this is the great sign given you by God that He is about to punish the world for its crimes by means of war, famine, and persecutions of the Church and of the Holy Father.

Mary delivered this message in Fatima on July 13, 1917, during World War I. Although World War 1 was called "the war to end all wars," Mary accurately predicted when another, worse war would come—something unimaginable to shell-shocked Europeans at the time. She also predicted the red aurora that

101

would appear all over Europe on January 25, 1938, signaling the onset of World War II.

After this warning about another, more horrific war, Mary then completed the Second Secret, but not, as one might expect, with a warning about the rise of Hitler and Nazi Germany. Instead, only a few short months before the Bolsheviks and Vladimir Lenin came to power in Russia, she said this:

> To prevent this, I shall come to ask for the consecration of Russia to my Immaculate Heart, and the Communion of reparation on the First Saturdays. If my requests are heeded, Russia will be converted, and there will be peace; if not, she will spread her errors throughout the world, causing wars and persecutions of the Church. The good will be martyred; the Holy Father will have much to suffer; various nations will be annihilated. In the end, my Immaculate Heart will triumph. The Holy Father will consecrate Russia to me, and she shall be converted, and a period of peace will be granted to the world [236]

Sister Lucia reportedly said later that she and her two cousins did not know the meaning of the word "Russia," and that they believed it was referring to a wicked woman whom the Virgin wished to convert.[237] Perhaps the Virgin Mary was focused on Communism rather than Nazism because she already knew which one would endure. Regardless, Mary accurately predicted the rise of Russia as a global superpower.

Part of this second secret appears to be the Virgin Mary's description of the coming Cold War. There is no doubt that, from the Christian point of view, Russia spread her errors throughout the world, causing wars, persecuting Christians, and martyring many people, including tens of millions in Russia alone. More Christians were martyred in the 20th century than in all other centuries combined.

Parts of the second secret, however, open up speculation that perhaps Mary was not describing the Cold War which has already taken place, but something worse yet to come: *the Holy Father will have much to suffer; various nations will be annihilated.* Some say this has not yet occurred, although Pope John Paul II himself suffered personally under communism, and the Catholic Church (along with Orthodox, Protestants, and all other religions) suffered enormously behind the "Iron and Bamboo Curtains." If the "annihilation of nations" refers to the re-drawing of borders, annexations and re-naming of nations, this certainly happened during and after World War II as the Soviet Union expanded and the Iron Curtain was drawn across Europe. On the other hand, if the annihilation refers to atomic destruction, then the world has been spared the fulfillment of this prediction thus far. It remains an open question whether these prophecies in the Second Secret of Fatima can be described as already fulfilled; as something from which humankind has been spared because history has been permanently altered with the dissolution of the Soviet Union; or as a prophecy that will be fulfilled in the future, as possibly predicted at Garabandal.

And what about the final portion of the Second Secret? *In the end, my Immaculate Heart will triumph. The Holy Father will consecrate Russia to me, and she shall be converted, and a period of peace will be granted to the world* [238]

The consecration of Russia to the Immaculate Heart of Mary—one of two conditions for peace in the world given during the messages of Fatima—remains controversial. In 1917, Mary's exact wording was "I will come" to ask for the consecration of Russia—which she apparently did in an appearance to Sister Lucia on June 13, 1929, saying: "The moment has come in which God asks the Holy Father to make, in union with all the bishops of the world, the Consecration of Russia to My Immaculate Heart, promising to save it by this means." [239]

By that time, persecution in Russia was in full swing and the Vatican knew it. Jesuit Father Edmond Walsh, a member of the American Relief Association, had been sent to Russia in charge of famine relief. He wrote to the Vatican Secretariat of State Cardinal Gasparri that executions, imprisonments, exiling, confiscations and "other savage manifestations of class hatred and revenge" made their work impossible. [240]

Pope Pius XI himself wrote on February 2, 1930, to Cardinal

Pompili, Vicar of Rome: "This past year during the Christmas holy days, not only were hundreds of churches closed, great numbers of icons burned, all workers and schoolchildren compelled to work, and Sundays suppressed, but they even compelled factory workers, both men and women, to sign a declaration of formal apostasy and hatred against God, or else be deprived of their bread rationing cards, clothing and lodging, without which every inhabitant of this poor country is reduced to dying of hunger, misery and cold."[241]

Sister Lucia's message from Mary to consecrate Russia had apparently been passed on to both the Bishop of Leiria-Fatima and Pope Pius XI in 1930 by her confessor, Jesuit Father Jose Bernardo Goncalves.[242] Although Pope Pius XI never consecrated Russia, it is curious that beginning in June 1930 he asked everyone to pray at the end of each Mass specifically for the conversion of Russia and to invoke the aid of the Virgin Mary and St. Michael toward this end.[243] Whatever his reasons, after Pope Pius XI failed to consecrate Russia in 1930, the "spreading of Russia's errors" began right away. In a striking connection between Garabandal and Fatima, the spreading of Russia's errors, from the Church's perspective, began in Spain when 1931 elections brought to power an anti-clerical government and led to the sacking and burning of churches, the dissolving and expulsion of religious orders, and the confiscation of the Church's goods.[244]

"Destruction was methodically ordered in all cities. On May 11, twelve convents and schools, including the University of Arts and Trades, were burned at Madrid. An equal number burned at Alicante. At Malaga, before the eyes of government troops and the police, who did nothing, the convent of Jesuits, the convent of Augustinians and the episcopal palace were burned in broad daylight. At Cadix, the convent of San Domingo, the Jesuits and Saint Francis along with the Carmel were burned. At Burgos the convents were pillaged. At Grenada, at Cordova, and at Seville churches were burned..."[245]

Over the course of several years of right-left political power struggles, Spain eventually descended into civil war between the Soviet-backed Republican government and the Nationalist rebels led by General Francisco Franco and aided by Hitler and Mussolini. In the end, Spain suffered more than 500,000 deaths, including the murder of thirteen bishops, more than seven thousand priests and other religious, and the destruction of 20,000 churches. Remarkably, all this took place during a period when Sister Lucia resided in a convent in Spain, where she expected to be martyred, "But it really seems to me that They (Heaven) did not want me there now."[246]

In 1937, the Bishop of Leiria-Fatima, alarmed by what was taking place in Spain, himself wrote to Pope Pius XI asking for the consecration of Russia to the Immaculate Heart of Mary as requested at Fatima. In 1938, the Portuguese bishops wrote to Pope Pius XI expressing their thanksgiving to the Immaculate Heart of Mary for having saved Portugal from communist rule after they consecrated the country to her in 1931, and begging the Pope to likewise consecrate the whole world to her.[247] On April 1, 1939, church bells rang out freely again in Spain with the defeat of the Republican forces, and, from one perspective, "the great Spanish cities returned from Stalin and Bakunin to Saint Teresa of Avila and Saint Ignatius of Loyola."[248] What followed, though, was the long dictatorship of General Franco.

A short two months later, in June 1939, Sister Lucia wrote this rather prophetic and heartbreaking letter to a Jesuit priest: *Our Lady promised to defer the calamity of war if this devotion (the First Saturday confession, communion, and rosary) were to be propagated and put into practice. We see her holding back this punishment as much as efforts are being made to propagate it, but I'm afraid we do not do as much as we can and God, being displeased, will withdraw the arm of His mercy and let the world be devastated by that punishment which will be horrible, horrible.*[249]

Although Pope Pius XI had spoken out forcibly against communism during this time, and he had been notified of the Fatima request by several parties, the consecration of Russia had still not taken place in 1940. Sister Lucia heard these words from Jesus during this time: *Pray for the Holy Father, sacrifice yourself so that his courage does not succumb under the bitterness that oppresses him...His Holiness will obtain an abbreviation of these days of tribulation if he takes heed of my wishes by promulgating the Act of Consecration of the whole world to the Immaculate Heart of Mary, with a special mention of Russia...*[250]

Perhaps the change in Jesus' words from "the Consecration of Russia" to "the Consecration of the whole world with special mention of Russia" was because Russia's errors had now reached the world. Accordingly, Sister Lucia wrote this letter to Pope Pius XII in 1940:

In several intimate communications our Lord has not stopped insisting on this request, promising lately, to shorten the days of tribulation which He has determined to punish the nations for their crimes, through war, famine and several persecutions of the Holy Church and Your Holiness, if you will consecrate the world to the Immaculate Heart of Mary, with a special mention for Russia, and order that all the Bishops of the world do the same in union with Your Holiness.[251]

Tuy, Spain, 2nd of December of 1940.

Maria Lucia de Jesus

Fascinatingly, in the same letter, Sister Lucia also wrote this:

Most Holy Father, if in the union of my soul with God I have not been deceived, our Lord promises a special protection to our country in this war (World War II), *due to the consecration of the nation by the Portuguese Prelates, to the Immaculate Heart of Mary; as proof of the graces that would have been granted to other nations, had they also consecrated themselves to Her.*[252]

The bishops of Portugal consecrated their country to the Immaculate Heart of Mary in both 1931 and 1938, and many Portuguese believed that was why they were spared tragedies like that of the Spanish Civil War, as well as the ravages of World War II. In fact, Portugal itself had just gone through its own revolution—including the sacking of churches and suppression of Christianity—not long before the Virgin appeared in Fatima in 1917, which perhaps explains why the bishops of Portugal were so quick to respond to the request.

By 1942, World War II was underway and the accuracy of Fatima's 1917 message had become painfully apparent. In an attempt to finally respond to the requests made by the Virgin Mary at Fatima, Pope Pius XII in 1942 consecrated the entire *world* (but not specifically Russia, and not in union with the world's bishops) to the Immaculate Heart of Mary. On May 4, 1943, Sister Lucia wrote a letter to her confessor Father Goncalves in which she stated: "He (Jesus) promises the end of the war shortly in answer to the act of consecration made by His Holiness. But since it was incomplete, the conversion of Russia will take place later."[253]

Why didn't Pope Pius XII consecrate Russia? Possibly because it was 1942, and the western democracies were now allied with the Soviet Union in the war against Nazi Germany: "At the request of President Roosevelt, the Vatican has refrained from all polemics against the communist regime, but this silence which weighs on our consciences has not been understood by the Soviet leaders, who continue their persecutions against the Church and the faithful in the USSR and the countries occupied by Red Army troops."[254]

Belatedly, in 1952, Pope Pius XII consecrated Russia specifically (*so now We dedicate and consecrate all the peoples of Russia to that same Immaculate Heart*),[255] but *without* the participation of the world's bishops. In 1964, Pope Paul VI renewed Pius's consecration of Russia but without the participation of the bishops, even though they were assembled for Vatican II.[256] (Some believe the Virgin was appearing in Garabandal at this time precisely to encourage the consecration of Russia by the pope and bishops during Vatican II.)[257] In 1967, Pope Paul VI called for renewed consecration to the Immaculate Heart in general.[258] So at least four attempts or versions of consecration were made, with apparently none of them fulfilling the explicit criteria of consecrating Russia to Mary's Immaculate Heart, specifically in union with all the bishops of the world.

Did John Paul Finally Consecrate Russia?

As far as we know, Pope John Paul II did not exhibit any burning need to rectify this situation until the fateful day of May 13, 1981. On that day, which was the anniversary of the first apparition at Fatima, he was shot four times in St Peter's square, lost three-quarters of his blood, and almost died. Mehmet Ali Agca claimed (but later denied) that he was working with the Bulgarian secret service and the KGB, who were worried about the Pope's influence in Poland (with good reason.) Yuri Andropov, who was KGB Director at the time, believed the Pope's election was part of a conspiracy to bring down the Soviet Union (again, quite prescient.) Andropov described the Pope as "our enemy," and sent a memo saying, "Because of the activities of the Church in Poland, our activities designed to atheize the youth not only cannot diminish but must intensely develop."[259]

But Andropov's frantic instructions had little chance against Pope John Paul II, who, on his first papal visit to Poland in 1979, drew not thousands, as the communist officials expected, but millions, and told them, "Christ cannot be kept out of the history of man in any part of the globe, at any longitude or latitude." The crowds' response? "We want God! We want God!"[260]

On May 13, 1981, in Rome, Pope John Paul bent down to look at a small girl who was wearing an image of Our Lady of Fatima when two bullets whizzed over him where his head had just been. Although he was subsequently shot four times, he believed that it was Our Lady of Fatima who saved his life. He was still recovering in his hospital bed when he reviewed the documents on Fatima. Almost immediately, he also began the strangely frustrating process of trying to consecrate the world, with special mention of Russia, to the Immaculate Heart of Mary in union with all the bishops of the world. In fact, he immediately wrote a prayer called the "Act of Entrustment," which, since he was still recovering from his wounds, he recorded and broadcast on June 7, 1981. In that Act, he entrusted the whole human family, and *also those whose act of entrustment you too await in a particular way.*[261]

Then, on May 13, 1982, Pope John Paul II invited the bishops of the world to join him in consecrating the world and Russia to the Immaculate Heart of Mary. John Paul emphasized the collegiality of the act, mentioning that the pastors of the Church were united for this occasion, just as Christ desired of Peter and the Apostles. Nonetheless, many bishops were unable to attend because the letters went out too late. Furthermore, the reference to Russia was oblique. Without naming names, John Paul simply consecrated the nations *which particularly need to be entrusted and consecrated.*[262] The consecration took place in Fatima, where the Pope thanked the Virgin for saving his life.

Pope John Paul II then made several more "renewals" of the consecration, in an effort to make sure the job was done. At the end of 1983, with many cardinals and bishops in attendance for the Synod of Bishops, the Pope renewed the 1982 consecration, adding, *"...in your presence and in union with you, I wish to repeat what I said on 13 May 1982."*

Finally, on March 25, 1984 at the Vatican, Pope John Paul II "convoked" the bishops beforehand,[263] asking them in a letter to join him in renewing both the 1942 consecration of the world and the 1952 consecration of *Russia* to the Immaculate Heart of Mary.[264] John Paul II then essentially renewed the 1982 consecration yet again before the statue of Our Lady of Fatima which was brought to Rome for the occasion: *"...repeating in substance the act that I made at Fatima on May 13, 1982. ..."*

Again, he took pains to emphasize the collegiality of the act. Yet again, the Pope did not specifically name Russia in his official remarks. Instead he made numerous indirect references to Russia, mentioning that Pope Pius XII had consecrated *the peoples for which by reason of their situation you have particular love and solicitude.* (Pope Pius XII had specifically consecrated Russia.)

Then, as if to make sure, he included everyone in the consecration: *The power of this consecration lasts for all time and embraces all individuals, peoples and nations.*[265] He made one last gallant attempt to consecrate the entire human family the next morning, *especially those in such need of this consecration, this entrustment.*[266] He also prayed, among other things, *From nuclear war...deliver us.*

Afterward, on more than one occasion, Sister Lucia confirmed that the 1984 consecration "took." Both the Bishop of Leiria-Fatima and the Apostolic Nuncio of Lisbon asked Sister Lucia (for the second time) if Russia was now consecrated. In 1982, she had said, "No," because an insufficient number of bishops had participated, due to the late invitations. But in 1984, she replied, "Yes. Now it is." The Nuncio then said, "Now we wait for the miracle." Sister Lucia answered, "God will keep His word."[267]

In a letter to Walter M. Noelker on Nov. 8, 1989, Sister Lucia said, *"Sim, està feita, tal como Nossa Senhora a pediu, desde o dia 25 de Março de 1984."* "Yes it has been done just as Our Lady asked, on 25 March 1984."[268]

She also wrote a letter on August 29, 1989, in Coimbra, Italy, to Sister Mary of Bethlehem confirming that John Paul II *wrote to all the bishops of the world asking them to unite with him. He sent for the statue of Our Lady of Fátima—the one from the little Chapel to be taken to Rome and on March 25, 1984 - publicly - with the bishops who wanted to unite with His Holiness, made the Consecration as Our Lady requested. They then asked me if it was made as Our Lady requested, and I said, "YES." Now it was made.*

She then went on to explain in the same letter that the Consecration needed to be made in union with the bishops of the world as a sign of the power of a unified church, *because this Consecration is a call for unity of all Christians...and as He asked the Father: "... that they also may be one in Us, that the world may believe that*

You have sent Me. . ." (John 17:21-23).[269]

All this energy has been expended either consecrating, trying to consecrate, or fretting over consecrating Russia to Mary's Immaculate Heart, because the Virgin said at Fatima that if her requests were heeded, Russia would be converted and there would be peace. A consecration means setting someone or something apart for a holy purpose by dedicating it to the service and worship of God, essentially transforming it from being profane to being sacred. And so the general idea seemed to be that if Russia was entrusted to God and belonged to God—rather than to communism and atheism—it would mean peace for the world. Jesus also seemed to be asking his Church to call on God and trust in God by obeying His request and uniting to consecrate Russia.

In fact, Jesus was showing humanity the shortcut to peace—not through politics and wars, bloodshed and suffering—but through God. Sadly, even His own Church was quite slow to respond in obedience and faith. But even if Jesus would naturally want Russia consecrated to God—why would He care so much about consecrating Russia to His *Mother's* heart? This was a sticking point for some theologians in the Catholic Church who believed a consecration could only be made to God, not to one of God's creatures, because it constituted idolatry.[270]

Apparently, Sister Lucia asked Jesus this exact question during an appearance to her. Sister Lucia wrote about her conversation with Jesus in a letter from her convent in Pontevedra, Spain on May 18, 1936 to her confessor Father Goncalves, after Father Goncalves asked if he should still insist on the consecration of Russia. Jesus had told Sister Lucia that he wanted Russia consecrated to his mother's heart "Because I want My whole Church to acknowledge that consecration as a triumph of the Immaculate Heart of Mary, so that it may extend its cult later on, and put devotion to this Immaculate Heart beside the devotion to my Sacred Heart."[271]

Based on this response, anyway, Jesus apparently desired that his mother be accorded special recognition and honor in her unique role as our advocate before the Son of God—a position she holds because her own heart is in perfect union with her Son's, and because of her great sacrifice in bringing the Lamb of God into the world and accompanying him all the way to the cross. It is neither James nor John who has been granted the honor of sitting beside Jesus in his kingdom, as they requested— but the Mother of Jesus upon whom this privilege has been bestowed. Because of this position of honor she holds, she is able to intercede for us in a powerful way—especially when individuals or nations are consecrated in a particular way to her loving care.

Nonetheless, there are those who argue that the 1984 act did not fulfill the explicit criteria of consecrating Russia in unity with all the bishops of the world, and they, too, offer various reports (including from a journalist and a cousin) of Sister Lucia insisting that the 1984 consecration was *not* acceptable. Some suggest that the 1989 letters from Sister Lucia, confirming the consecration, were written under orders from the Church because John Paul II was still being deluged with petitions to properly consecrate Russia and he felt that it had been accomplished. This view holds that Sister Lucia began reporting that the consecration was complete because she was under obedience to do so.[272]

A different perspective is that John Paul's 1984 consecration of Russia was confirmed by Sister Lucia in 1989 because the Soviet Union was about to fall and it was God himself who was inspiring her to share at the appropriate time. In a July 1989 interview which was subsequently published in Fatima Family Messenger magazine in October 1989, Sister Lucia said that "God accepted the Consecration of March 24, 1984 as the one that fulfilled all the conditions for the conversion of Russia." She went on to say, again: "God will keep his word."[273]

Another argument against the 1984 consecration's validity is that not all bishops participated. The Pope in 1984 invited ahead of time not just all the Catholic bishops (most of whom responded) but also Orthodox and Protestant leaders (some of whom responded). Sister Lucia said, "The Pope was united to all the bishops in 1984. Those who did not want to be united with the Holy Father, the responsibility is theirs. The request for the Consecration was always an appeal for union. The Mystical Body of Christ must be united! The members of the same Body are united!"[274]

Sister Lucia herself died in 2005, just shy of her 98th birthday. She confirmed that the consecration of Russia had been "accepted in heaven" as late as 2001, in an interview in her convent with Archbishop Tarcisio Bertone, Secretary of the Congregation for the Doctrine of Faith.[275]

The push and pull between the pro- and anti- "authentic consecration" camps continues. Those who insist the 1984 consecration was "good" point to the sudden crumbling of the Iron Curtain a few years later as proof. Those who insist the consecration has not been accomplished claim that Russia is presently in moral and spiritual shambles, still scarred from the bloody eradication of Christianity and violent imposition of atheism (Russia—the first country to legalize abortion—has one of the highest abortion rates in the world, a high alcohol-related death rate, and a sharp population decline). On the other hand, Russia also has a profound pre-Soviet history of Christianity which seems to be experiencing an unquestionable resurgence right now.

It seems clear that Pope John Paul II did indeed, on multiple occasions, consecrate the world to the Immaculate Heart of Mary in deliberate union with as many bishops as he was capable of mustering, and that Russia was certainly referred to, repeatedly, in a special way. Furthermore, Pope John Paul II invited the bishops in his 1984 letter to renew the consecration of Russia, and not simply the world. What Pope John Paul II apparently *didn't* do was publicly call Russia by name during the actual consecration. Why was that so difficult? What in the world did

John Paul or any of the previous popes think would happen if they dared to publicly consecrate Russia by name?

It's easy to be glib now about various popes' fear of angering the Soviet Union, which might have provoked reprisal against the many laity, religious, priests, and bishops who were already suffering in communist prisons. When Paul VI was pope, this certainly appeared to be a factor: "We knew that the Vatican was engaged in very delicate negotiations with the Soviets for the liberty of the Church beyond the iron curtain. This was the reason why the Vatican could not openly lend its support to protests against the persecutions and also why it could not openly endorse the Fatima apostolate as we would have hoped."[276]

In fact, Russian Orthodox clergy and Catholic bishops behind the Iron Curtain allegedly were only allowed to attend Vatican II on the stipulation that no condemnation of communism be issued by the Vatican II Council.[277] And indeed, the Vatican II documents never refer to the communism which was causing so much suffering for millions of the Church's own members at that time.[278]

In 1980, prior to the attempted assassination, John Paul himself was reported as saying, "Such a consecration would be seen by the Russians as an interference in their internal affairs, and this would have political consequences."[279]

After the attempted assassination, when John Paul certainly experienced a wake-up call regarding Russia's consecration, the Pope's own homeland, Poland, was at a fragile turning point: the Solidarity movement had formed in 1980 after John Paul's transformative visit, and in 1981 the communist government imposed martial law in response, followed by several years of trying to suppress the movement.

The memory of Soviet tanks rolling in to crush the Prague Spring and occupy Czechoslovakia must have weighed on the Pope's mind, especially since John Paul II was already considered the mortal enemy of communism. He might also have recalled how the Nazis retaliated against Dutch bishops, who protested the deportation of Jews in 1942, by rounding up 987 Jewish converts to Catholicism and sending them to Auschwitz. After the 1984 consecration, John Paul II told Msgr. Paul Josef Cordes that he had not explicitly named Russia for fear "that his words might be interpreted as a provocation by the Soviet leaders."[280]

Popes are merely human, and suffer from the same painful limitations as the rest of us. Because of their great responsibilities, their failures can wind up being tragic rather than simply sad. Maybe, despite all their good intentions and earnest efforts, the Holy Fathers were not always stronger than the forces around them. The one thing records seem to reveal is that several popes were very earnestly *trying* to consecrate the whole world, with a special mention for Russia, to the loving heart of the Virgin Mary—even if it was, as Pope John Paul admitted during the final consecration of March 1984, according to their "poor human ability."[281]

Has the consecration of Russia—with its procrastinating popes, its oblique language, and some foot-dragging, uncooperative bishops—been nonetheless accepted by a benevolent God gravely concerned about humanity—a God of leniency rather than legalism? Is that what triggered the overnight fall of the USSR, setting Russia free to re-discover the Christianity it once practiced? We can certainly hope so. In the May 18, 1936 letter to Father Goncalves, Sister Lucia reported that Jesus said this to her in an apparition: *The Holy Father. Pray very much for the Holy Father. He will do it, but it will be too late. Nevertheless the Immaculate Heart of Mary will save Russia. It has been entrusted to her.*[282]

The Virgin herself made the same distressing complaint to Sister Lucia: *They didn't want to pay attention to my petition. Like the king of France they will repent and do so, but it will be too late. Russia will already have spread her errors throughout the world, causing wars and persecutions of the Church. The Holy Father will have much to suffer.*[283]

If the conversion of Russia from communism back to Christianity has not been as rapid and thorough as some would hope, maybe it's not because the consecration wasn't accomplished by John Paul II, but simply because it was done so late. This obsession with whether or not the requested consecration has been fulfilled is linked directly to the belief that without this consecration, Russia will not be re-converted from atheism back to Christianity, but will instead continue to spread its errors throughout the world, replacing the true God with the totalitarian state once again, as predicted at Garabandal.

The prophecy at Garabandal given by Conchita in 1965 was that Russia would conquer the church and the world "when communism comes again." Mari-Loli also said that "Russia will unexpectedly and suddenly overrun and overwhelm a great part of the free world. God does not want this to happen so quickly. In any case the Warning will come when you will see that Holy Mass cannot be celebrated freely anymore; then it will be that the world will most need the intervention of God."[284]

In 1965, at the height of the Cold War, an attack by the Soviet Union was widely feared, yet Mari-Loli spoke of a time when Russia's onslaught would *not* be expected. Furthermore, that "God does not want this to happen so quickly" suggests that fifty years ago Mari-Loli did not see the world-wide communist triumph as imminent. Instead, Conchita and Mari-Loli linked together three future events: The return of communism, the abolition of the Holy Mass,[285] and the Warning.

In light of all this, it's important to remember that the conversion of Russia requires two parts: the consecration of Russia to the Immaculate Heart of Mary, *and* the faithfulness of all Catholics to First Saturday confession, communion, and rosary prayer. If Russia's conversion remains incomplete, perhaps the popes are not the only ones to blame.

A decade into the new millennium, how should we interpret the last two lines of the Second Secret of Fatima? *In the end, my Immaculate Heart will triumph. The Holy Father will consecrate Russia to me, and she shall be converted, and a period of peace will be granted to the world.*

Mary's certainty is comforting. But is the "conversion" of Russia limited to its overnight abandonment of communism? Is the "period of peace" limited to that magical evaporation of the Cold War threat which briefly dazzled the world before we almost immediately took it for granted?

One theory is that the dissolution of the Soviet Union and the absence of nuclear conflict between superpowers these past few decades is, in fact, the predicted period of peace—a period of peace which we have all taken for granted. Imagine if nuclear war *had* erupted in 1985 between Soviet hardliners and a flint-faced Ronald Reagan: The multitude of lives cut short, the children never born. Imagine how different and damaged the world would have been for the past thirty years.

Yet in Garabandal, Jesus told visionary Conchita that the purpose of the upcoming Great Miracle—which has not yet taken place—is to convert Russia, along with the whole world. This suggests that the "conversion of Russia" may have only just begun as a result of the belated 1984 consecration. Could a profound and radical re-conversion of Russia into deep and lasting Christianity also transform the world and change the tragic, bloody course of human history?

And that brings us to the Third Secret of Fatima—a secret which really *did* remain a secret for decades, and which, when finally revealed, managed to ignite more questions than it answered.

The Controversial Third Secret

The Third Secret of Fatima was given to the children on July 13, 1917. In 1944, Sister Lucia finally wrote it down under orders from the Bishop because she had recently fallen ill, and there were fears that she might die. Why had she waited so long to pass it on? She had great difficulty obeying the order and writing down the Secret. Was it because she didn't believe the Virgin wanted her to write it down yet? Was it because the Secret was so grave and so terrible that it was agonizing even to put it on paper? Was it because, as some have suggested, Satan tried to prevent her from exposing his plan to place his minions in the highest offices in the Church? Was it because, as others have suggested, the Third Secret exposed the sexual abuse scandal in the Church, something Sister Lucia was mortified to record?

Sister Lucia herself insisted that what thwarted her was "not natural."[286] Was this God or was it the Devil? Actually, the conflict may have been much more straightforward and human: At the same time that the Bishop of Leiria-Fatima was telling Sister Lucia to write the Third Secret down, the Archbishop of Valhadolid, who oversaw her diocese in Tuy, Spain, was telling her *not* to. Because of these conflicting orders, the Virgin Mary finally appeared to Sister Lucia and resolved her dilemma, telling her to write the secret down.[287]

Unlike the first two secrets, however, the Third Secret was not released to the world at that time. Why? Here is where the story takes its sensational turn into a topsy-turvy world of secrecy and intrigue. The mysterious Third Secret was sealed in an envelope, and Sister Lucia asked that it be opened no later than 1960, or upon her death, whichever came first. She told Cardinal Ottaviani that the Third Secret would be better understood by then.[288] In 2000, Sister Lucia of Fatima told Archbishop Tarcisio Bertone, Secretary of the Congregation for the Doctrine of the Faith, that her own "intuition" had been that the Third Secret would be clearer by 1960, but the date was not set by the Virgin Mary.[289]

In the meantime, on April 4, 1957, the sealed letter, which had been in the safekeeping of the Bishop of Fatima, was placed in, yes, the *Secret Archives*, which apparently really do exist in the Vatican.[290] At that time, the Third Secret remained sealed and unread by both the Bishop of Fatima and Pope Pius XII. Presumably, the sole human being on the planet who knew the secret and bore the burden was Sister Lucia. The momentous year of 1960 came and went, but no Third Secret was revealed. Why?

Sister Lucia said in the 2000 interview with Archbishop Bertone that her job was to write the secret down, but it was up to the Pope to interpret it.[291] Did this mean that Sister Lucia only meant for the *Pope* to read the secret by 1960, rather than the general public? This question of whether or not the Virgin Mary wanted the Third Secret released to the whole world by 1960 has been hotly debated.

On Feb. 8, 1960, a press release from the Portuguese news agency *Agencia Nacional de Informaçao* read: "Faced with the pressure that has been placed on the Vatican, some wanting the letter to be opened and made known to the world, others, on the supposition that it may contain alarming prophecies, desiring that its publication be withheld, the same Vatican circles declare that the Vatican has decided not to make public Sister Lucy's letter, and to continue keeping it rigorously sealed.

"The decision of the Vatican is based on various reasons: 1. Sister Lucy is still living. 2. The Vatican already knows the contents of the letter. 3. Although the Church recognizes the Fatima apparitions, she does not pledge herself to guarantee the veracity of the words which the three little shepherds claim to have heard from Our Lady."[292]

With two secrets already out in the open, what was so unsettling about those final words that the Catholic Church itself refused to take responsibility for releasing them to the public? Instead, the Third Secret remained safely locked away, and occasionally opened, read, and re-sealed, by various popes.

Some trace the sharp decline in devotion to the Virgin Mary in general, and to Our Lady of Fatima in particular, to that great non-event of 1960. "Simple folk waited up until May 13 when it was believed that the revelation would be made. Later, people felt a profound disenchantment and disappointment which did great harm to devotion to Our Lady of Fatima, both inside and outside Portugal."[293]

In addition to the non-release of the Third Secret in 1960, another reason which has been suggested for the great "falling-away" from rosary prayer is the fact that the Acts of Vatican II, perhaps in an attempt to build ecumenical bridges, never once mentioned the word "rosary," as if it were radioactive. Whatever the reasons for the decline in devotion to Our Lady of Fatima and the rosary, this devotion was the *other* part of the requirement for peace in the world and the conversion of Russia.

Rather than putting the matter to rest, the failure of the Catholic Church to release the Third Secret in 1960 stirred up a hornet's nest of questions. Were the Fatima apparitions fraudulent after all? The Church seemed to raise doubts, claiming to recognize the Fatima apparitions while at the same time refusing to guarantee the "veracity" of the shepherd children's words. Why else would the Church refuse to release the Third Secret? Well, there was one other possibility. Failure to release the letter ignited speculation that there was something in the Third Secret that Popes found unbearable to reveal. The theory of the final secret of Fatima as off-the-scale apocalyptic gained momentum. Catholic urban legends made the rounds about the Third Secret. Sensational versions of the Third Secret were published which predicted oceans inundating continents and washing away millions, based in part on some comments reportedly made by John Paul II to a group of German Catholics and reported in a German magazine.[294] (John Paul II's sensational comments, however, have also been disputed.) In any event, these catastrophic versions had nothing in common with the Third Secret that the Vatican finally released.

In fact, actual comments by a few key Fatima players before the Third Secret was released definitely veered away from global natural cataclysms, and instead, into matters of politics and faith.

The Bishop of Leira-Fatima in *Mensagem de Fatima* in

The Mystery of Garabandal

February 1985 said that the Third Secret of Fatima did not talk about nuclear bombs but about our faith. "To identify the secret with catastrophic announcements or a nuclear holocaust is to distort the meaning of the message. The loss of faith of a continent is worse than the annihilation of a nation; and it is true that the faith is continually diminishing in Europe."[295]

On May 13, 1982, John Paul II told Sister Lucia in Fatima that it was "neither necessary nor wise to reveal the contents of the Third Secret, seeing that the world would not understand it."[296] In August, 1984, Cardinal Ratzinger seemed to echo Pope John Paul's perspective that the world wouldn't "get it." Publishing the Third Secret, Ratzinger said, would mean exposing the Church "to the danger of sensationalism, exploitation of the content."[297]

Sister Lucia herself wrote a letter to Pope John Paul II in 1982, after he had read the Third Secret but long before it was released, in which she explained it like this: "The third part of the Secret refers to Our Lady's words: "If not, Russia will spread its errors throughout the world, causing wars and persecutions against the Church. The good will be martyred, the Holy Father will have much to suffer, various nations will be annihilated." (July 13, 1917)

"The third part of the Secret, which you are anxious to understand, is a symbolic revelation which refers to this part of the Message, conditioned by whether we accept or not what the Message itself asks of us: "If my requests are heeded, Russia will be converted, and there will be peace; if not, it will spread its errors throughout the world, etc." Since we did not heed this appeal of the Message, we see that it has been fulfilled, Russia has invaded the world with her errors. And if we have not yet seen the complete fulfillment of the final part of this prophecy, we are going towards it little by little with great strides."[298]

It's a fascinating exercise to apply these previous comments about the Third Secret to the actual Third Secret which was finally released in the Year 2000 by Pope John Paul II:

121

After the two parts which I have already explained, at the left of Our Lady and a little above, we saw an Angel with a flaming sword in his left hand; flashing, it gave out flames that looked as though they would set the world on fire; but they died out in contact with the splendour that Our Lady radiated towards him from her right hand: pointing to the earth with his right hand, the Angel cried out in a loud voice: 'Penance, Penance, Penance!' And we saw in an immense light that is God: 'something similar to how people appear in a mirror when they pass in front of it' a Bishop dressed in White 'we had the impression that it was the Holy Father.' Other Bishops, Priests, Religious men and women going up a steep mountain, at the top of which there was a big Cross of rough-hewn trunks as of a cork-tree with the bark; before reaching there the Holy Father passed through a big city half in ruins and half trembling with halting step, afflicted with pain and sorrow, he prayed for the souls of the corpses he met on his way; having reached the top of the mountain, on his knees at the foot of the big Cross he was killed by a group of soldiers who fired bullets and arrows at him, and in the same way there died one after another the other Bishops, Priests, Religious men and women, and various lay people of different ranks and positions. Beneath the two arms of the Cross there were two Angels each with a crystal aspersorium in his hand, in which they gathered up the blood of the Martyrs and with it sprinkled the souls that were making their way to God.[299]

With the release of the Third Secret in 2000, John Paul II made it clear that he believed it was a prophecy of the assassination attempt against him, and also that the Third Secret was now fulfilled. In response to objections that Pope John Paul II wasn't murdered by a group of soldiers with bullets and arrows, the Vatican explained that the Third Secret was essentially the entire 20th century struggle of the Church with atheistic, totalitarian communism compressed into one brief and symbolic vision.

And the fact that the pope wasn't killed was because, according to Cardinal Ratzinger, "the future is not in fact unchangeably set, and the image which the children saw is in no way a film preview of a future in which nothing can be changed...The purpose of the vision is not to show a film o₁ irrevocably fixed future. Its meaning is exactly the opposite: it is meant to mobilize the forces of change in the right direction. Therefore we must totally discount fatalistic explanations of the 'secret.' " [300]

Nevertheless, it turned out that John Paul and Cardinal Ratzinger were correct: The world didn't get it. In fact, the reaction of both Catholics and the world was underwhelming. What was all the fuss about? Why all the secrecy? Why all the delay? What about comets striking the earth, oceans inundating continents, and millions dying (as predicted in the Bible[301] and speculative versions of the Third Secret published before 2000)? What about the Anti-Christ taking over the Chair of Peter and denying the Christian faith, a popular theory about an impending widespread loss of faith reaching to the very top?[302] What about a prediction of nuclear war among superpowers? All this waiting and all this secrecy and all this fuss about a bishop in white in a mirror?

But the Third Secret is actually an intensely apocalyptic message which communicates a great deal. In the revealed Third Secret, an angel touches a flaming sword to the earth threatening to set it on fire—an image eerily reminiscent of the terrifying Chastisement predicted at Garabandal, as well as the fourth bowl of wrath the angel pours out on the sun in the Book of Revelation, scorching humankind. Whatever it is specifically, whether natural (solar?) or man-made (nuclear?), an angel setting the earth on fire with his sword is apocalyptic imagery. Which is why the next part of the Third Secret is a complete surprise. Rather than a world that goes up in flames, the menacing conflagration dies out in contact with *the splendour that Our Lady radiated.* In the Third Secret of Fatima, the intercession of the Virgin Mary is protecting the entire human race from fiery destruction.

For how long has she been interceding on our behalf and protecting the human race? For the entire 20th century?

Catholics believe that because of the profound part that Mary played in bringing the Lamb of God into the world and in accompanying Him to His cross, her Son will grant her anything she asks. Is her powerful maternal intercession for us the only reason that the Soviet Union collapsed, that the Cold War did not erupt into a white-hot one, that we made it safely past the Year 2000?

The next part of the Secret is the Angel crying out "Penance!" not once, but *three times*. This is also what the Virgin has come to ask of the human race at three critical Cold War junctures: first at Fatima, then at Garabandal, and now at Medjugorje. This is the role which Mary says humans have to play in staving off a scorching judgment: Acts of penance are an attempt, in our human and limited way, to make amends for the wrong we and others have done, amends that allow us to share in some small measure in the saving sacrifice of Christ.

After revealing Mary's intercessory role and our own penitential contribution in turning away God's end-times wrath, the Third Secret moves into a sobering vision of the persecution and martyrdom of the Church. First of all, there is the odd detail about how the pope and others were seen "as though in a mirror," and they are described in the same breath as seen "in an immense light that was God." Perhaps this is a nod to the moment in the Book of Exodus when God told Moses that no man could see God's face and live; thus, one can only look at God indirectly, "as though in a mirror." 1 Corinthians 13:12 also comes to mind, "For now we see indistinctly, as though in a mirror, but then face to face."

An even more provocative explanation of this strange mention of the mirror has been that the pope and the other figures appeared "as though in a mirror" because this was a glimpse into the future, and the future is never set in stone, as Cardinal Ratzinger said. Perhaps through the Third Secret we are allowed to peek behind the curtain, at a future partially unveiled, but we do not have the whole picture because the future remains in flux.

Others have suggested that this is a prophecy of the Warning: the revealing light of God, when every human being must face himself or herself as though in a mirror. Whatever the meaning of the mirror in the Third Secret, everyone is affected, from the highest to the lowest. Pope John Paul II can hardly be blamed for ascribing this portion of the prophecy to himself; the Holy Father of the Third Secret does indeed sound exactly like the frail Pope John Paul II suffering from Parkinson's in later years: *the Holy Father passed through a big city half in ruins **and half trembling with halting step**, afflicted with pain and sorrow, he prayed for the souls of the corpses he met on his way*

The city half in ruins might be in a literal Rome in an apocalyptic time, or it might be, quite frankly, a spiritual description of today's Church. Likewise, the corpses that the pope "met" on his way might be actual dead after some terrible slaughter, or might be the many who are spiritually dead in today's confusion and chaos—the "great apostasy" that was predicted in the Bible.[303] The corpses could also be the many victims of totalitarian political regimes during the 20th century, which is the Vatican's central interpretation.

Finally, *on his knees at the foot of the big Cross he was killed by a group of soldiers who fired bullets and arrows at him, and in the same way there died one after another the other Bishops, Priests, Religious men and women, and various lay people of different ranks and positions.*

Again, this might be a description of the persecution of the Church in the 20th century, in which case it's understandable that Pope John Paul viewed the failed assassination attempt against him, had it succeeded, as the potential culmination of that persecution. Bishops, priests, religious men and women, and lay people all were martyred in the 20th century. The Russian government itself issued a report in 1995 describing the ways in which 200,000 clerics were killed by communists in the Soviet Union including being crucified on the doors of churches, shot, strangled, and drenched with water in winter until they froze into blocks of ice.[304]

Nor did the murderous violence, in the heat of the Cold War, come only from the communist side, by any means. The assassination of Archbishop Oscar Romero as he was celebrating Mass, along with the murder of many other unarmed religious and lay people in El Salvador, are noteworthy examples of the persecution of practicing Christians at the hands of a U.S.-backed anti-communist regime, rather than a Soviet-backed communist regime. Churches and altars were sacked and desecrated—a prediction made at Garabandal—by the right wing in El Salvador rather than the left. The Salvadoran Jesuit priest Rutilio Grande, shortly before he was assassinated, lamented that "very soon the Bible and the Gospel will not be allowed within our country."

Yet the Third Secret vision of persecution could also be about a future violent persecution of the Catholic Church specifically, and Christians generally, as possibly predicted at Garabandal. Before the Third Secret was revealed, both Sister Lucia and Cardinal Ratzinger said that it aligned with Scripture: The intense persecution of the Church portrayed in the Third Secret is clearly and repeatedly predicted in Scriptures, particularly End Times persecution.[305]

Despite widespread disgruntlement—after all that secrecy and waiting—over how "tame" the Third Secret turned out to be, it is actually quite doomsdayish in its imagery. The revealed Third Secret also helps explain why popes hesitated to release it. It was a revelation of what would happen if the Church failed to heed the Virgin's words at Fatima: If the Holy Father and the Bishops did not consecrate Russia to the Immaculate Heart of Mary, and the faithful did not fulfill the First Saturday devotions, Russia would spread its errors throughout the world, causing wars and persecutions of the Church. The Second Secret warns of this, the Third Secret depicts it. Yet what happens at the end of the Third Secret? After the slaughter of so many Christians, including the Pope, the Third Secret ends not with a triumphant Church, but with a haunting image of the martyrs' blood being sprinkled on the souls making their way to God. It's a message that might have encouraged communist powers even as it disheartened Christians—especially if the general public interpreted the secret as a future set in stone. (Although it might also have awakened Catholics to the need for penance to avert disaster, as the Angel in the Third Secret requested.)

Sister Lucia's comment in 1944 that the prophecy would be clearer in 1960 also aligns with the history of the Cold War. In 1944, the U.S.S.R. was part of the Allied forces, and the great danger to Europe was the Nazis. But by 1960, Germany was about to be severed by the Berlin Wall; Poland and all of Eastern Europe were under Soviet domination; and the Cold War was reaching its peak with the impending Cuban Missile Crisis. The punishment envisioned in the Third Secret—violent persecution of Christians—also was well underway by 1960, not just in Europe, but in Asia and Africa, just as Sister Lucia predicted.

It makes sense, after the failed assassination attempt and the fall of the Soviet Union, that John Paul II believed that the communist powers would no longer be gleeful nor the faithful frightened about the Third Secret, and thus it was safe to release it. And in a remarkable demonstration of how blasé the world quickly became about the miraculous dissolution of the Soviet Union, many *weren't* frightened by the Third Secret—they were merely piqued that it wasn't more sensational.

And so, like children who don't want the story to be over, speculation began about the *rest* of the Third Secret. Some have suggested that only part of the Third Secret was revealed, and that the un-revealed portion portrays a coming "abomination of desolation,"[306] or a desolation that is already well underway, depending on your perspective: the succumbing of the Church at its highest levels to the powers of darkness. The rancid fruit of the sexual abuse scandal certainly seems like strong evidence of darkness in the Catholic Church. Was the abuse scandal predicted in the "unrevealed" Third Secret, as some continue to speculate? Interestingly enough, one of the two formal, public messages of Garabandal (to be examined in the next section of the book) was indeed a grave warning about the state of some members of the Catholic clergy, and the perilous course the Church was on.

Beyond the sexual abuse scandal, others speculate that this "suppressed" Third Secret predicts that the worst is yet to come in the form of church leaders who end up denying the divinity of Christ and abolishing the daily Sacrifice of the Mass,[307] in favor of a faith that is more accommodating and less offensive to modern sensibilities. This scenario doesn't seem particularly far-fetched in light of enormously unpopular Catholic positions on sexuality, contraception, abortion, married and women priests—as well as fragile Christian relations with Islam. Change in any of these areas would be wildly welcomed by many, a revitalizing development in a Church that has lost its credibility due to the sex abuse scandal. A cadre of reformers could start out on a seemingly commendable, compassionate path of change and ride the wave of adulation and enthusiasm all the way to the apostasy of betraying Jesus Christ—as some still believe the "real" Third Secret of Fatima predicts. In Garabandal, villagers actually claimed to hear the visionaries speak of some sort of coming rupture in the Church, when cardinals "would go against the pope."[308]

Despite this feverish speculation about the suppressed Third Secret, Sister Lucia herself said in a 2001 interview with Archbishop Bertone, "Everything has been published. There are no more secrets."[309] On another occasion, Sister Lucia "repeated her conviction that the vision of Fatima concerns above all the struggle of atheistic Communism against the Church and against

Christians, and describes the terrible sufferings of the victims of the faith in the twentieth century."[310]

Most of the "pre-release" comments do seem to correspond with the *already* published Third Secret. And this already released Third Secret is a haunting and sobering vision, either of the profound sufferings of the 20th century which the Virgin Mary had hoped to spare us from, or, if we're not as fortunate, of something worse which is to come.

Nonetheless, in yet another twist, a *new* Fatima document has recently been released, in which Sister Lucia mentions a vision she had of that angel's burning sword finally touching the earth, resulting in—get ready—apocalyptic earthquakes and tsunamis which sweep multitudes away. Sister Lucia describes "the point of the flame-like lance which detaches, touches the axis of the earth." The earth then shakes, cities are buried, waters overflow and sweep away an uncountable number. Not only does the flame-like lance sound suspiciously like the angel's fiery sword (a fire which the Virgin successfully extinguishes in the Third Secret), but the vision is disturbingly similar to the contested John Paul II comments in Fulda, Germany about oceans flooding continents and sweeping away millions. This devastating vision is included in the official biography of Sister Lucia published by the Carmelites of Coimbra titled "Um caminho sob o olhar de Maria" (*A Pathway Under the Gaze of Mary*).[311] The existence of this vision perhaps helps explain the confusion surrounding the released Third Secret amid persistent reports of another, more apocalyptic version. Even so, it's important to recall that in the Third Secret, human penance and the Virgin's intercession deflect looming disaster, and so we are not shown it. The take-away lesson is that this global apocalypse which Sister Lucia apparently glimpsed is not set in stone.

Someone else quite surprisingly threw gasoline on the speculative fires by essentially stating that there is more to come regarding the Third Secret. Cardinal Ratzinger had dutifully downplayed the Third Secret before its release, and adhered to

John Paul's party line in the Year 2000 that it was fulfilled. Yet as Pope Benedict in 2010, he made this remarkable statement:

"With regard to this great vision of the suffering of the popes, beyond the circumstances of John Paul II, other realities are indicated which over time will develop and become clear."

After admitting that there was more to come regarding the already released Third Secret, Pope Benedict, even more astonishingly, appeared to link the Third Secret with the sexual abuse scandal and all manner of conspiracy theories about powers of darkness at work inside the Vatican:

"In terms of what we today can discover in this message, attacks against the pope or the Church don't come just from outside the Church. The suffering of the Church also comes from within the Church, because sin exists in the Church. This too has always been known, but today we see it in a really terrifying way. The greatest persecution of the Church doesn't come from enemies on the outside, but is born in sin within the Church."[312]

And so the great controversy of the Third Secret continues, and thanks to Pope Benedict himself, has even received new life: However accurate and authentic the Third Secret was, perhaps it hasn't yet been *completely* fulfilled. The Third Secret certainly concludes in open-ended fashion. It leaves us hanging with this question: Has the Catholic Church perished for good? After all, Scriptures do state in several places that Christians will be *overcome* in the End Times. The Book of Daniel in describing the End Times in chapter 12 refers to "he who crushes the power of the holy people." The Book of Revelation in chapter 13 describes the Beast who is "allowed to make war against the saints and conquer them." And Jesus in the gospels talks about Christian believers in the last days being tortured, put to death, and "hated by all on account of my name."

This, of course, happened to the early Christians in the Roman Empire; it happened under 20th century communism; and it is happening now with a vengeance in various parts of the world. But does the Third Secret of Fatima predict a culmination of this crisis? In the Third Secret, with the Church in ruins, the Pope dead, and souls making their way to God via the blood of many martyrs—well, what then? Is the "bishop in white" who is assassinated the final Pope? Garabandal intersects yet again with Fatima at this point: Through the famous—or infamous—"last pope" prophecy of Garabandal.

The Last Pope Prophecy of Garabandal

The "last pope" prophecy did not originate with Garabandal. Instead, it's been a topic of speculation throughout the centuries. Most famously, the long line of popes, including their shocking finale, was supposedly predicted by St. Malachy, who had a famous vision during a trip to Rome. St. Malachy lived in the 12th century, and it's been disputed that he had the vision and wrote down the list of popes because the incident was not mentioned by his biographers or in any records prior to the 16th century. Supporters say St. Malachy's vision had been lost and forgotten in the Vatican Archives during those centuries. But in the 16th century, a Belgian Benedictine monk named Arnold de Wion published a book called *Lignum Vitae*, in which he included a list of "papal titles" that correspond with popes beginning in 1143. De Wion attributed the list to St. Malachy's prophecy, but some scholars say the list appears to be plagiarized from a history of popes that was circulating at the time. One theory is that this miraculously re-discovered list of predicted popes was manufactured solely for the purpose of ensuring a particular papal candidate's election (who went on to lose).

Skeptics also say that the prophetic papal descriptions are spot-on accurate up until De Wion's time, but become less convincing after that. The Latin titles are short and vague, and at times it feels like a game of making the pope fit the title. Nonetheless, because some of the recent papal titles seem somewhat accurate, and because *we are now on the last pope on the list*, the last-pope-prophecy simply won't go away. Our reason for considering this controversial prediction is because of Garabandal's very own "last pope prophecy," which, as we'll see, is different, and laden with its own controversy.

In looking at St. Malachy's prediction, we won't bother with popes from the distant past, but will begin with Pope John XXIII, who heralded and commenced Vatican II. The St. Malachy prophecy which corresponds to him is "Pastor et nauta", translated "shepherd and sailor." John XXIII actually was the Archbishop of Venice, the famous flooded city. More significantly, he was responsible for shepherding the Roman Catholic Church into a definitively new era.

After that came Paul VI, described in the prophecies as "flos florum" or "flower of flowers." His personal arms were three fleurs-de-lis, or "flower of the lily."

The next pope was the mysterious Pope John Paul I, who only reigned for 33 days before dying under conspiracy-theory-oriented circumstances. His prophecy was "De medietate lunae," which is translated "from the half moon." The correspondence to John Paul I seems to be that he was born in the diocese of Belluno (beautiful moon); that he was supposedly born on the day of the half moon (Oct. 17, 1912); and that his name was Albino Luciani, which means white light. He was elected pope on August 26, 1978, supposedly also on the half-moon, and his reign lasted roughly until the next half-moon.

We move from the moon to the sun with Pope John Paul II, whose prophecy was "De labore solis," or "From the labor of the sun." It's also a Latin term for a solar eclipse. Pope John Paul II was born during a partial solar eclipse and was buried on April 8, 2005, the day of a complete solar eclipse. Some say John Paul II's dramatic connection with Fatima is also contained in the short prophecy. The Virgin Mary is described as the "Woman Clothed with the Sun" who is in *labor* in the Book of Revelation (symbolizing the Virgin Mary's role in the End Times), and her labor on behalf of the human race may have even given birth to John Paul II himself. He was sometimes known as "Mary's pope," because John Paul II had entrusted himself to Mary since his youth, and his motto of devotion to her was, "Totus Tuus," or Totally Yours. As a young seminarian in Krakow, John Paul II was slated to be deported to the Soviet Union when a Soviet army officer who had come into contact with John Paul struck his name from the order.[313] In addition, the great miracle of Fatima was the Miracle of the Sun when it appeared to spin out of control and fall toward the earth, as witnessed, photographed, and reported in newspapers in 1917. Others point to the fact that the sun rises in the east and John Paul was the first pope from Eastern Europe, or that John Paul II introduced the Luminous Mysteries to the Rosary. Other connections, real or imagined, are that both John Paul II and Copernicus were from Poland and lived in Krakow. Copernicus was the first astronomer to pronounce that the earth revolved around the sun, a position the Catholic Church denounced. John Paul II reversed the Church's position in 1992.

That brings us to Benedict XVI, whose prophecy is "De gloria olivae" or "from the glory of the olive." Ratzinger was the Cardinal of Velletri-Segni, whose coat of arms features three olive trees. Furthermore, one of the orders within the Benedictines is specifically known as the Olivetans, named after the passion of Jesus which began on the Mount of Olives, in the Garden of Gethsemane. Cardinal Ratzinger is neither a Benedictine nor an Olivetan, but he was born on the feast day of St. Benedict Joseph Labre, and he took the papal name Benedict XVI. Pope Benedict also has been engaged in trying to bring reconciliation between the Catholic and Orthodox branches of Christianity: the olive is a symbol of Greece, while "extending an olive branch," of course, symbolizes reconciliation and peace. Finally, the Mount of Olives was where Jesus gave his great discourse on the End Times which includes the persecution of believers, the Great Tribulation, and the frightening signs in the sun and the moon and the stars before his return. There are those who believe that the early birth pangs of this apocalyptic upheaval began during Benedict's reign.

Although it's relatively easy to find connections between current popes and the St. Malachy prophecies, the prophecies are also vague enough and short enough to fit just about anyone.

There is only one pope remaining after Benedict XVI—on St. Malachy's controversial list, at any rate: *In persecutione extrema Sanctae Romanae Ecclesiae, sedebit Petrus Romanus, qui pascet oves in multis tribulation bus; quibus transactis, civitas septicollis diruetur, et Judex tremendous judicabit populum suum. Finis.* "In the last persecution of the Holy Roman Church, Peter the Roman will hold the see who will pasture his sheep in many tribulations: and when these things are finished, the city of seven hills will be destroyed, and the terrible judge will judge his people. The End."

One of the problems with this last prophecy is that while all the previous papal titles were numbered, this one was not. The final entry appears to be a longer, later, non-numbered add-on. Consequently, some say the text suggests a continuation of many popes between "Glory of the Olive" and "Peter the Roman." In other words, the author skipped ahead, exhausted, and stopped counting all the future popes—not unlike the Mayans bringing an end to their calendar, but not to time. This means that the final entry may simply be telling us *how* it all ends, but not *when*. Peter the Roman is a highly symbolic name which could be referring to the papacy in general, and not to a particular individual.

There is one tantalizing tidbit about the new Pope Francis's connection to "Peter the Roman": Although he was born in Argentina, his parents were Italian immigrants. Italian popes have historically been the norm, but this pope of Italian lineage is a departure from the recent lengthy tenures of a Polish and German pope. Just as the end of the Mayan calendar led to feverish speculation about the end of the world, a medieval monk brought us a sensational prediction of the end of the papacy. But this brings us to a more recent and less well-known "last pope prophecy"—the last pope prophecy of Garabandal.

On June 3, 1963, Pope John XXIII died in Rome, eight months after opening Vatican II on October 11, 1962. Meanwhile, in Garabandal, the village bells began to toll.

At that moment, Conchita reportedly said to her mother, "Now only three remain."

Conchita's mother, Aniceta, was surprised, to say the least. After quizzing her daughter, Conchita explained that the Virgin had told her this. Shocked, Aniceta asked if this meant the end of the world.

To which Conchita replied, "The Virgin didn't tell me "the end of the world," but "the end of the times."

Aniceta asked, "Aren't they the same?" and Conchita replied, "I don't know."[314]

This was not the only occasion that Conchita spoke of the last three popes. In another instance, Paquina de la Roza Velarde, the wife of Dr. Ortiz, mentioned that with the death of the pope, the Council might also end.

Conchita replied, "Another pope will come and the Council will continue."

Paquina began a little argument with Conchita, suggesting at least two more times that the Council might now come to its end if the new pope held different views.

Conchita's response was, "I'm telling you, and I repeat: another pope will come and the Council will continue. And I also tell you that only three popes remain . . .and then the end of times."

Conchita also reportedly repeated this same statement to Father Lucio Rodrigo, a professor at the Pontifical University. Conchita told him, *"Yes Father. It's true. The Virgin told me that after John XXIII only three popes remain, and this one,* (Paul VI) *is the first of those three."* [315]

When Conchita was a boarder in Burgos, Spain in October 1966 with the Sisters of the Immaculate Conception, she reportedly said virtually the same thing to Mother Nievas Garcias, who wrote Conchita's words down.

"One day I said to the Virgin, *'Will the end of the world be during the time of these events?'* And she told me, *'No, the end of the times.'* After Paul VI, there will be only two more popes; and then the end of the times will come."[316]

Furthermore, during the reign of Pope John Paul II, Conchita confirmed this account to film maker Harry Daley, stating, "Our present Pope is the third Pope."[317]

And there's the rub. John Paul II was indeed the third pope after John XXIII—but he wasn't, we now know, the *last*. Conchita's prediction, which she apparently made on numerous occasions, is simply wrong.

Or is it?

There are some reports that Conchita made the statement that there were actually *four* popes after John XXIII—and one of them would have a very short reign (*muy poquisimo.*) She reportedly made the "four-popes" remark to the German author Albrecht Weber, and the "muy poquisimo" remark to Santander businessman Placido Ruiloba, who made many tape recordings of the apparitions and the girls in ecstasy. If true, it's obviously referring to the 33-day reign of Pope John Paul I. If Pope John Paul I can't be counted because he didn't even have time to get his papacy up and running, then the third pope before the end of times commenced would be Pope Benedict XVI.

Another argument put forth in favor of Conchita's prophecy lies in her statement, "After Paul VI, there will be only two more popes; *and then the end of the times will come.*"

In other words, however Conchita or others might have *interpreted* the prophecy, the Virgin never said that there would be only three more popes *remaining*—but that there would be only three more popes *before the end of the times would commence (el fin de los tiempos).*

There's a vast difference between predicting only three more popes, *ever*, versus three more popes before the End Times arrives. Of course, if the latter is true, it's still unsettling news, because it means the end of times may have started under the reign of Benedict XVI (or Pope Francis, depending on if Pope John Paul I is counted or not!)

But that also does not mean the end of times will *conclude* under Pope Francis, or that he is literally "the last pope." The end times, as noted when examining the Warning and Chastisement, do not necessarily mean the end of the planet Earth and the human race. They may signal the end of an era, which is the current evil age, and the ushering in of an era of peace, if we're fortunate—whether through our cooperation with God's mercy (which is God's preference), or through a period of fiery upheaval and purification as a result of human resistance. Some Garabandal supporters believe that Conchita's prophecy of the last pope before the end times will only be understood in retrospect—when we will be able to look back and clearly see the pivotal hinge between the ages.[318]

One last explanation (other than sheer falsehood) remains for Conchita's apparently failed prophecy that John Paul II was the last pope before the End Times: If the Third Secret of Fatima was about the assassination of John Paul II—as he himself believed—*then history was changed*. In the Third Secret, the Pope is murdered and Christendom lies in ruins. Remember that Sister Lucia herself said that the Third Secret was a vision of what would occur if Russia was not consecrated and the First Saturday prayers of reparation were not offered. In fact, the First Saturday prayers have been faithfully offered by some Catholics even to this day, and the consecration of Russia was hopefully finally accomplished, albeit late and not exactly according to orders. So although the terrible Third Secret was in the process of being fulfilled, the worst in fact *was not realized*.

The assassination attempt seemed to convince John Paul that unless he acted on the consecration, the Third Secret would indeed be fulfilled. Pope John Paul II survived because—as he himself believed—the Virgin herself intervened. As a result of his survival, he finally consecrated Russia to the Virgin in 1984. The Soviet Union fell, and the Iron Curtain crumbled. Formerly Christian Russia was given a new chance to re-discover its Christianity. In other words, perhaps the world was given more time and more popes before the end times could commence. If the pope in the Third Secret was John Paul II, then both the Third Secret assassination and Conchita's last-pope prophecy were frustrated by divine mercy.

With this reprieve, might Christians everywhere finally embrace the Virgin's warnings, multiply their prayers of reparation, and turn the tide of history so that the whole world returns to God rather than war? Or, if humankind continues to sin, will there be a second onslaught of militant communism upon the world, as the seers of Garabandal suggest?

Looking at the sobering vision of a murdered pope and persecuted Church in the Third Secret of Fatima, at St. Malachy's contested list, at Conchita's controversial prophecy, and at the Bible's prediction of end-times persecution, what are we to make of the future of the Catholic Church? Is it doomed, to the delight of many and the despair of some? Or might we hope that the worst of the predictions, while partially fulfilled, have been altered through feeble human cooperation and the mercy of God?

There is more to consider regarding the prophecies of Garabandal and the future of the Catholic Church. As some have suggested, the Church after end-times-turmoil may no longer be based in Rome. Perhaps St. Malachy's vision while in Rome—if it occurred—was about the end of the papacy in Rome, but not the end of the papacy itself. The Church itself may profoundly change, and prophecies of "last popes" may indicate the end of our troubled era, but certainly not the end of Christ's Church on earth. The Catholic Church teaches that the Chair of Peter will exist until the actual end of time, when Christ himself arrives, and the pope is replaced by the Shepherd of shepherds. "Anti-popes" have existed before and could come again—rival popes who gather their followers and engage in a power struggle with the true pope. Yet ultimately, the Roman Catholic Church believes that false popes cannot succeed because Jesus himself said, "You are Peter, and upon this rock I will build my church, and the gates of hell will not prevail against it."

Chapter 6

Is Garabandal the Prequel to Medjugorje?

A great sign appeared in the sky, a woman clothed with the sun, with the moon under her feet, and on her head a crown of twelve stars.[319] **The Book of Revelation Chapter 12**

"When the sign comes, it will be too late for many." **The Virgin Mary at Medjugorje**

In the Third Secret of Fatima, an arsonist angel tries to strike a metallic match and set the world on fire. Luckily for us, the flames die out in contact with the "splendor" of the Virgin Mary.

This apocalyptic Secret, delivered in 1917, predicted that the Virgin Mary would play a crucial role in warding off global catastrophe during the 20th century. By the time the Third Secret was publicly revealed in the year 2000, the Virgin Mary had indeed been reported making dozens of dramatic appearances throughout the decades and around the world—too many, in fact, for the Catholic Church to investigate or even to count. The Church has not made a decision on the vast majority of these claimed contemporary apparitions. A few have been stamped with a decisive negative decision (although those decisions are sometimes reversed by later bishops, as in the case of apparitions in Amsterdam in 1945.)

A small number of 20ᵗʰ century apparitions have been approved. The Virgin Mary appeared atop a church in Zeitun, Egypt to hundreds of thousands of people from 1968 to 1971, an event that was photographed and broadcast on television. Zeitun is thought to be the place where Joseph, Mary, and the infant Jesus fled to escape King Herod and the Slaughter of the Innocents. The Virgin Mary has also been photographed and viewed by thousands atop other churches in Egypt in 1986, 2000, 2009, and 2011, all of them available for viewing on the internet.

One notable Catholic Church-approved 20ᵗʰ century case was the appearance of Mary to a group of children in Rwanda starting in 1981, some of whom died in the subsequent genocide. The apparitions included visions of a river of blood and decapitated bodies, with the Virgin urging repentance and the rosary, and stressing that the vision did not have to occur. *"My children, it does not have to happen if people would listen and come back to God."* [320]

Another 20ᵗʰ century Church-approved apparition was the appearance of Mary to Sister Agnes Sasagawa in Akita, Japan on Oct. 13, 1973 (the apparition site is near the 2011 Japanese earthquake). Consistent with the most frightening aspects of Fatima and Garabandal (and occurring on the Fatima anniversary), Mary in Akita stated that if humans don't "repent and better themselves…fire will fall from the sky and will wipe out a great part of humanity." Like at Garabandal, Mary also offered up stark language about the state of the clergy. In fact, at Akita, Mary voiced what some of the faithful expected from the Third Secret of Fatima: "The work of the devil will infiltrate even into the Church in such a way that one will see cardinals opposing cardinals, bishops against bishops. The priests who venerate me (Mary) will be scorned and opposed by their confreres." Mary also predicted that "the Church will be full of those who accept compromises and the demon will press many priests and consecrated souls to leave the service of the Lord. The demon will be especially implacable against souls consecrated to God." And in line with the vision of church persecution in the Third Secret, Mary at Akita says that "churches and altars" will be sacked. The final words from Mary at Akita are plain: "If sins increase in number and gravity, there will be no longer pardon for them."

Startlingly, Sister Agnes received a *new* message on October 6, 2019 (the opening day of the Amazon Synod.) The new message requested, "Put on ashes, and please pray the penitential rosary every day."

There are countless claims of Virgin apparitions in the 20th century, some of them quite fascinating, like the series of Virgin-on-the-roof appearances in Egypt viewed by millions. But Fatima, early 20th century; Garabandal, mid-century; and Medjugorje, late-century, are three major 20th century apparitions that bear some striking similarities. Each of these three times, the Virgin appears in a remote, rural area to a group of children at a pivotal Cold-War moment, with words that are an unsettling mixture of warning and love. In Fatima, it was just before the Russian revolution and World War II; at Garabandal, it was as the Berlin Wall was being built, on the cusp of the Cuban Missile Crisis and Vatican II. In Medjugorje, it was shortly before the Iron Curtain crumbled, Yugoslavia disintegrated, and war erupted. Mary appears at the beginning, at the apex, and at the end of the Soviet Union's 20th century domination.

Each time, Mary appears as a concerned mother, urging *all* her children—not just the visionaries—to try harder and do better. She also issues somber warnings about what will befall the entire world in the future if we don't mend our ways.

The differences, however, are also curious: Each time, the group of children is a little larger in number, and a bit older on average. At Fatima, it was two girls and a boy, ages 7 through 10. In Garabandal, it was four girls, ages eleven or twelve. At Medjugorje, the Virgin reportedly appeared to four girls and two boys, ranging in ages from ten to sixteen.

Significantly, the later in the 20th century the Virgin Mary has appeared, the longer she has stuck around, as if the urgency is increasing. The apparitions in Garabandal occurred dozens of times from 1961-1965, eclipsing the six appearances over six months which occurred in 1917 in Fatima. In Medjugorje, meanwhile, the Virgin Mary began appearing on June 24, 1981— on the Feast Day of John the Baptist—and she hasn't stopped.

That's right—the Virgin Mary is still appearing to the same six individuals almost *forty years later.* Even the youngest of the children –who was ten when the apparitions began—is now middle-aged. And yet, *still* the Virgin shows up daily to some of the visionaries, and to every one of the visionaries at various times. This is a Virgin-Mary-apparition marathon.

When considering the Virgin's visits to Medjugorje, two questions spring immediately to mind:

What the *heck* is she doing?

And is she *ever* going to stop?

The answer to the second question, ominously, appears to be "yes."

Based on the words of Mary to the visionaries of Medjugorje, when she finally stops appearing at Medjugorje, all hell is going to break loose on earth. When the apparitions at Medjugorje cease, it may signal the end of a special age in Christian and human history—the "Marian age." The conclusion of Medjugorje, this mother-of-all-apparitions, may be the final page in the breathtaking vision recorded in the Book of Revelation 2,000 years earlier (a vision quite reminiscent of those glowing Virgins atop churches in Egypt):

A great sign appeared in the sky, a woman clothed with the sun, with the moon under her feet, and on her head a crown of twelve stars. She was with child and wailed aloud in pain as she labored to give birth. [321]

The Woman Clothed with the Sun, who is in labor, may finally give birth to a new age in the Church and in the world. If true, then it turns out the labor pains have lasted a lot longer than one night in Bethlehem—but that doesn't mean this period of difficulty and distress will last forever. One of Mary's most compelling comments from Medjugorje was on May 2, 1982: "I have come to call the world to conversion for the last time. Afterwards, I will not appear any more on this earth." Mary's special intervention in human history may be coming to an end.

How It All Began

Garabandal and Medjugorje have in common the "classic" apparition features that were present at Fatima: the rocky terrain and the isolated, insulated children who, one fine day, are supernaturally surprised. In Garabandal, rugged mountains shielded the girls from the global transformations of the 1960s, at least for a time. In 1981, Medjugorje, Yugoslavia was a tiny communist village of about 95 families isolated behind the Iron Curtain. Ironically, in both cases, it was the appearance of the Virgin that put these places on the map almost overnight.

The story of Medjugorje is chock full of surprising coincidence and turbulent drama, especially at its outset. In 1933, the poor but deeply religious village of Medjugorje erected a towering cross on a nearby mountain in honor of the 1900th anniversary of the crucifixion. Then, in 1969, the small parish built an oversized church for no discernible reason. As if divinely ordained, both the mountain top and the church now frequently overflow with visiting pilgrims.

The six visionaries of Medjugorje are Marija Pavlovic who was sixteen in 1981, on the date of the first apparition; Vicka Ivankovic, who was sixteen; Ivan Dragicevic, who was sixteen; Mirjana Dragicevic, who was sixteen; Ivanka Ivankovic, who was fifteen; and Jakov Colo, who was ten. Like the young girls at Garabandal, the youth in Medjugorje immediately began to tell others in their village about the strange sightings. They were counseled by some old women to splash holy water on the apparition in case it was Satan; they splashed, and Mary stayed. Some of the first words of Mary were, "Peace! Peace! Peace! Be reconciled! Only peace!"

Only four days after the apparitions had commenced, fifteen thousand people gathered. By the sixth day, the children had already been transported to nearby Mostar for a medical check-up. After only one week, the powers that be began to interfere. The children were driven away from the village during the typical time of the apparition (around six p.m.), but they poured out of the car and met with Mary by the roadside anyway. The communist authorities had forbidden the children or other visitors from gathering for the apparition, but the apparitions continued anyway in various secret locales. The authorities subjected the visionaries both to intense questioning and to a battery of tests. The government officials believed it was a political plot, and disseminated cartoons of Mary with a machine gun.

The parish priest, initially a skeptic, became a defender of the apparitions, was arrested and served a prison sentence as a result. In contrast, the local bishop, a supporter in the early months, turned against the apparitions after reportedly coming under pressure from the communist government and from some disapproving members of the Roman Catholic Church.[322]

The Arguments Against Medjugorje

Like the Energizer bunny, the drama of Medjugorje has continued on and on—for nearly forty years. Government opposition to Medjugorje has subsided over time, but Catholic opposition to Medjugorje has not. In the Catholic Church today, critics of Medjugorje thrive on both the left and the right. Opposed liberals view Marian devotion as a relic of the pre-Vatican II Church, or dismiss Mary as a tool of the Catholic conservative agenda since she's anti-communist and anti-feminist (being both virgin and mother, she had all the work with none of the fun).

Disapproving conservatives, on the other hand, seem scandalized by how open-minded the Virgin is. Mary in

Medjugorje made this statement, frequently carved up into little pieces and taken out of context, in response to a Catholic priest's "confusion" over the healing of an Orthodox child in a region where Croatian Catholics and Serbian Orthodox were sworn enemies:

Tell this priest, tell everyone, that it is you who is divided on earth. The Muslims and the Orthodox, for the same reason as Catholics, are equal before my Son and me. You are all my children. Certainly, all religions are not equal, but all men are equal before God, as St. Paul says. It does not suffice to belong to the Catholic Church to be saved, but it is necessary to respect the commandments of God in following one's conscience. Those who are not Catholics, are no less creatures made in the image of God, and destined to rejoin someday, the House of the Father. Salvation is available to everyone, without exception. Only those who refuse God deliberately, are condemned. To him, who has been given little, little will be asked for. To whomever has been given much (such as Catholics), *very much will be required. It is God alone, in His infinite justice, Who determines the degree of responsibility* (for each person) *and pronounces judgment.*[323]

Mary's words, which have scandalized some Catholics, are actually in line with the Catholic Church's position. Vatican II in its Dogmatic Constitution on the Church "Lumen Gentium" says, *Those also can attain to salvation who through no fault of their own do not know the Gospel of Christ or His Church, yet sincerely seek God, and moved by grace strive by their deeds to do His will as it is known to them through the dictates of conscience. Nor does Divine Providence deny the helps necessary for salvation to those who, without blame on their part, have not yet arrived at an explicit knowledge of God and with His grace strive to live a good life. Whatever good or truth is found amongst them is looked upon by the Church as a preparation for the Gospel. She knows that it is given by Him who enlightens all men so that they may finally have life.*

The Catholic Church's position is that this does not negate the necessity of Jesus as redeemer of the world—rather it is the great sacrifice of Jesus which has made the salvation of all actually possible—even those who do not yet know or love him. *In the human nature united to Himself, the Son of God, by overcoming death through His own death and resurrection, redeemed man and re-molded him into a new creation.*[324]

Because Mary at Medjugorje includes the entire human race in her message of love and salvation, she has been accused of being a "universalist" or "New Age" Mary, who views all beliefs as equally true. Yet Mary has explicitly stated in her Medjugorje messages that Jesus is the only mediator between God and man, and that there is no reincarnation—human beings live and die only once, and after that enter heaven, hell, or purgatory.[325] In a message in July 1982, Mary also maintained her Catholic orthodoxy in Medjugorje by noting that a person who has done great evil in his life can still enter heaven upon death if he confesses before dying, has sincere regret, and receives Holy Communion.

Mary's message—in a region that was about to explode into bloody warfare among Catholics, Orthodox and Muslims—was simply that loving God and neighbor (which is the whole of the law) is far more important than belonging to a particular religion, and that automatic salvation is not guaranteed to those in the "right" church (and there are numerous religions, churches and groups which make this claim.) In 1987, Mary reiterated, *Love your Serbian, Orthodox and Muslim brothers, and the atheists who persecute you.*[326]

Jesus himself demonstrated on many occasions in the gospels that God cared about a person's deeds and heart, not about his identity, culture, or religion. Jews, Samaritans, centurions, gentiles, soldiers, rabbis, Pharisees, tax collectors, lepers, divorcees, prostitutes, cripples, thieves, young, old, rich, poor, sick, healthy, religious and not—Jesus always approved of those whose hearts were humble and responsive to God. Peter and Paul both subsequently confirmed that God shows no partiality among human beings, but accepts all who fear God and do what is right.[327]

But Medjugorje continues to have ferocious detractors within the Catholic Church who insist it is the work of Satan, or that it is simple fraud on the part of a group of young people who started something as a prank, came to realize their village depended on it, and therefore could not stop it. Critics describe the Medjugorje seers as "professional visionaries" who must perform to keep the local economy going.

As proof, some point to how the visionaries have benefited materially. Developers have built hotels, condominiums, and shopping centers for the millions of pilgrims who have brought their money with them. Bigger houses have also been built in Medjugorje, although renting rooms to pilgrims is, in fact, how many locals support themselves. The appearance of the Virgin has brought a bustling pilgrimage economy to the region, but this does not invalidate the apparitions. Well-off critics begrudge an impoverished area its modest prosperity, preferring that the visionaries lead lives as perpetually struggling peasants in order to "prove" the apparitions are true.

Another complaint about the "visionary lifestyle" is that—like the Garabandal visionaries—they all married and had children as opposed to entering religious life as priests and nuns. This is a strange objection, since marriage is one of the Seven Sacraments of the Catholic Church. The visionaries do seem utterly typical of their time (since most Catholics do not enter religious life) and as the Book of Joel predicts, God's Spirit is being poured out on everyone, including the young, the sons and daughters, the "servants and handmaids" (the unimportant, the unimpressive, the uneducated).

Yet focusing on the six visionaries' lack of religious vocations completely ignores the large numbers of religious vocations which have resulted from Medjugorje. Any one of the visionaries could have used the apparitions as a launching pad to another life and left the stress of the Medjugorje spotlight far behind, yet they all remain actively involved with Medjugorje, residing there either part-time or full-time.

Another criticism is that Medjugorje can't be true because Mary would never appear for such a long time, although that is also one of the most compelling proofs that it *is* true. After all—it is almost 40 years later. That's a long time to maintain and coordinate a fraud which now involves six married adults with children who are scattered all over the world. Not a single visionary has denied the apparitions or stopped experiencing them completely. Most groups of six have difficulty maintaining unity for thirty minutes, much less thirty years. If it's fraud, as numerous people believe, the longevity and consistency remain impressive.

Furthermore, the first Marian apparition to be approved in the 21st century, Our Lady of Laus, involved a young French shepherdess in 1664 and lasted for *fifty-four years*. Known as the "Refuge for Sinners," Our Lady of Laus urged women in the area to stop having abortions and vigorously promoted the Sacrament of Confession.

An additional controversy in Medjugorje has been a long-running dispute between the local Franciscans, who were involved in supporting the apparitions early on and who had a centuries-long history of serving the local Catholics even under Muslim rule, and the local bishop, who was viewed as an outsider and who eventually opposed the apparitions. Like Garabandal, Medjugorje has its own distinct aura of troubling doubt swirling around it due to opposition from some bishops.

One more reason Medjugorje has generated suspicion is because it shares with Garabandal the more sensational aspects of the Marian apparition phenomenon: secrets, warnings, "permanent signs," and chastisements. Some accept the Virgin Mary appearing to children out of concern and love, but don't believe she would be involved in an elaborate scheme of secrets, signs and warnings. What's with the childishness of Mary whispering secrets into seers' ears that no one else can know? One explanation for this strange phenomenon is that Mary is sharing devastating prophecies of the future which *can* be changed, as Cardinal Ratzinger noted regarding the Third Secret of Fatima. On the one hand, the Virgin wants us to be warned. On the other hand, she doesn't want individuals to become obsessed or despairing over sensational predictions that are never set in stone, when the focus should be on turning to God *today* in order to alter that frightening future. Human nature is easily titillated by the sensational, but much less enthused about the hard work of repentance, prayer, and fasting. Hence, the Virgin Mary's practice of selectively sharing the gruesome details with a handful of seers whom she keeps close, instructs, and brings to spiritual maturity so that they can warn and assist others about the urgency of returning to God.

Nevertheless, the Virgin in Medjugorje is also warning that if we don't return to God, at least some of the "secrets" will not only eventually be revealed to everyone, but will indeed come true. This was the case at Fatima. The "Second Secret" regarding World War II, Russia, and the Cold War came true. The "Third Secret" of 20th century church persecution was also fulfilled, but we were spared the assassination of Pope John Paul II.

The Strange Secrets of Medjugorje

If Garabandal's prophecies are believed by some to be a continuation of Fatima's secrets, then Medjugorje appears to be a more detailed elaboration on Garabandal (which some say points to the fact that the visionaries were copying Garabandal). But the intricacies of the Medjugorje messages are even more complicated than those at Garabandal—not surprisingly, since Medjugorje involves *six* visionaries, *ten* secrets, and now, 40 years. At Medjugorje, each of the six visionaries is in the process of being given, over these many years, ten secrets from the Virgin Mary. When all six visionaries receive all ten secrets, the Virgin will stop appearing, and the secrets will begin to unfold.

As of this time, three of the six visionaries have all ten secrets—Mirjana, Ivanka, and Jakov. The visionaries who have been given the ten secrets are still visited by Mary at least once a
150

year. Mary promised to appear to Mirjana on her birthday, March 18th, for the rest of her life, as well as other select moments. Mary will appear to Ivanka each year on the anniversary of the apparitions, June 25th. The youngest visionary, Jakov, has his annual apparition on Christmas Day. That leaves the three remaining visionaries experiencing daily visits from Mary, while waiting on the last secrets. Meanwhile, the first three visionaries still have their annual apparitions, often filmed before observers; the messages from Mary which are given on those particular dates are always released. All of this is tracked and recorded in detail on various Medjugorje websites.

The words and behavior of the visionaries once Mary stops appearing to them on a daily basis are compelling, and offer insight into how the apparitions may have been sustained, unbroken, for 40 years. For the visionaries themselves, this phenomenon is not chiefly about secrets and signs. It's about a relationship. Mirjana, the first visionary to stop having daily apparitions, broke down in tears when it happened. Mirjana describes that day as the worst day of her entire life, and says she thought she was going to die.[328]

The Virgin told her, *"Mirjana, I have chosen you; I have confided in you everything that is essential. I have shown you many terrible things. You must bear it all with courage. Think of me and think of the tears I must shed for that. You must remain courageous. You have quickly grasped the messages. You must also understand now that I have to go away. Be courageous."* But Mary also told Mirjana that she would continue to appear to Mirjana at difficult moments stemming from Mirjana's knowledge of the secrets. Mirjana said, "At times, I can hardly cope with it when I seriously think of it. In those moments, Our Lady appears and gives me strength and courage to go on with my life."[329] And in fact, five years later, Mary began to appear to Mirjana every month on the 2nd, specifically to pray with Mirjana for unbelievers.

Meanwhile, some *seventeen years later*, Jakov turned to Mirjana for support when he learned he was about to receive the tenth secret. Growing up without his mother or father, he has said that Mary's daily visits in his life meant everything to him. He also wondered how he would go on with his life without seeing the Virgin Mary every day and has said that he waits anxiously every year to see her on December 25th.

But if the Medjugorje phenomenon for the seers is about a consoling, lifelong relationship with the Virgin Mary, for many curiosity-seekers, it's still about secrets and signs. Whether the Medjugorje apparitions are fraudulent, demonic, or from God, here is what we know about what the Virgin Mary is revealing about the future of the world—about our future. Just as Conchita has been appointed to announce the Miracle at Garabandal eight days ahead of time, Mirjana seems to be the visionary who has been singled out to reveal the Medjugorje Secrets to the world. Mirjana, who knows the day and date of each of the secrets, has chosen a priest, Father Petar Ljubicic, who will reveal the secrets to the whole world. Ten days before the first secret is to be revealed, Father Petar will be given a parchment containing the Ten Secrets. But this is the strange twist—this parchment is *not of this world.* So each secret will only materialize on the parchment for Father Petar when it's time for it to occur—something like holding the flame under the paper to read the message written in lemon juice. (This magical parchment smacks of Harry Potter and is another reason that Medjugorje is difficult to swallow for some.) Both the priest and the visionary will then fast and pray for seven days. Three days before the event occurs, the secret will be revealed to the world.

Like Garabandal, the Medjugorje visionaries are allowed to offer a limited amount of information about the Secrets. The First Secret has been described in the following way.

Our Lady showed Mirjana the first secret – the earth was desolate: "It is the upheaval of a region of the world. In the world there are so many sins. What can I do, if you do not help me. Remember that I love you. God does not have a hard heart. Look around you and see what men do, then you will no longer say that God has a hard heart. How many people come to church, to the house of God, with respect, a strong faith, and love God? Very few! Here you have a time of grace and conversion. It is necessary to use it well."[330]

Think about some of the upheavals of recent years which left parts of the earth "desolate": The 2004 Asian earthquake and tsunami, the 2010 Haitian earthquake, the 2011 Japan earthquake, tsunami, and nuclear disaster, and now the 2015 Nepal earthquake (great earthquakes in diverse places, which Jesus said would be a sign of the end times.[331]) Hurricane Katrina, the 2008 cyclone in Myanmar, and the 2013 typhoon in the Philippines. (Nations in perplexity at the roaring of the seas is another sign of the end times offered by Jesus.[332]) For all parts of the world, natural disasters, man-made violence, and all manner of human suffering have occurred in the first ten years of the new millennium alone. (Nation rising against nation and kingdom against kingdom was also on Jesus' end-times list.[333]) It's sobering to consider that something more severe than any of these past disasters might be the "kick-off" to the Ten Secrets of Medjugorje. In any event, the first secret will be restricted to "a region of the world," but no doubt will be witnessed by all thanks to internet and TV.

The Third Secret, we're told, will be an indestructible, beautiful and permanent sign left on Apparition Hill in Medjugorje. This, of course, closely echoes the "permanent sign" that is predicted to be left at the Pines in Garabandal on the day of the Great Miracle. If Medjugorje is true, it seems unlikely that these similar signs will be left on different dates; it's much more likely that something global is going to occur, and both Garabandal and Medjugorje are going to play a part. Not only will their respective visionaries announce events ahead of time, but a lasting and miraculous sign is going to be left at both locations. (The other possibility, of course, is Apparition plagiarism and fraud.)

[334] *After the Joplin, Missouri tornado of May 22, 2011*

The point of all these secrets, signs and warnings is certainly to confirm the truth of the apparitions of Medjugorje, and to convert the whole world. However, the Virgin made this rather ominous statement about that time: *"Those who are still alive will have little time for conversion."*[335] One interpretation of this statement is that because the apparitions have continued for so long, many of the older people of 1981 Medjugorje will have already passed away by the time the secrets unfold.

What else do we know about the Ten Secrets of Medjugorje? The Seventh Secret has been described as an evil that was threatening the world; Mirjana and Vicka have both stated that part of the Seventh Secret no longer exists because of the prayers and fasting of people around the world responding to Mary's pleas at Medjugorje. Indeed, Mary has said in Medjugorje, *"You have forgotten that with prayer and fasting you can ward off wars, suspend natural laws."*

This is a clear repudiation of Christian fatalism which shrugs its shoulders and declares that the date of doom is written in scriptural stone and nothing can be done about it. In fact, Mary said in Medjugorje, *"If you think of evil, punishment, wars, you are on the road to meeting them. Your responsibility is to accept Divine peace, live it and spread it."*[336]

Mary says this is precisely the time when believers should pray, fast, repent, and do as much as possible to obtain God's mercy for the world. Human beings are not puppets, and prophecies have an infuriating habit of being perfectly prophetic only *after* the event. The prophecies in the Book of Isaiah that speak of a son being born, of a child being given, who will be called Mighty God and Everlasting Father seem obvious (to Christians, anyway) only after the fact of the coming of Jesus.[337] Likewise the prophecies in Isaiah regarding the Suffering Servant who is led like a lamb to the slaughter, pierced and crushed for our iniquities, and who justifies many.[338]

In his own day, Jesus spoke of destroying the temple and raising it up in three days[339] which only after the fact was clearly seen as referring to himself. Jesus also accurately predicted that the actual temple of Jerusalem would be completely and utterly destroyed. This event occurred forty years after Jesus died. That was enough time for many who heard this prophecy to die before its fulfillment. No doubt there were scoffers who gloated over Jesus' false words ten, twenty and thirty years later: *What about that prediction that the temple would become rubble?* Jesus was long-gone, yet the temple still stood—but only for a time.

Besides being crystal clear only after the fact, prophecies are also often just inexact enough to be applicable to more than one time and more than one event. The Third Secret of Fatima seems like just such a prophecy. Maybe it was referring to 20th century communism and Pope John Paul II—then again, maybe not. Perhaps this is a deliberate strategy on the part of God because it leaves enough wiggle room for last-minute repentance and mercy. Maybe God really did give the whole world a reprieve in the 1980s by saving the pope, who then consecrated Russia, which stopped a nuclear war.

God told the prophet Jonah to warn the great city of Ninevah that he was about to destroy it. Astonishingly, everyone in the city actually listened and believed, something that's hard to imagine happening today. The entire city repented, fasted and prayed, and God relented in his destruction, which injured Jonah's pride because it made him look like a liar and a fool. Fortunately, God was less concerned about protecting Jonah's ego and more concerned about saving the people of Ninevah (God even mentions wanting to spare the animals.) However, Ninevah was eventually destroyed, more than a century later, after it backslid and returned to its evil ways. The prophecy did eventually come true, but God clearly is always eager to relent. The greatest gift of God is human free will, which can make all the difference.

Another lesson from the story of Ninevah is that when it comes to prophecies of destruction, setting dates is deadly. "Prophets" who remain safely vague about dates have a better track record. But there are many who can't resist temptation and finally succumb to setting a date. YouTube is littered with prophecies of doom that have already passed their expiration date. Maybe the "prophets" needed to prove they were authentic; maybe they like the attention; maybe, occasionally, they are speaking the truth about a coming disaster, and God relents in his punishment, sacrificing the prophet's ego on the altar of God's mercy. But more often, human delusion seems to be at work, a disastrously wrong date is set, and the prophecy and reputation go down in flames.

Nonetheless, the Medjugorje and Garabandal visionaries expect to announce very specific dates and events just before these events occur. This will clearly be to prove that both the Medjugorje and Garabandal apparitions of the Virgin Mary—along with her pleas and warnings—came from God. The Medjugorje and Garabandal visionaries' very specific, dated predictions of significant global events have not yet been disproven because the visionaries have not announced them yet.

Unlike the failed YouTube prophets, the striking, decades-long silence of the Garabandal and Medjugorje visionaries is 100 percent accurate.

If the visionaries die without speaking up, or the predicted chain of events never occurs, it will discredit the so-called seers but be better for everyone else. No doubt someone will write a future book about the 20th century apparition hysteria and the cultural forces which produced it. If the day does come that all the seers get the ten secrets, and the visionaries of Garabandal and Medjugorje simultaneously start announcing dates, it might be time to sit up and take notice.

The description of the Ninth and Tenth Secrets of Medjugorje bring an involuntary shudder: They are "a chastisement for the sins of the world." The sequence of events at Garabandal is Warning, Miracle, Chastisement. The sequence of events at Medjugorje appears exactly the same—just revealed in greater detail. (The Chastisement of Garabandal was always described as conditional upon our prayers, penance, and response to God.)

The Ten Secrets of Medjugorje, seemingly a succession of grave and catastrophic events, sound a little too close for comfort to the Seven Seals, Seven Trumpet Blasts, and Seven Bowls of Wrath in the Book of Revelation. Is it possible that they are all of a piece—that the warnings, miracles, and chastisements prophesied by the Virgin Mary at Fatima, Garabandal and Medjugorje are merely the ancient Book of the Apocalypse in 20th-century Catholic wrap? The Medjugorje seers have at times made some spooky-sounding statements. Visionary Ivan said on June 24, 2011, "But one day when the time comes, when some things get revealed, you will understand why the apparitions are such a long time and every day...Later on, our eyes will be opened...When we see physical changes that are going to happen in the world...This is so important to understand...The time in front of us is the time of great responsibility."

And Mary said in Medjugorje on June 24, 1983, "I will pray to my Son not to punish the world; but I plead with you, be converted. You cannot imagine what is going to happen nor what the Eternal Father will send to earth. That is why you must be converted!"[340]

The Three Secrets of Fatima; the Warning, Miracle and Chastisement of Garabandal; and the Ten Secrets of Medjugorje hint at terrible events that have occurred or may be coming. Here is what the Book of Revelation contains: War, hunger, famine, religious persecution, the beheading of the saints, destruction of great civilizations on earth, signs in heaven, a murderous totalitarian global economic system, a global dictator possessed by Satan, a false prophet who runs the world religion, hail and fire mixed with blood, a burning mountain hurled into the sea, a burning star falling from heaven, bitter waters, darkening of the sun, moon and stars, a plague of locusts, a rampaging army of 200 million, the death of billions, a plague of sores, blood-red seas and rivers, the death of all sea life, a scorching sun, a global earthquake, darkness, and gnawing pains.

And yet the most disturbing aspect of the Book of Revelation is the constant refrain after each terrible cataclysm, whether the people are being burned by the sun or crushed by hundred-pound hailstones: *they cursed the name of God who had the power to cause such plagues, and they would not repent and praise him.* In Revelation 9:18, a third of mankind is killed by what sounds suspiciously like global nuclear war. This would have to be utterly traumatic for the surviving two-thirds, and surely such a cataclysm would trigger intense and widespread soul-searching— wouldn't it? Yet Revelation says specifically that the survivors do not repent of worshiping demons and idols of gold, silver, bronze, stone and wood, nor do the survivors repent of murders, magic potions, sexual immorality, or robbery.

Is it really possible that even after such widespread cataclysm, humankind would refuse to throw itself on the mercy of God? We do live in an age when belief in God is increasingly mocked and scorned, when even the mention of God is routinely censored and silenced because it has become so offensive. The United States has been very effective in banning the mention of God and Jesus from the public square, where both were once freely and frequently invoked—even as Russia has been set free to re-discover Christianity. In Medjugorje, Mary confirmed what she'd said in Fatima and Garabandal regarding the conversion of Russia: "The Russian people will be the people who will glorify God the most. The West has made civilization progress, but without God, as if they were their own creators."[341]

This Creator who no longer gets credit for our existence, this Savior who has become "he-who-must-not-be-named" in the once-Christianized West, is often the first to be blamed when tragedy strikes, just as the above verse from the Book of Revelation suggests. Then the hue and cry goes up: Why would a good God let this happen? Here's a possible, sobering answer: What if the outsized horrors of the Book of Revelation are the natural end of a nation, a planet, and a universe with no God? A universe empty of God not because God has abandoned his own creation—but because God has been evicted by the very creatures He has set free?

In the 1953 *War of the Worlds* movie, the human race doesn't stop the invading Martians until people fill the churches and begin to pray. But in the 2005 movie version, naturally no such prayer takes place. Hollywood wrote a triumphal ending for the human race anyway, just as it did in recent movies about earth-destroying comets and asteroids.

Reality, however, is not a Hollywood script, and the ancient Hebrew and Christian scriptures do not portray a human race that is able to save itself apart from God. Yet even in the terrifying Book of Revelation, a moment arrives when the world that has refused to repent and turn to God *changes*: In Revelation Chapter Eleven, after an earthquake kills seven thousand people, "the rest were terrified and gave glory to the God of heaven." Since earthquakes worse than that already occur with some frequency, the "seven thousand" figure is likely symbolic, seven often considered the number of God. In Revelation Chapter Sixteen, the earthquake is described as so violent that the human race has never before experienced anything like it. Not a comforting description, based on the havoc recent earthquakes have already wrought around the world. Whatever the details or dimensions of this earthquake, God somehow finally captures the attention and hearts of those who remain.

The Great Sign that is promised will apparently be a last-ditch effort to reach these unbelievers: *"This sign will be given for the atheists. You faithful already have signs and you have become the sign for the atheists. You faithful must not wait for the sign before you convert; convert soon. This time is a time of grace for you. You can never thank God enough for His grace. The time is for deepening your faith and for your conversion. When the sign comes, it will be too late for many."*[342]

How close is that day? Judging by the Medjugorje clock, entirely too close for comfort: Three of the visionaries know all ten secrets, but the three remaining visionaries already know *nine* secrets; Vicka, Ivan and Marija are waiting only for the Tenth Secret, and have been waiting for it for years. Either the visionaries are prolonging the fraud to keep the pilgrims coming—or God is prolonging this time of grace as long as divinely possible, hoping against hope that we will change.

If Medjugorje is a fraud, and the visionaries are doing it for money, that will surely become evident. One of the visionaries will write a book about the scam, go on a book tour, and be the toast of the talk-show circuit for about fifteen minutes. If, on the other hand, Medjugorje turns out to be true, we can only hope and pray that these three visionaries don't receive that last secret soon.

Are the Apparitions Almost Over?

Some events have occurred in recent years which have rattled the Medjugorje world. In 2012, for the very first time, after more than thirty years of messages from the Virgin Mary, the Virgin remained silent during an apparition while someone else spoke: Jesus. On Christmas Day, 2012, the Infant Jesus appeared in the Virgin's arms. Although this has occurred before (just as it did in Garabandal), never before during the Medjugorje apparitions has Jesus spoken instead of his mother.

The Medjugorje world was abuzz afterward with what this might portend. Did it mean the Virgin's appearances were coming to a close? Was it related to the fact that a commission investigating Medjugorje was supposed to issue a final report soon? Jesus' words were simply, "I am your peace. Keep my commandments." Commentators have noted that these words echo Jesus' discourse in John 14 shortly before he went to the cross, when he bequeathed his peace to his disciples and reminded them to keep his commandments.

In fact, some of the conclusions of the investigating commission were indeed "leaked" in 2017. The Ruini Comission ruled that the first seven apparitions were supernatural, while suspending judgment on the continuing phenomena.[343] And in 2019, Pope Francis officially authorized pilgrimages to Medjugorje. More recently, and more shockingly, the monthly apparition of Mirjana has come to an end. Each month since 1987 Mary would appear to Mirjana on the 2nd to pray for unbelievers, but in March 2020, she informed Mirjana that she would no longer appear on the 2nd each month. This news reportedly left Mirjana "shocked and saddened."[344]

Despite the sensational End Times predictions associated with Medjugorje, the bulk of Medjugorje's messages these forty years have been, like other Marian apparitions, somewhat simple and austere: To avoid tragedy, everyone should pray, fast, repent, do penance, confess your sins, receive communion. Draw close to God because God exists and God loves you. The Virgin in Medjugorje is quite clear about her role versus God's: *I cannot cure. God alone cures. Pray! I will pray with you. Believe firmly. Fast, do penance. I will help you as long as it is in my power to do it. God comes to help everyone. I am not God. I need your sacrifices and your prayers to help me.*

Like a good mother, she is always encouraging even as she asks of us difficult things. She said to the visionaries: *I would like all of you to become priests and religious, but only if you desire it. You are free. It is up to you to choose. If you are experiencing difficulties or if you need something, come to me. If you do not have the strength to fast on bread and water, you can give up a number of things. It would be a good thing to give up television, because after seeing some programs, you are distracted and unable to pray. You can give up alcohol, cigarettes, and other pleasures. You yourselves know what you have to do.*[345]

All the strident Catholic opposition, as well as bloody regional war for numerous years, have not stopped the apparitions in Medjugorje—and have not stopped an estimated 50 million pilgrims from visiting Medjugorje since 1981. There are countless stories of conversion and healing, including the healing of diseases like multiple sclerosis and leukemia. Some of the testimonies come from the least likely quarters. In the book *The Miracle Detective*, an atheist neurophysiologist, Dr. Marco Margnelli, visited the apparitions in an attempt to debunk them, but determined by the end that the visionaries were in a genuine state of ecstasy, in an altered state of consciousness. Yet he admitted that what really haunted him and eventually made a practicing Catholic out of him were *the birds* of Medjugorje: All the birds would gather in the trees and create a boisterous racket every afternoon, then suddenly go silent each day at dusk when the Virgin Mary appeared.[346]

The apparitions of Garabandal might very well be the link between the foundational, Church-approved apparitions of early-20th-century Fatima and the enormously popular (and hugely controversial) ongoing apparitions at Medjugorje. And yet, Garabandal has turned out to be the weak link. Along the way, the messages of Garabandal—possibly meant to be a bridge between the two—instead mysteriously collapsed into the apparition abyss.

Something went wrong at Garabandal. A shadow hangs over

the Spanish mountain apparitions that has effectively suppressed its story. Was it because the *messages* of Garabandal were too hot to handle at the time—and might be even today? In the final section, the Virgin Mary's central message at Garabandal will be explored in depth and detail, including what the Virgin Mary controversially predicted in 1965 regarding the Roman Catholic Church that has already come to pass, and what Mary said needs to be done in the future to change the course of human history and avert disaster.

Yet it may be the doubting *messengers* of Garabandal themselves who are the key to the mystery of Garabandal. After all, the message doesn't much matter if the visionaries made it up, and there are accusations of exactly that. How did the visionaries of Garabandal eventually come to doubt the apparitions, and what do they believe today about what happened to them 50 years ago?

PART 3

Solving the Mystery of Garabandal

347 *Garabandal, Spain today*

Chapter 7

Shocking Last Words from the Virgin Mary

Many cardinals, bishops and priests are on the road to perdition, and with them they are taking many souls. **The Virgin Mary during her last message in Garabandal.**

348 *Mari-Loli, Conchita, Mari Cruz, Jacinta—not in ecstasy*

Fatima, Garabandal, and Medjugorje are three Marian apparitions which occurred at pivotal Cold War moments in the 20th century. Millions of pilgrims stream to both Fatima and Medjugorje each year. Yet only a small trickle of visitors reaches the mountains of Garabandal. Soaring shrines and ample accommodations greet travelers in Fatima and Medjugorje. Only

Garabandal has remained relatively untouched in size and scale. There's an extra inn or two here and there, a few more homes, but that's about it.

The mysterious "disappearance" of Garabandal can't be blamed on the remote locale; Fatima and Medjugorje were tiny and tucked away as well. It can't be blamed on the passing of decades; Fatima occurred much longer ago. It can't be blamed on the material in the messages—Garabandal, like Fatima and Medjugorje, urged repentance and warned of impending global peril if the warnings were ignored. Garabandal's invisibility also can't be blamed on the messengers—Fatima and Medjugorje featured child-visionaries just like Garabandal did. It can't even be blamed on opposition and controversy. Medjugorje has thrived despite intense ambivalence about it within the Catholic Church itself.

Yet for all their shared components, Garabandal has some unique aspects that set it apart from Fatima and Medjugorje. Its most troubling characteristic is undoubtedly that of the denials and back-pedaling of its visionaries. The children of Fatima never denied the apparitions, even in the face of being threatened with boiling oil, although two of the three children died within a couple of years of the apparitions; remarkably, the youth of Medjugorje have never denied the ongoing apparitions even into their own middle-age, although unlike Garabandal, the Medjugorje appearances have never *stopped*.

But a gloomy prophecy about denial was given in Garabandal from the start. The Virgin Mary told the girls early on that a day would come when they would deny seeing her, would contradict each other, and their parents would not get along. The four girls, naturally, were shocked to hear this. At that time, in the throes of their daily ecstasies, they couldn't imagine ever denying the astonishing experience they were having in their little village. In fact, the girls at first refused to reveal what the Virgin had told them, insisting that they didn't understand it. Under persistent questioning, they finally reported that the Virgin had predicted future denials, contradictions and conflicts on the part of the girls. When pressed about whether the Virgin had said anything else, they brought forth this strange statement from the Virgin Mary in 1961: "In this way you will establish among yourselves the same confusion that exists in the church." A priest who was present immediately objected to the notion of "confusion in the church," attributing these words to the devil rather than the Virgin.[349]

But by early 1963, a short eighteen months after the apparitions had commenced, the denials began. Conchita's description of the denials in her diary is odd. She simultaneously denies and affirms the apparitions.

The Denials Begin

"We even went one day to confess it (that they had made it up). But we felt inside that the Angel and the Most Holy Virgin had appeared to us, since they had brought a peace and internal joy to our souls, and a great desire to love them with our whole hearts."[350]

If they felt inside such peace, joy and intense love for both Michael the Archangel and the Virgin Mary, why did they confess to making the apparitions up? The explanation is not very enlightening.

"We doubted a little, but a doubt of a type that seems from the devil, who wants us to deny the Virgin. And afterwards, we told our parents that we hadn't seen the Virgin; but that the calls and the Miracle of the Sacred Host were true."[351]

Conchita says she was "surprised" to be denying the Virgin when her conscience was at peace that she had seen her. So where was this denial coming from?

A commission of doctors then came to the village and questioned Mari Cruz, Jacinta, and Mari-Loli, who not only denied seeing the Virgin, but said that Conchita had performed the Miracle of the Host herself. In her diary, Conchita explained the betrayal this way: "Obviously, they didn't know what they were saying at the time. And they allowed themselves to be controlled by the devil."

The gaps in this diary narrative make it sound as though the denials sprang fully formed from thin air for no reason and with no explanation except as a trick of the devil. In reality, the fissures in the girls' relationships, along with their parents' rivalries, may be traced at least as far back to the Miracle of the Host, about six months earlier. After that time, a divide appeared more starkly between those who believed in Garabandal and those who did not. The believers, including those who were reduced to tears at the sight of the Miraculous Host, were more convinced than ever; the disbelievers were more skeptical than ever before.

On the skeptical side, Conchita in particular had come in for special scrutiny. There were those who said that Conchita had performed the so-called "Miracle" herself, that she had pocketed the host beforehand and deposited it on her tongue at just the critical moment. It's hardly surprising that this alternative to a genuine miracle was circulated, since it seemed like the likeliest explanation. Yet there was also the fact that dozens of flashlights and eyes were riveted on Conchita's bare and extended tongue before the host appeared. Had the host been sticking to the roof of her mouth and suddenly dropped? What were the precise logistics behind the fraud?

A villager who witnessed the host materializing on Conchita's tongue remarked, "If there had been a trick, I would like someone to explain it to me because as far as I am concerned, I really don't know how she could have done it."[352]

Conchita's own cousin was accused of conspiring to commit communion fraud. Instead, she insisted that she and Conchita were sitting by a window watching a village celebration take place. "Afterwards, we were accused of having prepared the Host at that time."[353]

The other three visionaries, along with the parents, also were being drawn into this disagreement. Perhaps resentful that Conchita was getting so much attention, they also began to suggest that Conchita had faked it. Or—if the apparitions were false—then Conchita hogging the limelight was finally bringing the whole charade to light.

In September of 1962, Conchita had a conversation with the Virgin Mary during an ecstasy that was tape recorded, and which no doubt added to the sense of Conchita being singled out for special favors while the others were being shoved to the margins. Conchita was recorded as saying to the Virgin, "*You say there's going to be a miracle? . . .And the miracle is going to be that? . . . And the Virgin will be seen?...And when? . . . So long away? . . . With me alone . . . No. I don't want that . . . Don't do that! Perform it with the four.*" [354]

This was reportedly a mention of the Great Global Miracle along with a new nugget of information that Conchita alone was destined to announce it. Since this pronouncement came from Conchita herself, it likely added fuel to the rivalry fires.

In the midst of all this, Mari-Loli all alone one day received communion from Michael the Archangel. In a rather poignant exchange, she reportedly asked Michael why all four girls hadn't been given the miraculous visible communion like Conchita had, since some villagers had suggested it was because the remaining three girls were bad. Michael dismissed the notion that the other three girls had been excluded from the miracle because they were bad. [355]

Ironically, both Jacinta and Conchita later exhibited resentment that *they* had been excluded from Mari-Loli's solitary communion experience with Michael. The girls were immature—they were barely in their teens. Even the disciples of Jesus, grown men, quarreled jealously and competitively over who was greatest among them. Father Enrique Valcarce Alfayate, a cardinal visiting from Madrid, took note of the rivalries between the girls, but saw it as proof that it wasn't an act they'd concocted. He also noted the girls' radiant expressions in ecstasy, while in their normal state they were "withdrawn and taciturn." His final word on what caused the ecstasies: *I don't know.*[356]

Still, by and large, the apparitions continued for all four girls as the summer of 1962 wore on. But for Mari Cruz, the apparitions were rapidly nearing their end. Mari Cruz had stopped praying the rosary every day with the other girls. Was it because of her parents' objections to the whole affair, their efforts to separate her from the other girls and shield her from the frenzied spotlight? Whatever the reason, Mari Cruz's visions also stopped. By September of 1962, Mari Cruz wrote in a letter: "The people don't like me because I see the Virgin less, but I want what She wants. It has been 18 days since I've seen her, but I love her as I do when I see her."[357]

Mari Cruz means Mary of the Cross, which, as some have noted, seems apt considering the strange, sad cross Mari Cruz carried as a result of the apparitions. Despite Mari Cruz's distress and her experience of being ostracized, she did not attempt to fake and prolong her ecstasies.

Mari Cruz was now completely out of the picture, apparition-wise, but the other three girls continued to have frequent apparitions of the Virgin Mary, numerous times each week. And sometime during the autumn of 1962, as Conchita had begged and hoped for, both Jacinta and Mari-Loli were given the promise of a miracle as well. But was it the same miracle—the great global miracle? Were they being allowed to participate in the great miracle after all, as Conchita asked of Mary on more than one occasion?

No. Instead, word spread through the village that Jacinta and Mari-Loli were expecting a miracle of their own. A miracle that was destined to occur before the end of 1962. Actually, followers of the Garabandal apparitions were expecting Conchita's Great Miracle to happen at any moment, much like the followers of Jesus expected him to return to earth almost as soon as he left.

As a result of both of these miracles—Conchita's Great Global Miracle, and the newly promised Loli-and-Jacinta

Miracle—surely the girls would at last be vindicated, the stresses and strains imposed on the village and the visionaries would be worthwhile, and all would believe. It would only be a short time now, and believers were full of eager anticipation. This was the atmosphere in Garabandal toward the end of 1962.[358]

It was "Loli and Jacinta's miracle," as it came to be called, that everyone was waiting on first, before the end of 1962. But as the days ticked by, and the end of December came and went, bitter disappointment set in. What happened? Nothing. Unlike the Miracle of the Host, the girls did not send out letters announcing the date of the new miracle and summoning the pilgrims to Garabandal. Nor did they bother to explain the delay, by attributing it to irreverent spectators or partying villagers, as had been the case before. In fact, the girls, for their part, were strangely silent. Conchita still insisted the Global Miracle would take place—she hadn't changed her mind about that—but of "Loli and Jacinta's miracle," *no one said anything.*

It turned out that "Loli and Jacinta's miracle" was a prank gone awry that morphed into a blame game. Conchita finally confessed that Loli and Jacinta were going to bury a statue and then "find" it under the Virgin's direction—perhaps a stunt concocted by two girls who were tired of hearing about Conchita's miracles, both big and small.

However, Jacinta claimed Conchita conceived of the prank and talked them into it. Jacinta would admit later that whenever she and Mari-Loli queried the Virgin about a miracle, Mary never promised one, but said, rather, "They will believe. They will believe." Jacinta insisted that Conchita had given them the idea of a miracle that they, too, would participate in.[359]

Was Conchita, self-conscious about her increasingly special status, trying to dream up a way to share the spotlight with her resentful friends? Conchita had said to the Virgin in a taped apparition on the night of September 9: *"When you perform the Miracle, perform it with all of us, I don't want to be alone by myself."*[360] Or was Conchita, who had been accused early on of instigating the

171

apparitions, continuing the deception by coming up with a new trick for the girls to play?

Whether it was Conchita or Mari-Loli and Jacinta who conceived the idea, the buried statue stunt had its origin in an earlier Spanish apparition that the girls had doubtless heard about. At the beginning of the 14th century, the Virgin appeared to a shepherd with instructions to dig at the site of the apparition. A statue of the Virgin was uncovered which had previously been buried by priests fleeing from the invading Moors. This re-discovered statue helped inspire the Christians to take back Iberia from the Moors. The statue, supposedly carved by St. Luke himself, depicted a dark-skinned Virgin of Guadalupe who became much more well-known when she later appeared in Mexico to unite the Spanish colonizers and the indigenous people.

But the buried statue wasn't the only prank the girls dreamed up. Conchita, playing her own prank, gave some toothpowder to Mari-Loli and Jacinta claiming that it would help them levitate. Conchita said she was only joking, but Mari-Loli, apparently hoping it was true, ingested so much powder that she got sick to her stomach. This incident does lend credence to the idea that the other girls followed Conchita's lead, and Conchita did in fact seem to be the mischief-maker of the group. At the end of an apparition, she would sometimes repeatedly make the sign of the cross wrong in order to force the Virgin to stay a while longer. Mary wouldn't leave until Conchita finally made the sign of the cross correctly.[361]

From these pranks that the girls were either plotting (the buried statue) or already executing (levitation powder), the unfortunate rumor of "Loli and Jacinta's miracle" began to circulate through the village. The rumor apparently gained a momentum of its own and the die was cast. At the time, the failure of Loli and Jacinta's miracle to materialize by the end of 1962 was sharply disappointing and was taken as evidence of the falsity of the entire affair—something which made the much-maligned bishops' skeptical pronouncements appear eminently wise and reasonable.

How could this have happened? A practical joke involving magic tooth powder (which Conchita played on her friends) and a buried statue (which the girls discussed but never actually performed), along with the failure of the girls to foresee the dire consequences of their foolishness, managed to call the entire Garabandal episode into question.

But the girls' penchant for practical jokes may not have been the only human dimension of this story that led to such unfortunate consequences. The Virgin had essentially presented a simple, almost mundane message at Garabandal asking people to become more prayerful and devoted to God—a message which many were not particularly interested in heeding.

More commonly, the pressing crowds arrived in this off-the-map village with high hopes and expectations of witnessing the miraculous. Conchita was attracting disproportionate attention, with her central role in the little Miracle of the Host and the coming Great Global Miracle. The girls struggled with jealousy, their families harbored old village rivalries, and the superficial crowds made pressing demands for miracles and passed harsh judgments on the girls who didn't produce. Witness young Mari Cruz's suffering. Is it any wonder, in such a climate, that the girls may have succumbed to the pressure to please the multitudes and out-perform each other?

Catapulted into the spotlight, immature and human, is it possible they tried to concoct their own miracle to supplement the Virgin's? Was this prank the result of Mari-Loli and Jacinta trying to best Conchita's special status with a "miracle" of their own, a hoax which spun out of their control? Or could it have been that an isolated Conchita was trying to share the spotlight with her friends, and planted the hopeful fantasy of Loli and Jacinta having their own special miracle? Or, when the girls weren't in ecstasy, did they forget the seriousness of their situation and the scrutiny they were under and decide to prank the pressing crowds? Or—perhaps most likely—had the "apparitions" been nothing more than teenage pranks all along?

³⁶² *Did gifts from admirers pressure the girls to perform?*

Like most 13-year-olds, the Garabandal visionaries were not saints. Contrast them with the three children of Fatima—two of those children died very soon after the apparitions, the third lived into venerable old age as a cloistered nun. The children of Fatima seemed like saints and martyrs from the get-go. But the four girls of Garabandal disappointed in this regard. They were more like the rest of us. In their early teens, they lacked an awareness of the responsibility that had been thrust upon them, and apparently engaged in foolish frivolity without thought for the greater consequences. And like most people, they had trouble coming clean when their deceit was exposed—they were reduced to maintaining a sheepish silence in the face of their missing miracle.

It's noteworthy that the girls never followed through on finding the buried statue. If the girls had concocted the apparitions on their own—faking all the apparitions and the Miracle of the Host—why not bury the statue? Everyone was now waiting with feverish anticipation for the next miracle, just as they had been before the Miracle of the Host. Why stop? Was it because the girls hadn't concocted the apparitions or the

Miracle of the Host, and when push came to shove, they weren't up to manufacturing a miracle copied from a past apparition?

In retrospect, this episode brings out a sharp contrast: On the one hand, the countless times the girls appeared to be in genuine unblinking ecstasy that awed the crowds and left people marveling. On the other hand, the limited number of times when the four girls were merely their own childish selves, playing pranks that went badly awry, trying to conjure up awkward miracles on their own, sowing nothing but confusion and disillusionment in their wake.

With fifty years of hindsight, the disappointing human side of the four visionaries only makes their many strange ecstasies more striking and unexplainable: The long nights when the girls were out in freezing rain and bitter blowing snow with no one to witness their hardship, except for the dutiful family members who accompanied them and the stray neighbor who saw them outside and called them in from the cold.[363] The grueling marches in the dark up and down rocky hills at high speed, backward, sitting down, and on their knees.[364] The long hours of praying the rosary in unified, musical cadence at dawn and midnight even in the village cemetery. (Many people grow restless just rushing through part of the rosary in the middle of the day.) The girls' insistence on waiting up, fully dressed, for their ecstasies because the Virgin would not wake them for an ecstasy if they had already gone to bed and fallen asleep.[365] The way they fell to their knees "as if struck by lightning," knees crunching, and held impossible physical positions, even for hours, without injury.[366] Their mature availability and generosity to the visiting throngs even to the point of exhaustion, their patient endurance while being scrutinized and mocked by villagers and strangers alike.[367] Their luminous joy and deep sorrow while in conversation with the Virgin, their passionate descriptions of her loving eyes and motherly kiss,[368] which apparently drew the girls like a magnet and sealed their devotion to her—in spite of the upheaval and suffering that Mary's appearance had brought into their village and their lives.

Still, at the time, many people, who had heretofore hoped and believed, reasonably began to doubt when Loli and Jacinta's fake miracle failed to materialize by the end of 1962. Among them were exhausted and humiliated family members, who began to pressure the girls, in the face of the failed miracle, to admit that they had been lying about everything. And who could blame them? All the families had paid a price. Conchita's mother recalled how the village shunned her and her sons when Conchita was summoned to Santander in the summer of 1961 to be interviewed by the bishop, because villagers believed Conchita's mother was trying to end the apparitions.[369]

Later, the village atmosphere veered from giddy belief to dark skepticism. Many people began to doubt the Miracle of the Host, and Conchita's own belief started to wilt in this pressure cooker atmosphere. Conchita's mother was so upset that she backed Conchita against the kitchen wall one day and demanded to know how Conchita had faked the Miracle of the Host. "Oh! Mamacita!" Conchita replied. "I didn't do anything!" Maybe the Miracle of the Host had never occurred, Conchita said, but she herself hadn't faked it. People must have seen what they wanted to see through "autosuggestion," Conchita told her mother. Conchita's mother thought, "The people could have been autosuggested, but not the camera."[370] Jacinta's father Simon was so disturbed because people said his daughter was sick and the bishop didn't believe in the apparitions that he went up on the mountain alone to cry, certain that he was going crazy.[371]

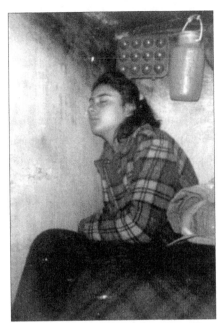

³⁷² *Conchita waiting up for an ecstasy*

Mari-Loli's father, who was also the mayor, seemingly lost patience with the phenomenon and the girls in the wake of the failed miracle and summoned the commission of doctors to the village. It was during these interviews that Mari-Loli, Jacinta, and Mari Cruz, under pressure from disillusioned villagers and family members, confessed the apparitions were not real, and accused Conchita of faking the Miracle of the Host—an accusation Conchita sadly attributed to the influence of the devil.³⁷³

And then comes one of the most poignant remarks in Conchita's diary: "And after that day, they didn't have any more apparitions. I had apparitions on the same night, and until the 20th of January (1963). After that I didn't see her again."

The Virgin Disappears

So there it was. The miracle failed, the girls confessed, and the Virgin, conveniently enough, stopped showing up. Had a hoax gone wildly awry finally played itself out? Did the girls start something that fateful day in the sunken lane with bitter apples that took on an astonishing and frightening life of its own? Were Mari Cruz's parents, by throwing up a barrier between their daughter and the other girls, the wisest of the bunch? And were the girls at last afforded a way out of the highly public trap they had ensnared themselves in?

Or had the Virgin stopped appearing because of mistakes made by the immature visionaries, the subsequent loss of faith of the villagers, the increasing resistance of family members, and the Peter-like denials of the girls themselves?

At the time that Conchita wrote her short, sad elegy in her journal, the Virgin Mary had indeed vanished. Garabandal had become an apparition-free zone. As Conchita wrote to a friend, "I don't know when the Virgin will appear to me again, since she didn't say goodbye, nor did she say anything to us. Here the people are very disappointed."[374] To a priest, Conchita wrote that hardly anyone believed in the apparitions anymore, even her own mother and formerly faith-filled aunt, who declared sorrowfully that nothing had been from God.

Conchita herself maintained she still believed and insisted that Mari-Loli and Jacinta had returned to their senses as well and believed again. Conchita declared, "Really, how could they not?" The rift in the girls' relationship also had mended. Mari Cruz, however, continued to deny the Virgin's appearance, and only a short while later, in another letter to the same priest, Conchita said she herself didn't believe, after all.[375] And yet, Conchita's fresh lack of belief was coupled with her mention of *no longer* seeing the Virgin, rather than *never* seeing her: "As I don't see the Virgin now, I don't know what to write...I miss you very much. Do you still believe so much? I don't believe anything."

The end of the apparitions certainly triggered a sense of loss for the girls. As late as 1965, Jacinta would comment, "Sometimes, I dream that the other three are in a trance and I am left out. It hurts me very much. But one day, Conchita said to me, "I was dreaming that you were in a trance, Jacinta." And this gave me great joy."[376]

During this time, with all traces of the Virgin gone from Garabandal, the girls, along with many villagers and followers, vacillated between belief and dark doubt. Yes, there had been *something*. No, it had been nothing. Then one day, in the spring of 1963, something happened to Conchita. She was doubting that day in her heart that the Great Miracle would ever come. And then she heard a voice:

Conchita, do not doubt that my Son will perform a Miracle.

This simple sentence restored Conchita's confidence and joy. She began to believe again, and became very devout, spending a great deal of time praying in the church. And thus was launched a new phase of Garabandal. Both Conchita and Mari-Loli would begin to have locutions of both Jesus and Mary—they heard voices inside themselves.

Conchita did not know there was an actual name for her experience until she began to tell others what she was hearing. In her journal, she expressed a strong preference for the voice over the apparition: "I prefer the locution more than the apparitions, since during the locution, I have her in my very self. Oh! What happiness, with the Most Holy Virgin within me! And what a shame, to be so bad! But that is the world." She also said that the locutions with Jesus were even more wonderful than those with Mary. In fact, she recorded at the time an entire conversation she had with Jesus that included mention of the Great Miracle.

"I asked Him to give me a cross since I was living without suffering—except the suffering of not having a cross. And he answered: *Yes. I will give you a cross.* And with much feeling, I went on praying . . .And I said to Him, Why is the Miracle coming? . . . to convert many people? He answered, *To convert the whole world.* Will Russia be converted? *It also will be converted; and so everyone will love Our Hearts.* Will the chastisement come afterwards? (He didn't answer me.) Why do you come to my poor heart, without my meriting it? *I certainly do not come for you; I come for everyone.* When the Miracle comes, will it be as though I were the only one who saw the Virgin? He answered me, *By your sacrifices, your patience, I will allow you to intercede for the accomplishment of the Miracle.* And I said to Him: Wouldn't it be better for me to be with all the others; or if not, that You don't use any of us to intercede? *No.* Will I go to heaven? *You should love much and pray to Our Hearts.* When will You give me a cross? (He didn't answer me.) What will I be? (He didn't answer me; He only told me that everywhere that I would be, I would have much to suffer.) Am I going to die soon? *You have to stay on the earth to help the world.* I am very small. I couldn't help in anything. *With your prayers and sufferings, you will help the world.* When does one go to heaven? . . .when one dies? *One never dies.* (I thought that we didn't go to heaven until we were resurrected.)"[377]

The conversation with Jesus accurately foretold Conchita's future in many respects. She asked, maybe out of naked human curiosity, if she would die soon, and Jesus said no. When she asked, "What will I be?" she was referring to becoming a nun, which she had asked and hoped for—but which in fact did not occur. She asked again that it either be all or none of the four girls when it came to involvement in the Great Miracle, but Jesus confirmed she had a particular role to play. (Indeed, since Mari-Loli has already passed away, who can say which of the remaining three visionaries will still be alive to see the Great Miracle?) Jesus also mentions that Conchita's *patience* would help accomplish the Great Miracle, and she has been patient for more than fifty years now. And finally, Conchita asked Jesus to give her a cross, and Jesus assured her that He would, and that she would have much to suffer. Conchita's role as the central Garabandal visionary—perhaps already a cross that she didn't yet recognize—would continue to be her burden in the years ahead.

In Mari-Loli's locutions, the Virgin Mary also spoke of suffering. When Loli pled with Mary to let her parents believe in Garabandal, Mary replied that *They do not believe, so that you will have more to suffer. Suffer with patience.* And again I said to her, *Why don't my parents believe?* And she said to me, *Because you have to suffer. You have much to suffer in this world.*[378] For Mari-Loli, the Garabandal experience also would be a cross she would continue to carry.

But Conchita was not only experiencing locutions, she was also going to experience apparitions again. The Virgin was going to appear again in Garabandal after all. At the tail-end of 1963, on December 8, the Feast of the Immaculate Conception, Conchita alone had an apparition just outside the church doors in the icy pre-dawn hours. It had been almost a year since the Virgin Mary had shown her face in Garabandal, a year marked by disappointment and controversy. During this new apparition, the Virgin made an unsettling future prediction about the young teenager whose life had been turned upside down in the previous two years: *You will not be happy on earth, but you will be in heaven.*[379] (As it turns out, this was the same prediction given by the Virgin Mary to Bernadette of Lourdes.)

Scattered locutions would take place involving Conchita and Mari-Loli during 1964, and visitors would still come, despite the relative quiet that reigned. There were no apparitions, no ecstatic marches up to the Pines, to the doors of the church, to the graveyard, to the sunken lane, to various villagers' homes. No chaotic days with the mobs pressing close, the flashbulbs popping, the doctors prodding and pricking. No solitary nights of making house-to-house visits in the village, crucifix in hand, lone parent in tow.

Then, an entire year after the last apparition, again on the December 8 feast day, Conchita would have a locution with the Virgin Mary. But this one was significant. The Virgin told Conchita that something important was going to happen in 1965, and an exact date was given—June 18. Back in 1961, when St. Michael had made his early appearances to the girls, he had flashed a sign giving the date of Mary's first "message to the world"—October 18, 1961. Now, the order was reversed. During Conchita's December 8, 1964 locution, the Virgin Mary gave a date when *St. Michael* would appear with an important message for the world: June 18, 1965. These would be the only two official, formal "messages to the world" that would come from the Garabandal apparitions, and they would serve as bookends to the event.

The First Message of Garabandal

The first message was hinted at in the strange sign that St. Michael was carrying in the summer of 1961 when he first announced that the Virgin was coming to town. Like a preview of a coming attraction, the sign reportedly read: "One must...XVIII-MCMLXI." Alternately, it has been translated as, "It is necessary to... XVIII-MCMLXI." In any event, what mostly caught the girls' eye was the strange lettering that they could not decipher. Later, they learned they had been looking at Roman numerals. The Virgin Mary subsequently explained to them that the sign was announcing the date and opening words of her first formal message at Garabandal. She then began to explain the entire message to the girls over the course of several apparitions, which apparently left the girls at times in tears.[380] Furthermore, visuals sometimes accompanied the script in case the words were not clear: The girls at one point described seeing a chalice filling with drops of either blood or tears, along with the Virgin, looking profoundly sad and saying in a low voice, *The cup is already filling.*[381] Twenty years later, Mari-Loli said the Virgin told them the drops of blood were falling from the heart of Jesus.[382] So the visionaries of Garabandal enjoyed a pre-screening of the First Message of Garabandal several months prior to its release date.

On October 18, 1961, close to fifteen thousand people descended on the village.[383] From early on, the crowds certainly seemed to crave a significant miracle as proof that the Virgin Mary really was appearing, something like the Miracle of the Sun at Fatima.[384] Dozens of people arrived in Garabandal on October 18 believing that this was the date when some wondrous, confirming miracle would finally occur. The girls reportedly tried to dampen this expectation, stressing that they were going to deliver a *message*, not a miracle. But it was to no avail. The crowd was on the scene and primed for a prodigy.

The weather was the first indicator that all would not be well. It had been raining continuously for a couple of days, and many of the pilgrims were forced to slog up the mountainside in slippery mud. The village priest, Father Valentin, was described as darting about through the crowds looking unaccountably nervous. Why? Had he deduced that the girls were frauds, and was he horrified at the stupendous turnout for their scam? He subsequently confessed to a few visitors that he already knew the message—the girls had finally told him the night before. His reaction? *The people aren't going to like it.* He even described the message as infantile—as from a little child.[385] But of course, maybe it *was*. If the girls were lying, they were about to make a serious misstep, since apparently the message they had cooked up was not a crowd-pleaser.

[386] *Pilgrims trek to Garabandal*

Meanwhile, the Commission investigating the apparitions interfered in how the night would unfold. Displeased with the

Virgin's instructions, Commission members began to pressure the village pastor with directions of their own. The girls had been told by the Virgin Mary to meet at the church doors at 10:30 at night to announce the message. The members of the Commission who were present that night squelched that locale because they didn't want it to appear that the Church was giving approval, and the new spot was shifted to the Pines. The Commission also said the time for the message should be moved up—no more waiting. It was 8 p.m., dark, and pouring rain. It was time to proceed.

So the jostling crowd surged up the muddy mountainside toward the Pines in the dark and rain, slipping and sliding the whole way. Many people were complaining bitterly by the time they reached the top. About that time, the rain stopped, and the moon shone through the scudding clouds. The girls arrived on foot with Father Valentin, accompanied by guards on horseback. The girls then handed the message to Father Valentin, who was supposed to read it to the crowd.

[387] *Rain on the day of the First Message*

Instead, he scanned the note and handed it back to the girls to read to the crowd themselves. Embarrassed by the childishness of the message he was about to deliver to the

184

stressed and expectant crowd, he evidently lost his nerve and rejected his bit part in that night's drama.[388] It might be easy to judge him for this, since he was also the priest who, plagued with doubt, would try to keep Conchita from spreading the word about her forthcoming little miracle. Yet these actions also make him appear appealingly human and sensible; furthermore, most of his behavior throughout the unfolding apparition drama, including taking detailed notes from day one, comes across as steadfast and sincere, if at times skeptical and severe toward the girls.

At any rate, Conchita read the message to the crowd, and after that, two men repeated the messages in booming voices because Conchita's voice was hard to hear. The language of the First Message has the same awkward, repetitive, sing-song cadence as the message from the Night of the Screams. It is indeed simple and childish. Unlike the more serious and more adult Second Message, the First Message really does sound like four girls' interpretation of what the Virgin Mary had said to them.

We must make many sacrifices, perform much penance,
And visit the Blessed Sacrament frequently;
But first we must lead good lives.
If we do not, a chastisement will befall us.
The cup is already filling up, and if we do not change, a
very great chastisement will come upon us.
The Blessed Virgin wants us to do these things so that
we may avoid God's punishment.

Despite the simplicity and childish tone, the message is grave. The second half contains a spark of the sensational in its warning of a filling cup and a great punishment on its way. But the first half, even for a religious crowd in 1961, was terribly anti-climactic and rather dull. Sacrifices? Penance? Visits to the Blessed Sacrament? *This* is what they had climbed the mountain in the rain for? Fittingly, the rain that had temporarily let up for the reading of the message now began to pour down again.

The crowd trudged down the mountainside that night full of bitter disappointment in the so-called apparitions of Garabandal. All the giddy excitement and raging wonder that had been building during the summer and fall of 1961 vanished on that dark and stormy night. Among those slipping and sliding their way down the hillside was the grief-stricken brother of Father Luis Andreu, the priest who had *died* thanks to the apparitions of Garabandal only two months before.

Father Ramon Maria Andreu later recorded his thoughts from that night: *What are you doing here? These girls are nothing more than poor sick children. And all this is a pathetic comedy of backward villagers.*[389] He decided, right there in the rain, to say goodbye to Garabandal and go somewhere far away, like America. He describes himself as so depressed about the meaninglessness of his brother's death that he comes to a stop on the mountainside, unable to move or continue his descent, even as the other pilgrims surge around him down the hill, "flashlights going up and down like a nightmare."[390] A furious thunderstorm had by this time unleashed itself, and some in the crowd were terrified by it, while others turned surly. *The girls to the butcher! And their parents with them!*[391]

While Father Ramon plotted his escape to America, even as he was too paralyzed by despair to get off the mountain and out of the rain, matters took a surprising turn. A younger sister of Mari-Loli tugged at his sleeve and announced to him that he was being summoned: Mari-Loli had a message for him. It turned out that the four girls, after imparting their message on the mountain, had gone into ecstasy as they made their way down. The girls were turned in the direction of the Pines, where the Virgin was apparently hovering, and thus made their way down the dark slippery mountain backward while in ecstasy, winding up at the church doors—the place where the message was supposed to have originally been read, which would have spared the crowd the frightening climb and descent in the stormy dark.

Mari-Loli proceeded to tell Father Ramon that the Virgin Mary had given a message just for him: "Call him and tell him not to doubt anymore—that it is really I, the Virgin, who is appearing here. And in order for him to believe better, tell him: *When you went up, you went up in joy; when you came down, you came down in sorrow.*" The Virgin had also told the girls that Father Ramon was thinking of going to America.[392]

The grieving Father Ramon was rescued from his bitter disillusionment by a personal message from a profoundly compassionate Virgin Mary. Yet for most of the pilgrims, there was no miracle that night. Furthermore, the message was a tremendous let-down. Much of the crowd missed the apparition which occurred after the message was read. Would the apparition have occurred before the entire gathering if the Commission members hadn't insisted on changing the time and place? Many stopped believing in Garabandal on that night, while others, even steadfast believers, mistakenly assumed that night marked "the death of Garabandal."

If the girls were lying, they had botched it. They had not even come close to giving the crowd what it had come for. And if they were telling the truth, then the Virgin Mary was giving some incredibly unglamorous and mundane instructions to Catholics. What was the point? Well, possibly the point was the future. In 1961, instructing traditional village Catholics to sacrifice, do penance, and visit the Blessed Sacrament might have seemed embarrassingly obvious—sort of like telling the children of Fatima that there was a hell. But maybe the Virgin Mary was looking further down the road than anyone dreamed—even fifty years down the road. In 1961, it appears that the Virgin Mary saw the great Catholic crisis coming down the track like a runaway train. She saw that it was going to jump the track, and she knew a terrible train wreck was going to result. And that brings us to the Second Message of Garabandal.

The Second Message of Garabandal

On January 1, 1965 (also the Feast Day of the Mother of God), two shepherd boys came upon Conchita alone on the mountaintop beneath the Pines, on her knees, face turned upward, in deep ecstasy.[393]

[394] *Conchita in ecstasy at the Pines*

She would later admit that she had been having an apparition of the Virgin Mary who had said another message would be given to the world on June 18, 1965—because the first message of October 18 had essentially been ignored.

Apparently, the Virgin also took the opportunity on January 1 to explain the World-Wide Warning in detail to Conchita. And despite the fact that the physical-event-in-the-sky has never been clearly explained, both Conchita and her aunt with whom she shared this information seemed to be watching for something after that. Conchita's aunt told Conchita that she was now obsessively searching the sky, and Conchita made this remarkable admission: "I too, and when I go to bed, I look and have great fear. Though on the contrary, I have a desire for it to come, to see if we amend our lives, since we don't understand the offenses that we make against the Lord."[395]

During this time of waiting for the June 18th 1965 message, many outsiders began to make plans to visit, and attempted to find places to stay. One of these was an American in her thirties from Brockton, Massachusetts named Maria Saraco. Not only would her journey to Garabandal change the course of Saraco's life, but it would also lead to a lifelong friendship with visionary Mari-Loli.

"I decided to go when the prophecy came that St. Michael was going to appear on June 18, 1965," Saraco told me in 2009. "I had read a small article one year earlier but it didn't have information about where the apparitions were happening. Then a year later I read an article with more information." A priest then sent Maria Saraco the Garabandal messages in French, which she had to get translated.

At the same time, the locals continued to doubt, discuss and debate whether or not the apparitions had been genuine. Mari-Loli's own father, a respected leader and businessman in the village, called the upcoming apparition "pure lies," and Mari-Loli herself questioned Conchita's prediction of another apparition.[396] The local pastor—still wrestling with his inner doubting Thomas—had pressed Conchita on whether she was certain that this 1965 message was going to be delivered or not.[397] Conchita, perhaps affected by the surrounding skepticism, seemed to lose her nerve at the last moment and wrote a letter to a priest asking him not to come, and to spread the word that no one else should come, either:

It is possible that the people—almost all of them—will leave very disillusioned. Something evil could result from it, because many people will expect some kind of miracle to happen. And this will not be the case.

Conchita knew she was going to see the Angel and receive a message, but that no splashy miracle was going to occur. Instead, she said that people should plan to come to Garabandal for the Great Miracle, rather than for this message that only she would hear. She stated in the letter that if visitors came instead for the June 18, 1965 message and were disappointed by it, no one might bother to show up for the all-important Great Miracle. (In fact, this was one of the Garabandal predictions—the Virgin told Conchita on December 6, 1962 that something would happen a short time before the Great Miracle which would cause many people to stop believing in the Garabandal apparitions.[398]) Perhaps Conchita was beginning to fear that June 18, 1965 would be the Great Disappointment which would finally shatter faith in Garabandal.

This letter also reveals how much more worldly-wise Conchita had become since the apparitions had begun. She had seen the bitter disappointment of the surly crowd after the First Message in October 1961. She had also seen that the Little Miracle of the Host had not persuaded everyone, and that many people's belief evaporates immediately after any sign or wonder. Jacinta's own mother believed in the apparitions when Jacinta was in a trance, but didn't believe if Jacinta wasn't in a trance.[399] Furthermore, Conchita had lived through a time of great disillusionment and disbelief on the part of herself and everyone around her. So it must have alarmed her to see the apparition buzz building to a crescendo—even in the era before electronic social media. Or it alarmed *someone*, anyway. The letter's recipient suspected that Conchita had been directed to write the letter since some of the language did not sound like hers (*"so as to avoid promoting such an environment,"* etc.) Maybe it was the rattled village pastor—who had already been through so many traumatic ups and downs—who was trying to tamp down expectations.

I fear very much that something will happen on June 18. I think it is rather risky. It is up to you (the priest) to discourage people from coming so as to avoid promoting such an environment...If people come on June 18, I fear an indescribable something that could be harmful.[400]

But Conchita's snail mail letter was prior to e-mail and texting, and the visitor had already departed for the journey to Garabandal and did not receive the letter in time. By that time, the cat was already out of the bag, and the crowds began to pour in.

On the day of the predicted apparition, Conchita was bedridden with a high fever. Some suggested that this was Conchita's way to escape her latest lie—as if she were still trying to back out after the last-minute letter didn't work.[401] None of this stopped hundreds of pilgrims from many different countries from descending on the village, sleeping everywhere, indoors and out, including Maria Saraco from Massachusetts, who admitted she had a fantasy that she would actually catch a glimpse of St. Michael the Archangel.

"I went there and I couldn't get up the road except in an old, old Jeep. The roads were so rocky. Thousands were there. No bathrooms, no phones."

June 18th 1965 was a return to the glory days of Garabandal, although this time Conchita alone basked in the spotlight and bore its burden. Despite her illness, she rose and stood in the doorway of her house. The pilgrims from other countries, like Maria Saraco, appeared mostly serious and prayerful, no doubt because the lengthy journey required real motivation. Some of the Spanish visitors that showed up seemed more intent on enjoying an entertaining day.[402]

[403] *Crowds return to Garabandal for the Second Message*

The atmosphere at times was reminiscent of the height of Jesus' ministry, with people asking Conchita for prayers and healing, thrusting religious medals and rosaries at her for blessing, and even asking for her autograph on holy cards and taking her picture. The day wore on, and then the night. Conchita withdrew back into her house to rest without announcing a time for the apparitions. Still, the pilgrims prayed, sang and waited.

"Conchita was sick. She couldn't come out," Maria Saraco confirmed. "Then someone came out of Conchita's door and announced something in Spanish." The announcement which Maria Saraco couldn't understand was that the apparition would take place in the sunken lane, where the Angel had first appeared four years earlier. The throng moved toward the *calleja* in response, with some people being knocked down and even trampled upon.

[404] *Conchita greets pilgrims*

"But I didn't understand what they said, and there was no one to ask, so I just stayed where I was," Maria Saraco told me.

The response of the masses continued to resemble a scene out of the gospels, with friends helping a blind man get to a safe spot atop a wall, while others helped the lame navigate the rocky path.[405]

At this point, signs in the sky were reported. This wasn't the first time that strange cosmic phenomena had been described by various visitors to Garabandal. Stars showering down and fire in the clouds had been reported heralding the Virgin's appearance on some days. Early on, the four visionaries had reported that the Virgin and St. Michael had "come down from the stars," accompanied by large stars with long tails. At another time they described "seven stars" with tails.[406] On June 18, 1965, at least two bright stars were reported: The brightest star made a circle in the sky and returned to its starting point, while the smaller star floated from above Conchita's house toward the Pines.[407]

Finally, Maria Saraco saw Conchita emerge from her house. Just before midnight, Conchita appeared in the sunken lane and crashed to her knees. After a long dry spell, Conchita was once again in ecstasy mode in Garabandal.

"I was right behind her when she had the ecstasy," Saraco said. "There were floodlights all around from cameras. It was dark out there. Floodlights were shining in Conchita's eyes. She never blinked or showed distraction. She didn't know anyone else was there. She was holding a crucifix. Her head was way back. A French priest named Father Pel was behind her. She didn't know he was there, but she swung the crucifix behind her so he could kiss it."

Conchita's face in the many photographs of this event is upturned and luminous and undisturbed by the pressing crowd, by the microphones thrust close to her lips, and by the blinding glare of camera lights. She starts out laughing, and then tears begin to run down her cheeks.

"Conchita was crying a little bit, but she didn't reveal the message that night," Maria Saraco said. "There were very soft tears running down her face, not sobbing."

408 *The final message*

It was about this time that it became apparent that not all the news in the message was good. Conchita protested, "No! . . . No! . . . Still no! . . Pardon, pardon!" She was then heard to say, somewhat ominously, "Priests? . . . Bishops? . . . July 2nd?"409

Immediately afterward, Conchita's comment was that the message was "very sorrowful"—and that she would reveal it in its entirety the next day.

The following morning Conchita appeared energized by the apparition, even as many villagers and visitors slept in, exhausted. After Mass, Conchita, who had been fasting, finally released the handwritten message to a priest. It was subsequently read in Spanish, French, English and Italian. The message was from the Virgin Mary, but had been delivered by St. Michael because, Mary later explained, she found it too painful to deliver in person.

"The next day around ten a.m., I heard about the message," said Maria Saraco. "It was like she (Mary) was giving me another chance. I couldn't get over it. It was like she was talking to me. I met 15 to 20 people who spoke English. We all prayed by the church."

After that moment, Maria Saraco's life was never the same.

"After I got home, I didn't want all my coats and dresses anymore. I gave everything away that I could. I didn't care about anything anymore—money, property. All that I cared about was giving out the message of the Blessed Mother and saving souls.

We had a French convent near us. A young French-American sister who was a teacher came to the door—I gave her the messages to read. She was dumbfounded. The next thing I knew, a week later she called me up and asked me to go to someone's house to share the messages. The lady wanted me to show slides I had of Garabandal. I went over there and I showed them. The house was full of people. I was scared at that time. I wasn't sure what to say. The woman had told me, "I'm a Catholic, but my husband is not—is that O.K?" I said, "It's for everybody."

After watching the slides and hearing Maria Saraco's talk, the non-Catholic husband was the first one to come over and kiss the rosary.

"From then on, I got more and more invitations. I went all over the world. My husband tried to set some limits on me. He said I couldn't speak more than four times a week, and I needed to be home by a certain time, because he had to get up early and go to work the next morning. Sometimes I gave talks two times a day on Saturday and Sunday. I had one son at that time—he was about seventeen."

Maria Saraco, health permitting, has been travelling to Garabandal annually ever since. "I meet people from all over the world. The Virgin Mary told us when she appeared in Garabandal that she'd give us time to make the message known."

This is the final public message that Maria Saraco and thousands of others heard on June 18, 1965:

As my message of October 18 (1961) has not been complied with, and has not been made known to the world, I tell you that this is the last one. Before, the cup was filling up; now it is flowing over. Many cardinals, many bishops, and many priests are on the road to perdition, and are taking many souls with them. Less and less importance is being given to the Eucharist. You should turn the wrath of God away from yourselves by your efforts. If you ask his forgiveness with sincere hearts, he will pardon you. I, your Mother, through the intercession of Saint Michael the

archangel, ask you to amend your lives. You are now receiving the last warnings. I love you very much, and do not want your condemnation. Pray to us with sincerity, and we will grant your requests. You should make more sacrifices. Think about the passion of Jesus.

Mary's Message for the World

The first and most important point of both of these messages was that trouble was coming if the world didn't change. From the First Message in 1961: *The cup is already filling up, and if we do not change, a very great chastisement will come upon us.* And from the Second Message in 1965: *Before, the cup was filling up; now it is flowing over...You should turn the wrath of God away from yourselves by your efforts...I love you very much, and do not want your condemnation.*

But the second point is that the Virgin appeared to be placing a great deal of responsibility on Catholics to keep the world from sliding into darkness. The two main messages of Garabandal were deeply Catholic—less universal than the messages at Medjugorje, for example. Words like penance, Blessed Sacrament, and even Eucharist would have little meaning for non-Catholics, although it's easy to grasp the general thrust of the two messages. And while Mary spoke of great global events in Garabandal meant for the world, her appearance there coincided almost exactly with Vatican II, and her two main, public messages were inescapably meant for Catholics.

Mary's Message For Vatican II

Some believe this means the "Garabandal Virgin" was anti-Vatican II. But Conchita had more than one conversation with Mary about the momentous Vatican II Council, and in both of those conversations Conchita appeared to be infected by the excitement and optimism that surrounded the new Council. The Second Vatican Council was genuinely groundbreaking in numerous ways, not the least of which was a stunning new Catholic openness toward other Christians, as well as other

196

religions. The fresh breeze of Vatican II was an emphasis on mercy and open windows, rather than condemnation and closed doors.

[410]*The Final Message in writing*

In September of 1962, about a month before Vatican II officially opened, Conchita reportedly spoke with Mary about the Vatican Council. The conversation was overheard by others, although naturally it was one-sided. Conchita said: *The Council, is it the greatest of all? . . . Will it be a success? . . . How good! . . . That way they will know you better, and you will be very happy.*[411]

Mary may have told Conchita that Pope Paul VI would proclaim Mary "Mother of the Church" during the Council, or that the Virgin herself would be included in the Vatican II documents. Originally, an entire conciliar document had been proposed regarding the Virgin Mary. However, that became a matter of controversy, at least partly due to a desire to build ecumenical bridges, and in the end a chapter was devoted to Mary, re-affirming the Catholic Church's long-standing view of the Virgin.

197

Then, on November 18, 1962, another, somewhat mystifying conversation between Conchita and Mary was recorded in which Conchita seems to want to reveal a secret involving Vatican II, but is asked not to. *...shall I tell...Oh?...Good! That with the Council and the Miracle the world is going to be converted?...and afterwards the world will be forgiven? Oh, that is good...What?... and I can say that with the Council and the Miracle there will be conversion.... I'll tell it after the Council and...eh? Then I want the Council to end now.... I won't say anymore, nothing more, eh?....When the Council ends I won't say a word...oh, goodbye.*[412]

Mary *appears* to be telling Conchita that after the Council and the Miracle, the world will be converted and forgiven, which apparently leads Conchita to hope that the Council will end soon. This explicit connection between the Vatican II Council and the Great Miracle may lie in the Council's passionate emphasis on ecumenism. On more than one occasion, the Virgin reportedly told some of the visionaries about the coming unity of all the Christian churches—Catholic, Orthodox, Protestant, and even splintered sects.[413]

Could this be the great ecclesiastical event which will coincide with the Great Miracle? Such unity among Christians would be an unimaginable miracle, in itself. The biblical basis for this hope lies in Jesus' prayer for his disciples before he went to the cross: *so that they may all be one, as you, Father, are in me and I in you, that they also may be in us, that the world may believe that you sent me.*[414] In other words, according to this scripture, the unity of Christians leads to the conversion of the world.

Since the Council has been over for fifty years now, and the Miracle hasn't yet occurred, Mary's statement that the Council and Miracle would precede the world's conversion (if that was what she said) is still factually correct. But Mary also seems to stop Conchita from making a sweeping assertion that will be misunderstood. At first Conchita says, *I'll tell it after the Council..,* but then she backpedals and says, *When the Council ends I won't say a word...*

Perhaps Conchita was on the verge of proclaiming that after the Council and the Great Miracle, the world would be converted. At that time many were still assuming that the Great Miracle was imminent (and Conchita herself likely thought this until the Virgin gave her the date), so many would have naturally expected the conversion of the whole world almost as soon as Vatican II ended. The result would have been even more bitter disillusionment and disappointment in Garabandal, and more damage to its credibility.

This seems to be an occupational hazard for visionaries. Even the saintly children of Fatima mixed up the Virgin's message about the "soldiers coming home shortly" by proclaiming that the war would end on October 13, 1917, which was actually the date of the Virgin's final appearance in Fatima. World War I ended a year later, on November 11, 1918. At the time, this wrong prediction was considered enormously damaging to the credibility of Fatima.[415]

At Garabandal, the girls passed along messages as they understood them to others, and the listeners added their own interpretations as well. The "last pope" prophecy may be an example of just such a chain of misunderstanding, as well as the predicted "new eyes" for Joey Lomangino. The Virgin Mary may have averted another misunderstanding in the form of a premature prediction that the world would be converted shortly after Vatican II.

Conchita still managed to pass on the accurate prediction from Mary that the Council would continue despite the death of John XXIII. And not only did the Virgin *not* appear to be anti-Vatican II, but twenty years later, neither was Conchita. "With the changes in the Mass after Vatican II, I had a very difficult time, since I was so used to following along with my own missal. But I survived. I knew many people who would not go along with the changes. This is not right. I would not call these people Roman Catholics."[416]

Yet even if Mary was not anti-Vatican II, there is certainly some evidence that the messages at Garabandal were meant partially for the Council. In the last Garabandal message in June 1965, Mary said, *I, your Mother...* This was surely no accident. Pope Paul VI had proclaimed Mary "Mother of the Church" in 1964, on the final day of the third Council session, after the Council itself had failed to ratify such a title for her.[417] A power struggle of sorts had erupted during Vatican II between those who wished to highlight Mary's role in the Church and further develop Catholic doctrine about her, and those who did not want Mary to have an elevated, cultish status which would upset other Christian sensibilities, particularly the Protestant view of a much tamer and more invisible Virgin Mary.[418]

By claiming the title which Pope Paul VI had conferred upon her—Mother of the Church—Mary at Garabandal was emphasizing who she was precisely when some during Vatican II were hoping to lower the Virgin's profile in order to build ecumenical bridges with Orthodox and Protestant churches.[419] (Pope Francis recently addressed Mary as "Mother of the Church" when he welcomed her statue from Fatima and consecrated the whole world to her on Oct. 13, 2013.)[420]

One consequence of downsizing Mary's role during and after Vatican II involved the diminishment of the rosary and other private devotions to Mary, as the emphasis shifted toward public, communal liturgies. It's hard to escape the impression that Mary's appearance at Garabandal coincided with Vatican II at least partially to counteract some of these "anti-Marian" trends. Downplaying the rosary after Vatican II, and failing to release the Third Secret of Fatima, doubtless contributed to the abandonment by many of the First Saturday Fatima devotion—a devotion which was one of the requirements for the conversion of Russia. What if the Church *had* released the Third Secret of Fatima in 1960, with its haunting images of persecution, and then gone on to consecrate Russia to the Immaculate Heart of Mary during the Vatican II Council? The First Saturday devotion might have been reinvigorated rather than sidelined in this alternative version of history.

Another reason to believe that Mary intended to speak to the Vatican II Council was because in Mary's Garabandal message of June 18, 1965, she specifically addressed cardinals, bishops, and priests three months before they gathered for the last Council session on September 14, 1965. There is no evidence that Mary objected to the *updating* which Pope John XXIII had hoped for during Vatican II. Hearing the Mass in one's own language instead of a long-dead language, for example, was an enlivening change for many Catholics (though not all). Instead, Mary in her two messages seemed to be warning against excessive swings of the pendulum that could lead to the wholesale abandonment of truth—throwing the baby out with the bathwater, as it were.

The point of Vatican II was to bring the Catholic Church into the modern era (update it), making it more vibrant and engaged in the modern world—and thus more effectively evangelistic as well. The point was never to deny the truth of who Jesus is and His real presence in the Eucharist, nor to abandon traditional practices such as Adoration of the Blessed Sacrament.

During a Catholic Mass, the bread and wine are consecrated and transformed into the Body and Blood of Christ. In the past, the Body of Christ (the consecrated bread not yet consumed) resided in a special tabernacle that occupied a place of supreme honor on the altar at the front and center of every Catholic church. In the years after Vatican II, that tabernacle, along with the Body of Christ, was literally moved into a small side room in church after church, although there were no directives in the Vatican II documents to do so.

One reason given was that since Christ is present in each believer, the body of believers should reverence Christ in one another during Mass rather than revere what amounts to a "fancy breadbox." The Vatican II perspective zeroed in on Christ's presence in the body of believers (including the laity and not just the clergy)—and not exclusively in the consecrated bread and wine. The Catholic Church was opening up in ways which were "old hat" for Protestantism, by placing more emphasis on the full participation of Spirit-filled lay people, on the Bible, and on a more modern and accessible liturgy.

Yet the risk was that this new and invigorating openness might come at the expense of what beat at the heart of Catholicism but not Protestantism: the real presence of Jesus Christ in the Eucharist. For this reason, the removal of Christ from the front of His own church appeared to some as a deeply significant, and profoundly negative, development. There were those who believed this dismantling process was simply a stripping away of the trappings of a tradition in order to make way for something new and better. But for others it appeared that God himself was being abandoned, ignored, and displaced within his own church.

Private devotions to the Eucharist collapsed like dominos as communal participation in the Mass was emphasized instead. Hours of Adoration before the Body of Christ fell by the wayside. Confusion began to spread about whether or not Jesus was actually present in the bread and wine.[421] At Garabandal in 1961, as Vatican II began, Mary said, *It is necessary to visit the Blessed Sacrament*, effectively announcing ahead of time that emphasis on communal celebration of the Mass in no way precluded private adoration of the Eucharist as well. In 1965, before the last session of Vatican II, Mary in Garabandal warned, *The Eucharist is being given less and less importance.*

Many have argued that the way Vatican II was implemented was not always consistent with the actual documents, partly due to honest confusion in a time of transition, but partly due to those who took advantage of Vatican II to try to change the Church to fit their own image.[422] Despite post-Vatican II confusion surrounding the Eucharist, Vatican II had declared that the "Eucharistic sacrifice is the source and summit of the Christian life."[423] The miracle which Mary had given as a "sign" at Garabandal was the miracle of Conchita receiving Holy

Communion—a miracle which led some onlookers to sob and reform their lives at this glimpse of "the true God." Furthermore, St. Michael showed up on days when there was no priest in the village to ensure that the girls received *frequent* communion—which was also very much a part of the documents of Vatican II.[424] The message of Garabandal, as well as the message of the Vatican II Council, unquestionably revolved around frequent reception of the Eucharist—the Body and Blood of Christ. In this sense, the Virgin Mary and Vatican II were completely in sync.

If the Eucharist is only a symbol, rather than food, there is no reason to distribute it every day, as the Catholic Church does. And there's certainly no reason to "adore" the Eucharist if it's not actually the Body and Blood of Christ. The Virgin at Garabandal was urging that reverence for and adoration of the Blessed Sacrament not be tucked away in some side room and forgotten like a dusty, pre-Vatican II artifact, as if Jesus were no longer present there. It was imperative that the Body and Blood of Christ not be treated like one more church statue locked in the closet after Vatican II.

A remarkable footnote to Mary's Garabandal message to the Vatican II Council took place years later. During Vatican II, two future popes, Bishop Karol Wojtyla and Joseph Ratzinger, were part of the progressive reformers' camp. Yet fifteen years later, in 1980, Pope John Paul II apologized for any harm which was done to the Eucharist, and the Church, after Vatican II. "I would like to ask forgiveness...for everything which, for whatever reason, through whatever human weakness, impatience, negligence, and also through the at times partial, one-sided and erroneous applications of the directives of the Second Vatican Council, may have caused scandal and disturbance concerning the interpretation of the doctrine and veneration due to this great Sacrament. And I pray the Lord Jesus that in the future we may avoid in our manner of dealing with this sacred mystery anything which would weaken or disorient in any way the sense of reverence and love that exists in our faithful people."[425] Despite efforts to silence Mary's voice in Garabandal, Pope John Paul II still got her message about the Eucharist.

A More Widespread Crisis

But the Garabandal message was not just meant for the Vatican II Council. Mary appeared prescient about the reality that much of Western Christianity was about to take a sharp turn away from the Cross of Jesus. In the first Garabandal message of 1961, Mary had said it was necessary to do much penance and make many sacrifices. She ended the 1965 message with, "You should make more sacrifices. Think about the passion of Jesus." In Catholicism, practices such as fasting, penance (turning away from sin and making amends for it in some specific way), and the Catholic sacrament of confession were being increasingly neglected and abandoned by many; consequently, awareness and concern about personal sin were more and more diluted.

Other corners of Christendom also were beginning to turn their backs on notions of sacrifice: The prosperity gospel and the general linkage of Christianity with rip-roaring success in life would come to dominate the American airwaves. What was emerging was an all-Easter, no-Cross Christianity. In society at large (Christian or not), responsibility and sacrifice for the sake of one's marriage and family also were about to be widely abandoned, which has proven devastating, especially to the poorest children.

It's not as if the Virgin was advocating self-flagellation for our sins. In Garabandal, when the Virgin recommended penance, the girls began wearing "penitential belts" under their clothes at someone's recommendation. One day, while they wriggled uncomfortably in front of Mary, hoping she would notice their sacrifice, the Virgin asked them to take the belts off, saying that's not exactly what she meant by penance, and stressing that they should never harm themselves. Instead, she asked them for faithfulness in ordinary life,[426] encouraging them to offer to God the material of their daily lives with love and faith, such as giving up an enjoyment like a piece of chewing gum or some other pleasure, or trusting God with physical or emotional suffering. The point was to remember throughout the day that one was living for God.[427]

This direction is consistent with what Fatima seer Sister Lucia wrote on Feb. 28, 1943, about a vision she had in which Jesus begged for more penance. "From Thursday to Friday, being in the chapel with my superiors' permission, at midnight, Our Lord told me: *The penance that I request and require now is the sacrifice demanded of everybody by the accomplishment of his own duty and the observance of My law.*"[428] Sister Lucia explained, "And He desires that this way be clearly made known to souls, for many give to the word "penance" the sense of great austerities, and as they feel neither the strength nor the generosity for that, they get discouraged and let themselves go into a life of lukewarmness and sin."

Jesus was not calling for exacting score-keeping or for saintly heroism in penance, which only served to discourage many who then gave up on the struggle against sin altogether. Instead, this holistic approach to penance—making one's whole life a gift of love to God, including the practice of abstaining from ordinary pleasures or offering up daily sufferings for others—seemed to reveal a Jesus who was filled with the spirit of Vatican II twenty years before it occurred.

The most critical reason for the emphasis at Garabandal on sacrifice (going the sometimes painful extra mile for others) and penance (in some way making up for one's own sins or for others') was because *the cup was overflowing.* In a world that was growing increasingly evil and which was increasingly threatened by grave dangers, God needed extra effort on the part of the good to counteract it. The Virgin of Garabandal called for penance to avoid a great chastisement, and the Angel in the Third Message of Fatima also called for penance to avert global conflagration. It was not business as usual, when people could spend their lives focused largely on themselves and their own well-being. The requested penance was not a loveless, joyless tallying up of merit points to offset one's faults and failings in the hopes of squeezing through heaven's door. Instead, people were being asked not only to offer themselves each day to God with love, but also to exert themselves at some cost so that souls would not be lost—in other words, out of love for their neighbor. The primary way people could do this was by being faithful to their particular duties in life and following God's law of love while doing so.

Conchita later expanded on the sacrifice-and-passion part of the message using mystical sci-fi language. The Virgin, Conchita explained, wished us to meditate more on the passion of Jesus because in this way we would "feel closer to God's portals," which in turn would help us accept our crosses with love.[429] Some Christians take issue with Catholic notions of penance and sacrifice because human works cannot take the place of Christ's sacrifice. Yet Christ has invited us to participate in his saving work, in both the cross and the resurrection, in order to help ourselves and others. The concept of taking up one's own cross comes straight from scripture,[430] as does the notion of working out one's salvation with fear and trembling,[431] of being part of a holy priesthood offering up spiritual sacrifices,[432] and of joining our own small sacrifices to the perfect sacrifice of Jesus: *Now I rejoice in my sufferings for your sake, and in my flesh I am filling up what is lacking in the afflictions of Christ on behalf of his body, which is the church*[433]

In the First Message at Garabandal, Mary said, *It is necessary to make many sacrifices, to do much penance...* In Message Number Two, she said, *You should make more sacrifices. Think about the passion of Jesus.* A central concern at Garabandal seemed to be that the world was in dire need of the Catholic practices of sacrifice and penance precisely when many Catholics were abandoning them.

Was the Virgin Addressing the Sex Abuse Scandal?

But it wasn't just the world in need of sacrifices and penance—it was also the Catholic Church. If the sharp de-emphasis of the Eucharist and the Cross were two disasters Mary foresaw and was trying to forestall, a third was inextricably linked to the first two: the profound crisis in the Catholic clergy. In fact, the "priest crisis" was actually mentioned *first* by Mary in the June 18, 1965 message, and this was indisputably the most shocking pronouncement she made. "Many cardinals, many bishops, and many priests are on the road to perdition, and they are taking many souls with them."

Conchita's initial hand-written message, which has been reproduced many times, contains the word *los sacerdotes*. Conchita later confirmed that St. Michael spoke specifically of cardinals and bishops as well, which she later included, but that first night she reasoned they were all included under the umbrella term "priests." When asked why she didn't write cardinals, bishops and priests in the original note, she confessed that it seemed too controversial and she didn't have the nerve. Years later, Conchita said that back in 1965 a priest was almost like God Himself, which made it extremely difficult for her to relay what she'd heard. "Back in the village in those days, nothing of what is happening with priests today was heard of. This is why (some individuals) called me a liar and said they were going to kill me."[434] Nonetheless, she had a change of heart, and decided in subsequent copies to write down what St. Michael had actually said.

The specificity of Mary warning cardinals, bishops and priests now appears significant for several reasons. First, because cardinals, bishops and priests were meeting at that time for Vatican II, and Mary was warning the Council about post-Council missteps that could diminish reverence for the Body and Blood of Christ and otherwise damage the faith of the People of God.

Another obvious reason for this dire warning was surely the sexual abuse crisis. Most of the abuse in the U.S., for example, did in fact occur in the 60s, 70s, and 80s, immediately after Vatican II. Four percent of American priests were accused as abusers, but those abusers did widespread damage, reportedly abusing more than 10,000 victims in 95 percent of Catholic dioceses (80 percent of the victims were males, and 75 percent were ages 11-17).[435]

But the problem did not lie only with a relatively small number of abusive priests. Rather than exposing and expelling the abusers from the priesthood—or at least sealing them up behind the walls of a monastery—some bishops arranged for treatment for the abusers on the recommendation of psychologists, re-assigned the abusing priests to new locales in the hopes that they were now cured, and concealed past abuse from police and parishioners to protect the Church's reputation and resources—all of which led to more abuse.

By the time the Church got around to recognizing the full horror of what had occurred and responding to it, it was like locking the barn door after the horses had bolted. Also, the barn had already burned down and lay in smoking ruin. Cardinal Ratzinger—who was accused of acting too slowly in some cases but who also implemented reform—spoke on Good Friday 2005 of the filth in the Church, "even among those who, in the priesthood, ought to belong entirely to (God)." He went on to say, "The soiled garments and face of your Church throw us into confusion. Yet it is we ourselves who have soiled them! It is we who betray you time and time again, after all our lofty words and grand gestures." Ratzinger described the Catholic Church in 2005 as "a boat about to sink, a boat taking in water on every side."

At Garabandal, the Virgin Mary had been trying to warn about gashes in the boat forty years before Cardinal Ratzinger spoke those words. In retrospect, it would have been much better for some cardinals, bishops, and priests to have taken to heart the Virgin's stark, simple warning at Garabandal that they were on the road to hell, than to follow the tragically wrong legal and psychological advice they received from the professionals of the day.

Division in the Church

But there's yet another reason Mary may have been specifically warning cardinals, bishops, and priests during Vatican II: because of division in the Church. If the theme of penance to avert disaster flowed seamlessly from the message of Fatima to Garabandal, then Garabandal's warning to the hierarchy flowed forward into the Church-sanctioned messages of Akita ten years later. On Oct. 13, 1973 (a Fatima anniversary date), at Akita, Japan, the Virgin Mary repeated the most terrifying themes of both Fatima and Garabandal: If people don't repent, "Fire will fall from the sky and will wipe out a great part of humanity."

But the Virgin Mary at Akita also went on to speak of a great and damaging division in the Church among the hierarchy, and she saw some of this unyielding divisiveness centered around devotion to the Virgin herself: "The work of the devil will infiltrate even into the Church in such a way that one will see cardinals opposing cardinals, bishops against bishops. The priests who venerate me will be scorned and opposed by their confreres."

The tragic fall-out from Vatican II has been the terrible divide that has split the Catholic Church—although perhaps Vatican II only exposed fault lines which already existed. Fifty years later, the bitterness has not dissipated, even though, of course, a house divided cannot stand for long. On one extreme end of the spectrum are those who insist that only the pre-Vatican II Church is legitimate, who reject Vatican II and everything which came after it. On the other extreme end are those who want to sever the post-Vatican II Church from everything prior, attacking the Church's authority, traditions and teaching, including not just devotion to the Virgin Mary, but even the divinity of Jesus and His real presence in the Eucharist.

A telling example of the seemingly unbridgeable gulf is how some in the Church responded to John Paul II. Undoubtedly, the charismatic, globe-trotting papacy of John Paul II was born of and embodied the "Spirit of Vatican II." He himself participated in and came of age at Vatican II, and his dynamic global and ecumenical outreach had never been seen before in a Catholic pope. Yet some liberal Catholics criticized Pope John Paul II for destroying the Church by turning the clock back to pre-Vatican II, *at the exact same time* that some traditional Catholics accused him of ruining the Church by being a post-Vatican II "aggiornamento" pope. The Spirit of Vatican II—which surely was intended by God to set His Bride on fire with love—devolved into a tussle over which side should steer the Church, much like the disciples who were always jockeying for power and missed the big picture completely.

In response to the changes of Vatican II, a traditional wing of the Catholic Church broke away in 1988 with Archbishop Marcel Lefebvre. Then, as the post-Vatican II pendulum swung the other way, some in the liberal wing also argued for breaking away, for sloughing off the tradition-bound hierarchy and forming local churches that govern themselves democratically—which Protestants have been doing for centuries.

The animosity of some liberals toward Pope Benedict was near its breaking point (or "breaking-away" point) when Pope Francis took the helm, and now the new pope seems to be alienating some traditional Catholics—although both popes seem to be on the same page, doctrinally speaking.

Pope Francis also seems to be in tune with both the Fatima and Garabandal messages. In an historic first, Pope Francis led a world-wide Hour of Eucharistic Adoration, and he requested that his papacy be consecrated to Our Lady of Fatima on May 13, 2013.[436] In the footsteps of John Paul II, he also consecrated the whole world to the Immaculate Heart of Mary on Oct. 13, 2013 in the presence of the statue of Our Lady of Fatima, which traveled from Portugal to Rome for the event.[437] As part of his private prayer, Pope Francis has said he prays the rosary daily and spends an hour in Eucharistic Adoration every evening.[438]

All Catholics, wherever they lie along the "conservative-to-liberal" spectrum, might heed the words of John Henry Cardinal Newman who in the 1800s declared that "looking at early history, it would seem as if the Church moved on to the perfect truth by various successive declarations, alternately in contrary directions, and thus perfecting, completing, supplying each other. Let us have a little faith in her I say. Pius is not the last of the popes. The fourth Council modified the third, the fifth the fourth...Let us be patient, let us have faith, and a new Pope, and a re-assembled Council may trim the boat."[439]

Both "sides" have gifts and blind spots which they bring to the table, which means both sides need each other for the Body of Christ to be whole. (Just as Catholics, Protestants, and Orthodox need each other for the Body of Christ to function as God intended it to.)

There were likely several reasons that the Virgin gave such a provocative warning at Garabandal—the warning that many cardinals, bishops, and priests were on the road to hell, and were dragging many souls along with them. If the words were unbelievable at the time, tragically, no one can say they sound unbelievable now. The destruction of children, both body and soul, by those who were supposed to protect them and lead them to God is an almost inconceivable betrayal of trust, and the worst years of this betrayal took place immediately following the apparitions in Garabandal.

In addition to this most obvious reason for the grave warning was the distortion of the Spirit of Vatican II, particularly in the de-emphasis of Eucharistic Adoration, and the unforgiving division among brothers and sisters in Christ which weakens the Church to this very day.

Skeptics argue that the Virgin Mary would never deliver such an excessively harsh message. After all—*many* priests? On their way to *perdition?* Any practicing Catholic knows many sincere and dedicated priests. But the Virgin Mary did *not* say that most shepherds were destined for hell. She *did* warn in 1965 that many (not a majority of priests, but still a lot) were currently on the wrong path, were headed in the wrong direction, and as shepherds of souls, were responsible for the lambs as well. Her purpose was to try to turn them in the right direction. She understood that priests, since they were merely human, were as likely to be affected by the times they lived in as anyone else.

The Virgin's last message in Garabandal was not a blanket condemnation of the Roman Catholic hierarchy. But her strong words were as attention-getting as a pealing fire alarm, warning that the house was in danger of burning completely down.

Mary's Love for Priests

The spirit and tone of Garabandal was not anti-clerical or anti-priest, just as it wasn't anti-Vatican II. The girls at Garabandal were repeatedly told to pray for priests. One of the phenomena of Garabandal was the girls' ability, while in ecstasy, to name the number of priests who were in the crowd that day watching. This almost always included priests who were not in their clerical garb. Some priests came to observe the proceedings anonymously; some were on the scene without permission.[440] When the girls stated there were twelve priests in the village, and only nine men wore collars, the game would begin of tracking down those disguised as laymen.

Mary at Garabandal repeatedly expressed her love for priests and her desires for priests in her apparitions and messages. Conchita wrote down a list of Mary's requests for priests in response to one priest's letter. The requests included fulfilling his vows out of love for God, leading by example and prayer, being sacrificed out of love for souls, retiring in silence to hear God, meditating frequently on the passion of Jesus in order to be more united with Christ, speaking about Mary who leads souls securely to her Son, and speaking about both heaven and hell.[441] Jesus, in his conversation with Conchita, also gave her His to-do list for priests, asking Conchita to pray for priests to be holy and fulfill their duties, to make others better, to make Jesus known to those who do not know Him, and to make Jesus loved by those who know Him but do not love Him.[442]

And Conchita herself—taking responsibility for the state of the Church rather than casting blame on the hierarchy—declared that "we ourselves are to blame for many of the priests who are on the road to perdition, because we do not pray enough, because we do not sacrifice ourselves…" She went on to paint a poignant picture of priests who had desired to give themselves to God but failed because they lacked both strength and friends.[443]

The Virgin Mary also told Mari-Loli almost fifty years ago to offer up the sufferings of her life for priests. Indeed, Mari-Loli once confided to a priest in a letter that "the Virgin has made me know when a priest is in sin. She has helped me to know that he needs many prayers and sacrifices." When Mari-Loli specifically asked for a cross to bear for priests, Mary told her to bear everything with patience and to be humble.[444]

The importance of priests was a core theme of the Garabandal messages because their role is linked absolutely to the Eucharist and the Cross. Vatican II confirmed this: "The Eucharistic sacrifice is the center and root of the whole life of the priest."[445] Is it any wonder, then, that if one decays, so does the other, and is it any surprise that the decline in devotion to the Eucharist went hand in glove with the decline of integrity in the priesthood?

In Catholicism, only a priest has the power from God—passed down apostolically from Peter "the Rock" (and before that, from Jesus himself)—to transform ordinary bread and wine into the Body and Blood of Christ. As Vatican II said, the Eucharist, or Holy Communion, is the essential rite of Catholicism—all other fruits spring from this vine. People can support each other and help others under many different auspices and names. But the fundamental mission of the Roman

Catholic Church is to provide this daily, transformative manna from heaven—bread that saves souls by bringing them into daily (and eternal) union with their Creator and with the Body of Christ. This is why the Eucharist matters, and this is why the priesthood matters.

Some insist that the sex abuse crisis was caused precisely by the overemphasis on the Holy Eucharist and the exaggerated importance of the priesthood. That the clerical culture consisted of a club of men who viewed the preservation of their own status as paramount even at the expense of the victims, and that the laity also placed the priesthood on this dangerous pedestal. Obviously, there were shepherds who stopped following the Shepherd and subsequently lost their way, leading many lambs into the present darkness and crisis—just as Mary warned about in 1965 at Garabandal. *Many cardinals, many bishops, and many priests are on the road to perdition, and they are taking many souls with them.* Mary's prophetic words punctured the inflated image of the priesthood long before it became fashionable to do so. But Mary was also insistent at Garabandal about the centrality of the Eucharist, and the priesthood has a vital role to play in this indispensable sacred mystery.

These are three interlocking themes hidden under the humble words of Mary in her final message at Garabandal: the priesthood, the Eucharist, and the Sacrifice of Christ on the Cross. These are three crucial elements of Catholic faith that Mary warned were under siege.

This final message has been criticized as inaccurate, since Mary said that because the first message was ignored, *this would be the last.* But June 18, 1965 was indeed the last public apparition and great gathering of Garabandal. Elsewhere in the message, Mary says we are receiving the "last warnings." One interpretation is that the Virgin was referring to Lourdes and Fatima as the earlier warnings (at Lourdes, Mary's message was "Penance! Penance! Penance! Pray to God for sinners." At Fatima, the Angel also cried, "Penance! Penance! Penance!")

Garabandal was the first of several urgent Marian pleas for penance issued in the last half of the twentieth century, which also include Akita, Rwanda, and Medjugorje.

If we have now crossed the threshold into the new millennium, we might be grateful that God's mercy, along with these "last warnings," have continued during this time. Jesus warned that the temple in Jerusalem would be destroyed—a warning that took forty years to fulfill, but which unfortunately occurred just as he said.

"The Lord does not delay his promise, as some regard "delay," but he is patient with you, not wishing that any should perish but that all should come to repentance. But the day of the Lord will come like a thief, and then the heavens will pass away with a mighty roar and the elements will be dissolved by fire, and the earth and everything done on it will be found out."

(2 Pet. 3:9-10)[446]

Opposition from the Church

If Mary's warnings at Garabandal weren't heeded, what would be the result? The answer is sobering: The cup, she said—rapidly filling between 1961 and 1965—was now *overflowing*. And it was overflowing for two reasons—because the message was not heeded, certainly.

But Mary said the cup was also overflowing because the message *had not even been made known*. Mary seemed to be holding the Church hierarchy responsible for failing to simply clear the path and allow the transmission of the message. She seemed to be criticizing their resistance to Garabandal and their suppression of its message which took the form of negative pronouncements by some bishops, the ban on priests visiting, on Masses being celebrated, a prohibition on promoting and publishing about Garabandal, and the request that pilgrims refrain from visiting. In other words, the refusal to simply let Garabandal be and allow it to flourish.

There are many sites throughout the world where the Virgin Mary is said to have appeared which the Church has never ruled on one way or another, has never encouraged but also never restricted. In fact, Jesus counseled to let the weeds grow alongside the wheat, lest excessive zeal in uprooting the bad plants lead to the destruction of good plants as well. The Church hierarchy—those with both responsibility and authority regarding Garabandal—need not have made a positive pronouncement yet, but they also didn't have to take a stand against it, discouraging both the clergy and the faithful from paying any attention to Mary's words.

One of the pronouncements that there was no evidence of the supernatural at Garabandal was issued by the bishop just prior to the opening ceremonies of Vatican II. Conchita actually went into ecstasy as the radio began to broadcast the opening ceremony. As the Conciliar fathers solemnly processed in, Conchita, on a different wavelength, took advantage of the apparition to ask the Virgin why the bishop had just issued that negative Nota on Garabandal. The Virgin, apparently unruffled, "didn't answer. She only smiled."[447]

The Roman Catholic Church has an almost impossible task in evaluating the many Marian apparitions of the past 100 years, and there are undoubtedly numerous fakes, which can be devastating. In a world with far more lies than truth, the Church's skeptical attitude toward apparitions is understandable. Garabandal may be one of those lies. It may in fact be a weed. Yet if Garabandal turns out to be genuine, the opposition it has experienced places it in good company.

A time of darkness and denial often seems to be the lot of those the Church later recognizes as genuine—Jesus himself being the prime example. Joan of Arc, another girl visionary, was burned at the stake. Saint Faustina was a Polish nun who passed on a Plea for Divine Mercy given to her by Jesus on the eve of World War II, a prayer which was furtively circulated throughout concentration camps. When one reads the beautiful plea, it's difficult to fathom why it was suppressed for a time and placed on the Church's list of "banned books." Padre Pio is another who was harassed and silenced before he was sainted. Padre Pio reportedly wept upon hearing about the first decree issued against him by the Holy Office, but he explained that he wasn't weeping for himself, but "for all the souls who will be deprived of my witness by those very ones who should be defending it."[448] For that matter, the Fatima apparitions met with much stiff opposition from priests and theologians within the Church for many decades.[449]

When one examines these two messages from Garabandal, they seem thoroughly Catholic and quite traditional. In retrospect, they also seem spot-on accurate: It's 1965, as the transformative Vatican II Council is drawing to a close and the turbulent, hedonistic Sixties are about to explode. Mary is worried about the declining importance of the Eucharist, about the need for more Christ-like sacrifice on the part of all Christians, and about priests in peril, which puts others in jeopardy as well. She makes it clear that the listeners can make a difference in turning away God's punishment, for both themselves personally but more importantly for the community at large. (*You should turn away the wrath of God by your efforts...You should make more sacrifices...I want to tell you to amend your lives.*) She promises that God pardons those who sincerely ask forgiveness. These are hardly controversial words from a Catholic viewpoint. Today, it's hard to imagine what was so disturbing to some bishops about Mary's quite conservative, deeply Catholic words at Garabandal. Except, of course, for her dire pronouncement that many of them were on the road to perdition.

Word quickly spread that the message was about priests, and within a few days a group had gone to complain to the bishop about the message.[450] The local Spanish hierarchy may have thought the Virgin Mary was singling them out for blame and shame—hence, their resistance and resentment toward the message. And they even had reason for feeling this way: Twenty-five years earlier, Sister Lucia of Fatima had delivered a message from Jesus to the bishops of Spain, calling on them to resume their practice of meeting together in retreat to address the laxity and lack of zeal among clergy, religious, and laity.[451] Jesus seemed worried about strengthening the Spanish Church in 1941, no doubt because Spain had just emerged from a bloody civil war which had decimated the Church and the country. So there was some precedent for the Spanish hierarchy feeling singled out by a heavenly apparition. Yet it's undeniable that fifty years after Garabandal, Mary's dire warning about the state of various cardinals, bishops, and priests reverberates painfully throughout the global Church. The Garabandal message was never meant just for Spain.

Fifty years later, it's also possible to see a distinct change in the bishops' positions toward Garabandal. At the time the Garabandal apparitions began, Spanish Church officials had legitimate reason for concern about Marian apparitions, which had a long history in Europe. Specifically, the Ezkioga apparitions had occurred thirty years earlier, in 1931, just before the Spanish Civil War broke out. There were allegations that the Ezkioga apparitions, which were later condemned both locally and by the Vatican, were used for political purposes by Basque nationalists promoting visions of a polarizing Virgin Mary who wielded a sword. Any bishop of Santander had legitimate fears, especially in the early days, about the Garabandal apparitions stoking violence in this area which bordered the Basque region. In fact, the Basque separatist group known as ETA launched its first attack in July 1961, as the Garabandal apparitions were gaining momentum.

The two original Ezkioga visionaries of 1931 claimed to see Mary as the Mother of Sorrows (who typically has swords piercing her heart) weeping without words. At the time there was deep anxiety in the region due to mob violence against the Catholic Church which had erupted when the anti-clerical Spanish government came to power. The initial vision of the two children watching Mary weep quickly spread like a contagion into literally hundreds of people who said they were having visions of the Virgin, sometimes bearing a sword along with angels wielding bloody swords. Visionaries also reported seeing a witch in the sky, a headless figure, a monkey who turned into a witch who then threatened to kill them, a girl in a low-cut dress, short skirt, painted face, and peroxided hair, a parade of coffins, and a red-haired devil dressed in black with long teeth.[452]

Some speculate the events were indeed supernatural, but a demonic imitation designed to foment violence and damage authentic appearances of the Virgin Mary. Others saw the apparitions as perhaps initially genuine with some authentic visionaries, until the phenomenon was hijacked for political purposes during perilous times. Needless to say, like Garabandal, some thought the entire episode was a sham.

Because of reported visits to view the Garabandal apparitions by Ezkioga seers and Basque nationalist priests,[453] as well as fears of mass hysteria and violence, the earliest bishops apparently had good reason for wanting Garabandal to be off-limits to priests and pilgrims alike. To prevent an Ezkioga-like episode, members of the investigative Commission arrived on the scene early in Garabandal hoping to spirit the girls away from the village. The Commission told Mari-Loli and Jacinta's fathers "the longer the girls remained here, the more people would come and that other people in the village would start having visions, apparitions."[454] But the fathers refused to send their daughters away, the apparitions continued, and the only other visionary to emerge from Garabandal was Father Luis Andreu, who didn't survive the experience.

On July 8, 1965, shortly after the last public message in Garabandal, the Bishopric of Santander issued its fourth "nota" in as many years on the matter. Maria Saraco said that after the June 18, 1965 apparition in Garabandal, she herself went to the bishop to talk with him about what was happening in Garabandal.

"When I went to see the bishop, there were only two pilgrims left in the village after the apparitions. The boy came with me and there was also a girl still in the village. He was an American living in France at that time. I don't know if he is still alive or not. The girl who was also still there spoke many languages. She later died in an earthquake," Saraco recalled. "I met with him (Bishop Eugenio Beitia Aldazabal) and he told me he was going to write something to the people about Garabandal. The bishop also told me to read the New Testament every day. I have kept that promise."

The bishop did indeed write to the people about Garabandal, and this fourth nota agreed with the previous three, that "*there is no evidence of a supernatural character in the phenomena*" of Garabandal. Nonetheless, Bishop Aldazábal was more positive than negative in his pronouncement, stating that "*we have not found any reason for ecclesiastical censure with regard to condemning either the doctrine or the spiritual recommendations that have been promulgated in this affair… Rather they contain exhortations to prayer and sacrifice, to Eucharistic devotion, to devotion to Our Lady in traditional praiseworthy forms, to the holy fear of God offended by our sins. They simply repeat ordinary Church doctrine in these matters.*"[455]

Then, only a month later, in August 1965, a new bishop was appointed. Bishop Vicente Puchol Montis had a reputation for being decisively opposed to the apparitions and set to work to quash the spread of Garabandal.

In the early days of the apparitions, at least one attempt had already been made to extinguish Mary mania in Garabandal. The steadfast pastor Father Valentin was sent packing on an extended "holiday" in late 1961, ostensibly to treat his frayed nerves but more likely because he was seen as too supportive of the apparitions and was even suspected of being an instigator.[456] He was replaced by an unbelieving young psychologist priest who told the villagers the apparitions weren't true and the Virgin was no different than any other saint.[457] The plan hit a glitch, however, when the new priest also began to believe in the apparitions.[458]

The bishop reportedly complained, "I sent you to de-mystify the affair and the result is that you come back more convinced of the reality of the apparitions than the girls themselves."[459] Soon afterward, Father Valentin was back at his old post.

But in 1965, the new Bishop Puchol Montis finally removed Father Valentin for good and forbade him to even visit, replacing him with another young priest whose job it was to put a stop to the Garabandal phenomenon once and for all.[460]

Conchita, meanwhile, had entered convent school in Pamplona where she was deeply shaken as she began to face the reality that she had no vocation to become a nun. She was seventeen years old and away from home for the first time in her life. She thought she had crossed the threshold into her future as a missionary nun in Africa, and now she no longer had any idea about what awaited her in life. At the same time, she began to have doubts about the presence of Jesus in the Eucharist. And finally, she met up in Garabandal with Mari-Loli during the Easter holidays in 1966, only to learn there that Mari-Loli was having doubts about the apparitions which she had been discussing with the new Garabandal pastor. Conchita, already in a confused and fragile state, also spoke to the unbelieving young priest during this time.

Then Conchita returned to the convent school in Pamplona where a three-day retreat was conducted by another young priest who was also a disbeliever in the apparitions. Conchita—grieving over the crumbling of her religious vocation, filled with anxiety about her future, tormented by spiritual doubt about the presence of Jesus in the Eucharist, and fresh from meeting with doubting Mari-Loli and the unbelieving young Garabandal pastor—unburdened herself to the skeptical priest in confession that she herself now had doubts about the apparitions as well. But how could anyone know what Conchita said in the confessional? The young priest responded by refusing to give Conchita absolution unless she confessed to the village and the pilgrims that she had deceived everyone.[461]

In order to fulfill this condition, Conchita made arrangements to meet with the Bishop. On August 30, 1966, Bishop Puchol Montis, his Vicar General, a secretary, and the young Garabandal pastor arrived on the doorstep of Conchita's school. The interview with this intimidating entourage lasted seven hours, with a break for lunch. During this interview Conchita said that she no longer remembered seeing the Virgin, but her diary was true, the Miracle of the Host was true, the Messages of Garabandal were true, and the Great Miracle would come.[462] In a 1980 BBC documentary, Conchita said that she spoke with the bishop for "many hours," and although she admitted to the Bishop that she couldn't remember seeing the Virgin, she also told him that she didn't know who had given her the June 18, 1965 message: "I didn't invent the message."[463]

Father Valentin gave a feisty interview years after he was exiled from Garabandal (when he was finally permitted to speak about the events) in which he makes this exact point: Conchita's 1965 message that cardinals, bishops, and priests were on the road to perdition—given by a 16-year-old girl in a remote village that revered priests—"has been fulfilled to the letter. It was impossible for the girls to know about it, because at that time not even I knew such conditions existed."[464]

A strange shadow had fallen over Conchita's memory of seeing the Virgin and St. Michael, but she still maintained that the *essence* of the Garabandal message remained intact. (Conchita's confusing contradictions will be examined in greater depth in the next chapter.) The Bishop absolved Conchita after her confession, and told her, in light of her confusion, that it was better not to speak of the apparitions anymore.[465]

But this latest rip in the fabric of Garabandal would not stop there. The unraveling was just beginning. Due to Conchita's contradictions in her interview with the bishop, the other three Garabandal visionaries were summoned for interviews with the bishop as well. This wasn't the first time the girls had been interviewed by a bishop, and the results of the interviews with various bishops were hardly ever positive for the cause of Garabandal.

During these interviews, alternative possibilities were suggested to the girls, such as that the apparitions were a dream, a "collective hallucination," or were caused by "excitability."[466] During an interview in 1965, Mari Cruz was told by Canon Odriozola, clerk of the investigative Commission, that she was essentially a victim of the atmosphere in the village—that the influence of villagers and visitors pressured her to "produce" the apparitions. This could certainly explain why the girls continued the apparitions—but why did they start them? At least one of the doctors appointed by the bishop to examine the girls concluded that the children suffered from hysteria and had imagined and hallucinated the apparitions as a result of their poverty and isolation from big cities.[467]

But the skepticism about Garabandal couldn't just be blamed on a sinister authority figure whispering corrosive doubt into the visionaries' ears. The visionaries themselves injected the doubts. During an interview with the bishop in June 1965, Mari Cruz had actually demonstrated how they had simulated ecstasies. Then she added this comment: "When the ecstasies were genuine, we saw and heard nothing of what was going on around us. When the ecstasies were false, we saw and heard everything."[468]

Conchita explained the fake ecstasies in her diary this way: In the early days of the apparitions, the girls sometimes had already received two calls and wanted to stay together for the coming apparition, but were forbidden to be out on the streets after dark by their parents. Consequently, the girls would "look above as though we were seeing the Blessed Virgin. In this way we were able to stay together in the streets. Then the Blessed Virgin would appear to us while we were together."[469] The girls would stumble and trip when they kept their eyes fixed heavenward while faking it (unlike the genuine ecstasies), and they were rebuked by the Virgin Mary for pretending to see her as soon as she really did appear.[470]

But that wasn't the only occasion when the girls simulated ecstasies. Villager Pepe Diez recalled some "extremely rare" instances when pilgrims traveled long distances, arrived exhausted, and were deeply disappointed when no apparitions were forthcoming. Some of these pilgrims relentlessly badgered the girls to kneel and pray and attempt to "bring on" an ecstasy for them.

"It was, on the part of the little girls, a kind of compliance toward these people," Pepe Diez noted.[471]

The girls were essentially reduced to performing for "apparition tourists." Yet Pepe noted the striking differences between the real and simulated ecstasies.

"In fact, when the ecstasies were false, the girls had to move along flat roads, where they could walk easily, whereas in real ecstasies, they would go over all kinds of terrain without stumbling over any objects frontwards or backwards, in very difficult positions, with an ease...Moreover, the false ecstasy never lasted more than five minutes, maybe ten...the real ecstasies lasted sometimes four to five hours, on very difficult roads...without any sign of fatigue."[472]

Still, this admission by the girls to occasional faking was devastating—something which Conchita was painfully aware of. When asked if she realized that her "inventions" and "little deceits"—along with her own doubts—clouded the truth about the apparitions of Garabandal, she replied: "It is very possible that could be. Don't think that I haven't thought about it."[473]

And then came this damning development: All four girls, after the interviews with the bishop in the fall of 1966, agreed to "recant." The text that they signed was: "I did not see the Virgin." Meanwhile, the parents also were told to sign, but Conchita's mother, livid about the seven-hour interrogation, yanked her daughter out of the convent school and refused to sign: "I saw what I saw, I am not signing."[474] Jacinta's mother—who had screamed uncontrollably the first time she saw her daughter in ecstasy—said she would only recant if Jacinta could fall into an ecstasy right then and there in front of the bishop. When Jacinta said it was impossible, her mother also refused to sign.

Nevertheless, the Bishop had finally gotten the goods— enough to put Garabandal once and for all on the chopping block. In March 1967, Bishop Puchol Montis published the following memo: that neither Mary nor Michael had appeared in Garabandal, there was no message, and all the events had a natural explanation. He then launched a media campaign against the apparitions as a follow-up.[475] He was also considering a prohibition of the sacraments in the village of Garabandal, a severe measure known as an ecclesiastical interdict.[476]

Tragically, Bishop Puchol was killed soon after issuing this memo, on May 8, 1967, in a car accident.[477] It so happens that May 8 is a feast day commemorating an appearance of St. Michael to a bishop. This odd coincidence has led some to speculate that the bishop was perhaps slain by the fiery archangel himself for the crime of dissing Jesus' mother.[478] Conchita, however, burst into tears and said, "I am so sorry about what has happened! He was very good and very young. The poor man! He did everything with good intentions. Now the Bishop knows everything." [479]

This intimidating development of a possible angelic assassin did not stop Church objections to Garabandal, although the opposition mellowed as the years went by. Bishop Juan Antonio del Val Gallo was the bishop of Santander for twenty years, from 1971-1991. Bishop del Val Gallo had served as a member of the original 1961 investigative Commission for a brief period of time before resigning, and had observed the girls in ecstasy. Over his years as bishop, Bishop del Val Gallo gradually lifted restrictions that had been imposed in earlier years. And despite the fact that it says all over the internet that Garabandal has been "condemned" by the Church, both Bishop Aldazábal and Bishop del Val Gallo were quite clear decades ago that the apparitions, though not declared supernatural, have never been condemned.

Bishop Aldazabal said in 1965 that *we have not found any reason for ecclesiastical censure with regard to condemning either the doctrine or the spiritual recommendations that have been promulgated in this affair...* Bishop del Val Gallo affirmed this position in a videotaped interview in 1992: "The previous bishops did not admit that the apparitions were supernatural but to condemn them, no, that word had never been used," he said in the interview, which is available on-line both in video and transcription.[480] He went on to say that the Garabandal messages had never said anything against the doctrine of the Church—an important point since the abrogation of Canons 1399 and 2318 by Pope Paul VI in 1966 lifted all restrictions on publishing about apparitions and visits to those sites, whether approved by the bishop or Holy Father or not—as long as "faith and morals" are not endangered.[481] Garabandal passes this test, although Bishop del Val Gallo did admit in the interview that he himself was bothered by Mary's "severe" pronouncement that many cardinals, bishops and priests were on the road to perdition. However, in light of what has occurred since 1965, the Virgin Mary's unflinching warning appears more like a loving attempt to prevent tragedy rather than an angry condemnation.

Bishop del Val Gallo went on to say in the filmed interview that Christians should live the messages of Garabandal since the Virgin may truly have said these words. "But I'm not saying that she did since this would be admitting the apparitions are true and I cannot do that because the Church has not said so yet." In 2007, Apostolic Administrator Carlos Osoro Sierra confirmed that all priests were authorized to "go to Garabandal and celebrate Mass there at whatever hour they desire, and to administer the Sacrament of Reconciliation to as many people who desire it there."[482]

Bishop del Val Gallo wasn't the only member of the original 1961 investigative Commission to speak up about Garabandal in later years. Dr. Luis Morales Noriega, a psychiatrist, altered his position as time passed. In 1979, he even had his cancer-ridden wife kiss a crucifix that had been kissed by the Virgin in Garabandal, which took away her pain and suffused her with peace until she died. "Now I see the existential reality of Our Lady in Garabandal," Dr. Morales said, comparing Garabandal to Lourdes and Fatima.[483]

The Roman Catholic Church understandably takes an extremely cautious approach toward present-day claims of visions and messages from the Great Beyond, and there were numerous reasons to be skeptical in the case of Garabandal. The Virgin's tough-love message for clergy was no doubt a factor in the Church's negative stance toward the Garabandal apparitions because the message seemed excessively harsh at the time—but that wasn't the only reason for Church skepticism. Add to this the early concern about the Ezkioga apparitions, as well as the Garabandal visionaries' own inconsistencies, and the Church's lack of approval of Garabandal is not surprising.

Conchita was once questioned by some Americans about the difficulty Catholics experienced in wanting to please the Virgin and spread the message of Garabandal while also wanting to obey those in authority in the Church.[484] Conchita replied that the Virgin wished people to spread the messages of Garabandal, but that it glorified God more to obey the Church. When an English pilgrim asked how she could spread the Garabandal messages when bishops opposed their propagation, Conchita replied, "Sacrifice oneself and practice the messages."[485]

The Virgin also said that there would be time for the message to be spread with the permission of the Church. Indeed, it's been forty-five years since Pope Paul VI lifted all restrictions on both visiting and publishing about apparition sites—even the unapproved ones—as long as the faith and morals of the faithful are not harmed. That move, in addition to the relaxing of restrictions by subsequent Garabandal bishops and the explosion of the internet, have certainly afforded much greater opportunity to spread the message of Garabandal.

But even if some bishops have spoken more positively about Garabandal and lifted restrictions as time has passed, the true wild card in this story is the visionaries. Did the doubts that opened up in the visionaries come to an end or continue? If the visionaries are the wild card in this story, they are also the key to it. In the next chapters, we'll look at the last remaining evidence for and against what happened at Garabandal, particularly the visionaries' own words as adults—including a final conversation with visionary Mari-Loli shortly before her death in 2009, and interviews with her children in 2020.

Chapter 8

A Visionary's Last Word

"Loli, if in the future I do not appear to you again, it is that your hour of suffering has come." **The Virgin Mary's farewell to Mari-Loli in 1965**

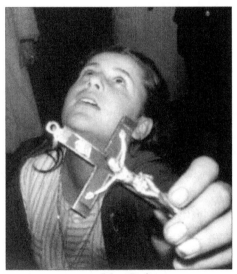

486 *Mari-Loli*

None of the four visionaries would remain in Garabandal. In a few short years, they would all be gone from the small mountain village where they were born, where they spent their childhood, and where—they claimed—the Virgin Mary had come and changed the course of their lives.

All four girls had spoken to each other of becoming nuns after the apparitions started in 1961, and more than one of them took steps in that direction after the apparitions ended in 1965. Jacinta had been accepted into a Carmelite convent where she hoped to retreat behind the iron grille and atone for the world, but at the last moment, her father forbade her to go. Instead, she joined Mari-Loli and made plans to go to a boarding school run by nuns.[487] Conchita, for her part, at the tender age of sixteen entered the Missionary Sisters of the Discalced Carmelites with the full intention of becoming a nun and going to Africa.[488]

"My mother has allowed me to enter into the convent. For me, it is a great thing to be able to consecrate myself completely to Christ like this — from my 16th year — for the rest of my life."[489]

Before entering the convent, Conchita would have one last apparition with the Virgin Mary, after Jacinta and Mari-Loli had left the village. It would be on November 13, 1965, at the Pines, where Conchita would go alone, and would include some fascinating last comments from the Virgin. Conchita would bring a handful of rosaries and medals to be kissed by the Virgin, who then asked Conchita to distribute them because through them, her Son would "perform prodigies." (Seven years later, the two mothers involved with the lost airplane in the Andes would pray that their sons be saved using just such a rosary from Garabandal.)

The Infant Jesus was also at this apparition, in his mother's arms as he'd been for some other apparitions in Garabandal. It was during this last private apparition that Mary would tell Conchita that she had not come just for Conchita. She would remind Conchita that the girl would suffer on earth, and told her to offer everything to God for the good of others. Mary then poignantly said, *This is the last time you will see me here. But I will always be with you, and with all my children.*

This apparition, rather than being the last public message which had occurred on June 18, 1965, seemed to be Mary's farewell to the four girls. The Virgin Mary specifically mentioned the other three girls by name, and did not seem the least bit disappointed or perturbed by anyone's failures or denials. *Do all that you can on your part; and we will help you, and also my daughters, Loli, Jacinta and Mari Cruz.*[490]

Mary also took this last opportunity to drive home the heart of the Garabandal message, urging Conchita to overcome her sloth and visit Jesus in the tabernacle more often, where he was "waiting for her day and night." Conchita, for her part, begged Mary to take her with her and Mary replied, *When presenting yourself before God, you have to show your hands full of works done by you for your brothers and for the glory of God. Now, your hands are empty.*[491]

Conchita wrote movingly about the last apparition: "That's all. The happy time that I spent with my best friend, my Mother from heaven, and with the little Jesus, is all over. I no longer see them, but I still feel them. Once again they have spread peace and joy in my heart with a great desire to conquer my faults and to love with all my strength, the Hearts of Jesus and Mary who love us so much."[492]

Conchita was not the only visionary who was granted a personal farewell from the Virgin. Mari-Loli, whose full name Maria Dolores means Mary of Sorrows, had a locution just before she left Garabandal: *"Loli, if in the future I do not appear to you again, it is that your hour of suffering has come."*[493]

But if you can take the girls out of Garabandal, it's been far more difficult to take Garabandal out of the girls. The apparitions of Garabandal—in all their wonder and controversy—would follow the four visionaries wherever they went. Their witness to these amazing events would continue in various forms as the years passed, but their doubts and confusion also would recur.

A Veil of Darkness

After the girls left Garabandal, the first post-apparition crisis struck Conchita in 1966 while she was in the convent discerning about becoming a nun. First, she was afflicted with intense spiritual doubts that Jesus was present in the Eucharist. After that, she confessed to the young doubting priest, and then the poor, doomed bishop, that she had doubts about having seen the Virgin. She also spoke very honestly to a sister at the convent school during this period of doubt and distress. Although only seventeen, Conchita sounded like someone in middle-age looking back with regret and wisdom at what had occurred, lamenting the "stupid" things they had said to the Virgin, things without importance. "From time to time I see more clearly that what happened to the four of us girls was true, but we wasted it...Our denials are our own doing. Sometimes, although very briefly, I see this very clearly."[494] Yet her periods of clarity were fleeting. More common was seeing everything that had happened "as if in a dream—the apparitions, the people...I'm sorry that many doubt the apparitions because of my denials."[495]

[496] *Conchita and Mari-Loli at the Pines in Garabandal*

Throughout Conchita's "confession" of doubt and denial, she spoke, often within the same sentence, as if she believed. "When I think about the Virgin, I picture her as something I dreamed...It isn't necessary to be perfect to see her. I have been a girl with many faults. On the day on which the Angel appeared to us, I had just fought with Jacinta."[497]

Also, during this period of doubt, Conchita talked about the insults and lies they had had to endure, and she listed all the accusations people had made which weren't true, insisting that the four girls had not been playing a game, had not tried to deceive, had not conspired to come up with a story, and had not made dough to create the "miraculous" communion host.

But Conchita admitted that the four had also done stupid things which were apparently read to Conchita by Cardinal Ottaviani in a visit to Rome, including the matter of the levitation powders and the statue of the Virgin they were going to bury.[498]

The official disapproval did not, however, dismay Conchita. "I don't feel rancor or hate toward anyone. When the priests of the Commission or those in charge of us attacked us, and the others became angry because of this, I did not. I thought that they had to act like this; and I loved them."[499]

Conchita then went on to make an odd remark about possibly becoming a nun "after the Miracle."[500] During this time in the convent, she had become aware she would not be a nun, not through some gradual process of discernment, but because Jesus actually spoke to her in what turned out to be a painful, life-changing locution: *I want you in the world, to stay in it to face the numerous difficulties you will face because of Me. All this, I want for your sanctification and offering for the salvation of the world. You must speak of Mary to the world...I emphasize, Conchita, that you will have much to suffer, from now until the Miracle, for there are few who believe you...Do not waver; in suffering you will find Me, and also Mary whom you love so much.*[501]

Remaining in the world rather than fleeing to a convent was a source of suffering for Conchita, who described her village as a prison in the aftermath of the apparitions. "I acted by the command of others who constantly advised me, *Go to Mass...Pray the rosary...Do this...Give up that.* At times I thought I would be happy to be in a hermitage away from everyone, and to work there alone for God, and see what I was capable of without their forever telling me."[502]

During this locution, Conchita asked Jesus if Rome would believe her about the apparitions of Garabandal. His reply? *Don't worry whether they believe you or not. I will do everything; but I will also give you suffering. I am near to those who suffer for Me.*[503]

But why did Conchita imagine that she would become a nun "after the Miracle"—which she herself supposedly already knew would be decades away?[504] Perhaps because it was still a dream she harbored, and Catholic history is full of older and widowed women who entered convents late in their lives—including St. Rita, and Fr. Luis Andreu's mother.

After she left home in 1966, was plunged into doubt, and recanted to the bishop, Conchita seemed to have her eye on the Miracle as the final answer to all her doubts. If the Miracle occurred, then obviously the apparitions were true. If the Miracle didn't occur, the apparitions were false. Seven years later, Conchita confessed in a filmed 1973 interview that she was looking to the Miracle to confirm the truth of the apparitions. "Since then, up to this time, I have a confusion and doubt within me. I am waiting for the Miracle to confirm whether this is true or not. To see if I saw the Virgin or not." But she had no doubts, she added, that the Virgin had indeed told her the date of the Miracle, as well as what it would consist of![505] This was almost exactly what she had told Bishop Puchol Montis in 1966—that everything was true, none of it was a lie, but she could not always remember seeing the Virgin.

Maria Saraco has described the doubts as many others have described them—as some sort of mystical darkness or veil thrown over the visionaries' memories, clouding their faith and afflicting them with doubts. The Virgin Mary said the four visionaries would pass through the same confusion and doubt as the Church itself.[506] Also, the darkness and veil will supposedly lift and be cleared once the Great Miracle occurs.

It was on June 29th, 1972 that Pope Paul VI made his famous (or infamous) comment that the "smoke of Satan" had entered the Church. (A more intriguing translation is "satanic breath.") He lamented that the "day of sunshine" the Church had eagerly anticipated after Vatican II had instead become one of clouds and storms and darkness. "...each day we separate more one from another. We are digging abysses, instead of filling them...Doubt has entered into our conscience, and it has entered across windows that should have been open to the light. Doubt has come with respect to everything that exists, to everything that we know..."[507] This is the widespread darkness of doubt and cancerous crisis of faith which some claim the visionaries of Garabandal were destined to prefigure and share in.

It's true that the visionaries in many subsequent interviews over the years have frequently (though not always) responded, "I don't know" or "I don't remember" to many questions about the events. (At other times, they have responded openly and in detail to various questions.) Perhaps their doubt and uncertainty are indeed some sort of mystical suffering that parallels the Church's confusion. On the other hand, there may at times have been other, less supernatural, reasons for the visionaries' avoidance of questions about Garabandal.

For one thing, over the past fifty years, the visionaries *have* given many interviews. Both print and video interviews of the adult visionaries litter the web. But the frequency of those interviews has also naturally tapered off as time has passed. The visionaries feel that they have said all there is to be said.

The visionaries have also noted as the long years have rolled by that they sometimes recall what they have *said* about the events more clearly than they remember the events themselves. Many people carry around vivid childhood memories that they're certain they will never forget. Yet commonly, when these memories are aired, another family member remembers crucial details of the same event quite differently. In an interview in 1978, a priest asked Conchita about the message that the ghostly

Fr. Luis had delivered to his still-living brother Fr. Ramon. Although that message was recorded in detail in the early 1960s, sixteen years later, in 1978, Conchita admitted she couldn't recall the message, although she did remember the deceased Fr. Luis teaching them the "Hail Mary" in Greek. By 1983, she said about the apparitions, "I can hardly remember. That is one of the reasons why I do not like to discuss the events...The future holds the answer."[508] Conchita's anxiety about the accuracy of her own memories places her in good company. Bernadette of Lourdes said this at the end of her life: "It is already far away...very far away...all these things: I do not remember them; I do not like to speak too much about them, in case, my God! I have been mistaken."[509]

The visionaries have also been asked to respond to what *others* have said they did. Much was written regarding the events and the girls' words almost from the first day. When the visionaries have been interviewed about Garabandal, they have frequently been asked questions about what others said about them rather than what they themselves actually said.

Another reason for avoiding questions about Garabandal is that the four visionaries, like all others who have been thrust into the spotlight in the age of mass media, have experienced being misquoted, misled, and misunderstood. Conchita admitted in 1983 that she had been too trusting in the early years, and had gotten burned by it. She explained that it was important to love all people, but to trust God, since it takes time to truly know people.[510]

Understandably, the visionaries are gun-shy about interviews. Conchita even admitted that some of the reporting was her own fault. "Sometimes, like everyone else, I would venture to state my opinion of what a certain thing meant, not realizing how many people would put more credence in what I said than anyone else's interpretation of the Virgin's words."[511] And Father Ramon Andreu recalled people pushing the girls "until they were exhausted, and in a state of confusion they would answer...Just listening to the way these people would repeat their questions in order to obtain the answers they wanted to hear also confused me. The girls were never left alone."[512]

This means literally. Mari-Loli confided to Dr. Ricardo Puncernau that in the early days of the apparitions she had felt greatly oppressed by people following her everywhere she went, even to the village's lone outhouse.[513]

Another view is that the visionaries are reclusive about interviews because they are being obedient to the Church or to their bishop. The Church's official skepticism toward the events at Garabandal has no doubt affected the four visionaries. Since they have remained devout practicing Catholics their whole lives, the visionaries may have feared offending God by not speaking up about what happened in Garabandal. But they may also have feared committing sin when they *did* speak up—because what if they were (unwittingly) lying? What if they were misremembering events? What if they were misunderstanding or misquoting *the Virgin*? What if they were misleading thousands with the terrible lie that the Virgin Mary had come to Garabandal? On the other hand—what if they were failing the Virgin by *denying* the truth of Garabandal? Conchita expressed this concern very clearly in a documentary produced by the BBC in 1980. She described the intense confusion she experienced in 1966 when she told Bishop Puchol Montis of her doubts. He asked her not to talk about the apparitions since she had these doubts.

When the other three seers signed their retractions in 1966, they were also reportedly instructed not to speak about the apparitions.[514] After that, when pilgrims came to the village and Conchita said she no longer believed in the apparitions, she felt like she was "talking against the Blessed Mother. I didn't feel right inside...I didn't know what to say to (the people). If I said everything was true, I felt like I was fooling the people. If I said it's not true, I was hurting the Blessed Mother."[515] This 1980 interview echoed exactly what she had expressed in 1966 after meeting with the bishop and denying the apparitions: "When I deny, I feel inside—deep down—something that doesn't leave me in peace."[516] Conchita also expressed profound anguish at the thought of seeing the Virgin again after having denied her during the fateful 1966 meeting with the bishop. "It would be painful for me now because of my denials..."[517]

[518] *Mari-Loli and Jacinta on an ecstatic walk*

The recurring "memory loss" and sporadic tongue-tied misery of the visionaries could very well be explained by this unbearable tension of feeling torn between the Virgin Mary and Church authorities while under the constant scrutiny of questing pilgrims. In fact, Conchita admitted that this painful predicament forced her to finally leave Garabandal.[519]

Do They Doubt Today?

Conchita fled Garabandal because of inner torment and outer scrutiny—and moved to the United States. If the apparitions were a charade concocted by Conchita which got out of hand, the escape to America afforded her the perfect opportunity to leave the past behind and start anew. Yet it was in this sudden calm, where no one knew who she was, away from the fishbowl of Garabandal, that the storm of doubt Conchita had been plunged into since 1966 began to lift, and her memories of seeing the Virgin Mary re-surfaced. "I started to remember the Blessed Mother again. I started to remember her voice." In the 1980 BBC documentary, Conchita said she can't explain the apparitions. "I know I saw the Blessed Mother. I saw her. I talked to her, I saw the angel."[520]

On the other hand, consider the difficult case of Mari Cruz, the one who is most often described as denying the apparitions occurred. When the other three girls at various times over the years renounced their denials, Mari Cruz reportedly stood fast and insisted that she had never seen the Virgin or the angel. In the early years, some observers believed Mari Cruz was under family pressure to deny the apparitions since "Mari Cruz, while denying, was constantly looking fixedly at her mother." At the same time, her mother was explaining away the apparitions as "arising from illness."[521] Yet years later, Mari Cruz still denied the apparitions. In a 1984 interview, Mari Cruz said that Conchita suddenly went into ecstasy that first time and put it into the other three girls' heads that they had also seen the angel. This echoes the Commission's belief that Conchita was the charismatic instigator who cast a spell on the other, more impressionable girls.

Mari Cruz also agreed with the Commission's suggestion that the crowds pressured the girls into continuing their charade. In the 1984 interview, she said that the girls were forced to continue the apparitions because miracle-hungry crowds began to descend on them almost instantly, badgering the girls for a message similar to Lourdes or Fatima.[522] (Due to this crowd pressure, the girls had repeatedly pressed the Virgin Mary to give "proof" as she had done at Lourdes and Fatima. The Virgin's response was the Miracle of the Host.)

Since Mari Cruz had the fewest number of apparitions and hers ended the soonest, it's quite likely that she felt pressured to perform long after she had stopped experiencing apparitions, while the other girls were still having visions. We've already seen how Mari Cruz was taunted when her own visions trickled away to nothing.[523] Her own mother, near tears, complained about the "slander" in the newspapers which suggested the family wasn't religious enough.[524] The temptation to feign ecstasies and avoid shame must have been great, and it's to Mari Cruz's everlasting credit that she didn't try to escape her lame duck status after September 1962 by faking ecstasies.

But if star visionary Conchita eventually doubted and complained of clouded memories—even with numerous apparitions and locutions under her belt over the span of several years—it's perfectly plausible that Mari Cruz's abbreviated apparitions (which lasted a little over a year) led her to forget even sooner and to doubt even more. Perhaps Mari Cruz—under pressure from judgmental believers, a skeptical Church, and disbelieving family—struggled to answer persistent questions about what she couldn't explain or clearly remember, and felt the sting of rejection because she had stopped having apparitions. It's understandable that she took refuge in the Commission's theory that a fanciful Conchita drew the girls into her fantasy and the clamoring crowds trapped them into a lie.

And yet—Mari Cruz's explanation of events could very well be the truth. After all, immediately preceding the angel's first appearance, the girls had been hurling stones at Satan for tricking them into stealing apples. In their passionate playacting, it would have been a natural segue into the next scene: Conchita falls to the ground, gasping in shock at the sudden appearance of an otherworldly being. Conchita was indeed the first one to spot the angel, and the other girls were alarmed by her strange behavior—until they, too, saw the angel. Maybe, instead of seeing an angel, the other girls simply followed Conchita's theatrical lead that first night. Giddy and giggling, flushed with forbidden excitement from stealing apples and throwing stones and staying out late, the girls infected each other and then others with their game. What they didn't count on was being instantly swarmed by eager believers—and by then it was already too late to back out. The Miracle of the Host—rather than being the Virgin's response to the demanding crowd—was *Conchita's* response. Wracked by guilt and even panic-stricken over what they had unleashed, the girls were forced to play their parts and follow the script to its bitter and unpredictable end. This would explain the retractions, the "memory loss," the "doubt," as the girls' falsehoods crumbled over time. In this scenario, Mari Cruz—rather than being branded with a scarlet D for denying and doubting—is the sanest and strongest of the four, who chose to walk away from the spectacle rather than continue the ruse.

Garabandal believers dealt with Mari Cruz's inconvenient truth by insisting that her perspective was an "attack of the devil" which would have a dramatic resolution: It was predicted that Mari Cruz would finally, at long last, "deny her denial" on the day of the Great Miracle. In actuality, neither Mari Cruz nor the rest of us have had to wait that long.

Twenty-two years after that 1984 interview, Mari Cruz was interviewed again, in 2006. And just as Conchita's memories of the Virgin re-surfaced miles away from the pressure cooker that was Garabandal, Mari Cruz evidently experienced a resurgence of memories of the Virgin with the buffer of—not distance—but time. Why? Conchita exiled herself to America where, physically distant from the events and people of Garabandal, her memories of the Virgin Mary bubbled up. Maybe forty-four years after Mari Cruz had experienced her last apparition, she was able to re-claim her role in this turbulent drama through the calming distance of time. Perhaps the stresses imposed on her by dubious villagers, suffering family, zealous pilgrims, mocking critics, an insatiable media, and a skeptical Church had finally waned.

In the 2006 interview, true to Garabandal form, Mari Cruz replied "I don't know" or "I don't remember" to several questions. But she also responded in detail to other questions such as feeling confused when St. Michael first appeared, and feeling emotional but not anxious when the Virgin would appear. Mari Cruz said she felt relaxed in the Virgin's presence and was told by Mary that it was O.K. to cry. This is curious since villagers recalled that Mari Cruz cried a lot: "She cried almost every time she had an ecstasy. I don't know what was happening to make her cry."[525]

During the 2006 interview, Mari Cruz also made this intriguing comment: "It was as though I was experiencing the present, the past and the future all at the same time." She said seeing the Virgin always seemed "natural," but she was nervous about what other people would say. She described her impression of the World-Wide Warning as more like a gentle father-son scolding than an ominous threat. Mari Cruz had married a Catholic Spaniard and remained devoted to the Virgin Mary in 2006, belonging to a weekly prayer group which invoked the Virgin's intercession. Mari Cruz never, during the interview, denies the apparitions occurred. She does, however, ask herself if it really occurred or not because "it is all like a pretty dream."[526] Mari Cruz can't be referring to the turmoil the apparitions brought to the girls' lives. So what is she referring to? Fifty years ago, during an apparition, young Mari Cruz rocked the baby Jesus in her arms and murmured, "Listen, tomorrow I shall bring you some caramels and some cakes."[527] Maybe it all seems like a "pretty dream" to mature Mari Cruz because just such shimmering, elusive memories flash now and then to the surface: of a young Mari Cruz cooing gently and rocking the infant Jesus to sleep.

⁵²⁸ *Mari Cruz in ecstasy*

Mari Cruz's case is quantitatively but not qualitatively different from the other visionaries—she simply had fewer apparitions and, as a result, was plagued with more persistent doubt. The other three visionaries also at times confessed doubts and uncertainty about what happened at Garabandal, and at times spoke with clarity and conviction about the events. Sometimes, they professed *both* doubt and belief not only in the same interview—like Mari Cruz in 2006—but even in the same sentence, like Conchita in 1966.⁵²⁹

If the Garabandal apparitions were a tall tale fabricated by a twelve-year-old girl one restless summer evening, Conchita had the chance to let her fantastic falsehood die a well-deserved death after she moved across the Atlantic. Instead, in the 1980s, she gave a videotaped interview stating that her memories of the Virgin Mary had returned—although she herself would only be completely convinced that the Virgin Mary had actually appeared if the Great Miracle occurs.⁵³⁰

More recently, Conchita also had the option to remain silent and let the 50th Anniversary of the Garabandal apparitions pass her by. She is no longer a young girl being summoned by the

bishop or chased by the crowds. Nor has Conchita or any of the
visionaries spent the past fifty years writing books and collecting
royalties on Garabandal—in essence, depending on the
apparitions for their livelihood. Conchita could have let the
anniversary pass without comment, and been left to live her life
in relative peace.

Yet on May 17, 2011, Conchita sent this note to the pastor of
Garabandal:

Dear Father Rolando,

I join with you in the celebration of the fiftieth anniversary of
the events of Garabandal. It is for me fifty years of
contemplating the most beautiful thing in the world. I give
thanks to God for having been a part of those experiences,
impossible to describe adequately, but which have pressed upon
my soul the secure assurance of faith and hope.

I thank you, Father Rolando, for granting me the opportunity to
recite the Message of Our Mother in the village yet again. Father
Rolando, there is nothing of greater importance that I can speak
about than this Message of Our Mother.

*October 18,1961-We must make many sacrifices, perform much
penance, and visit the Blessed Sacrament frequently. But first, we must lead
good lives. If we do not, a chastisement will befall us. The cup is already
filling up, and if we do not change, a very great chastisement will come upon
us.*

*As my message of October 18 has not been complied with and has not been
made known to the world, I am advising you that this is the last one. Before,
the cup was filling up. Now it is flowing over. Many cardinals, many bishops
and many priests are on the road to perdition and are taking many souls
with them. Less and less importance is being given to the Eucharist. You
should turn the wrath of God away from yourselves by your efforts. If you ask
His forgiveness with sincere hearts, He will pardon you. I, your mother,
through the intercession of Saint Michael the Archangel, ask you to amend
your lives. You are now receiving the last warnings. I love you very much and
do not want your condemnation. Pray to us with sincerity and we will grant
your requests. You should make more sacrifices. Think about the passion of*

Jesus.
In Union of Prayer,
Conchita

[531]*Mari-Loli, Conchita, and Jacinta in ecstasy*

Are the four visionaries of Garabandal vacillating flakes? Are they suffering saints? Despite being tormented at times by doubts, they have also spoken as adults with certainty and belief.[532] What are we to think about the truth or falsehood of Garabandal?

The visionaries themselves offer a different take on all of this. They claim that they themselves, and the accuracy of their memories, are not the point. Conchita said this in 1983: "The main reason for the apparitions was to give the world the messages. The messages sometimes get lost as people become involved in the sensationalism of the apparitions."[533] In 1968, Conchita summed up the Garabandal messages as, "Devotion to the Blessed Sacrament and prayer for priests."[534]

Joey Lomangino described a lunch meeting he had in 2000 with Conchita, who was a teenager when he first met her, and was now a grandmother. Joey said they discussed "the acceptance of every kind of suffering and the importance of the Holy Eucharist." Conchita said the answer to all questions was to sit in silence before the Blessed Sacrament and listen to Jesus.[535] In effect, Conchita affirmed the two Garabandal messages.

Visionary Jacinta met with Bishop del Val Gallo in 1971 to officially retract her 1966 denials.[536] She also said in a filmed 1983 interview—twenty years after her apparitions had ceased—that it was important to focus on the message of Garabandal, which she said was prayer, particularly for priests, and emphasis on the Eucharist. For those who were concerned about Church approval, Jacinta said that it wasn't even necessary to mention Garabandal; it was only necessary to fulfill the message.[537]

This is why the Virgin Mary came. The demanding, unglamorous message of Garabandal: Pray, ask forgiveness, change your lives, sacrifice more for others, help make up for the world's sins through love and faithfulness in your daily duty, adore the Blessed Sacrament, hunger and thirst for the Eucharist. Live these disciplines faithfully because in the background is that hovering, filling cup. The visionaries' philosophy about the apparitions has been expressed on various occasions like this:

If you believe the Virgin appeared in Garabandal but you don't live the messages, your belief does no good. Furthermore, if you live the messages, it's not necessary to believe in the Virgin's appearance.[538]

The apparitions at Garabandal turned the anonymous lives of these four children and their families upside down. The girls themselves seemed to experience only joy when the Virgin Mary was present, and sadness and disappointment whenever she left. But the swirl of events surrounding the appearances of the Virgin seemed, at times, cruel. If these events did in fact occur, then these four young girls did not ask for this destiny—it was thrust upon them. Christians who are falling in love with Jesus gradually understand that the cross is what awaits them. This is the paradox of Christianity. These four young girls were falling in love with the Mother of their Savior—a Mother who was leading them to her Son, whose cross awaited them as well.

The intrusion of Christ into the world two thousand years

ago also upended many lives. It set off shock waves. Just ask the unwed Mary, or her fiancée Joseph, or members of their families. Ask the cold, tired shepherds who were minding their own business, or the astrologers from the East who made a long, uncertain journey in search of a king. Ask King Herod. Ask the parents whose toddlers he murdered to preserve his power. Ask Peter who was just out fishing for a living and discovered in the bitterly defining moment of crisis what he was really made of. This dimension of Christianity—the transformative power of the cross—has always been the rock that causes stumbling.

After the upheaval that accompanied the Virgin's appearance in Garabandal came the doubts, denials, and contradictions of the visionaries which have thrown the events into question ever since. Every word and gesture of four immature girls was placed under microscopic scrutiny. They were examined often mercilessly and were under immense strain as the secluded world they lived in was invaded and irrevocably changed. They were under great pressure from doubting authorities, but also from those who believed. When apparitions didn't occur, others were disappointed. Others *wanted* to believe and wanted the apparitions to be "proven." When the Virgin Mary didn't materialize, the girls were questioned, and sometimes taunted. The public skepticism of the authorities inevitably followed, just as it did in Jesus' time. And the girls themselves, like the disciples, also began to doubt and deny.

Many have speculated that the doubts and denials of the Garabandal visionaries are meant as a sign of the parallel darkness and confusion in the Roman Catholic Church, and Christianity in general, in this age. In any case, once denials are expressed and doubts are aired, they cannot be erased—at least in the modern age. They are on record. But the greatest denial in human history also was recorded in painful detail, indelibly, for the ages—the denial of Peter. And yet he was the rock upon which the church was built. The Christian church is well aware that even denial can be redeemed and transformed, for the greatest good.

Conversation with Mari-Loli

In 2009 I contacted Mari-Loli, who had agreed to an interview through her friend Maria Saraco. Maria Saraco had prepared me for the interview by describing the visionary's condition.

"Mari-Loli can't breathe. She wears a tube in her nose 24 hours a day. She can't go to Garabandal. She can't go to daily Mass. Her husband brings her communion. She's coughing all the time. She says it's not suffering for her but I feel it is. She's a wonderful girl. She feels like she has to keep praying for priests."

Mari-Loli answered as soon as the phone rang. She had been diagnosed with pulmonary fibrosis and lupus, and our conversation was punctured by her painful and prolonged coughing spells. She struggled both to speak and to breathe. Nevertheless, Mari-Loli was extremely kind to me. At one point, in the early 1960s, Mari-Loli had asked the Virgin Mary for a cross that she could suffer for priests. Mary replied: *"Endure everything with patience, be humble, recite the rosary every day, and pray for priests."*[539]

Mari-Loli bore my tedious questioning with perfect patience, despite the fact that she was quite ill and frequently lapsed into bouts of coughing. As was the case in some previous interviews, Mari-Loli told me repeatedly that her memory was bad and there was much that she could no longer remember. She also frequently declined to offer her personal opinion on many topics. Her most frequent answers to specific questions I had about the apparitions were, "I don't remember." When I asked for her personal opinion on various Garabandal-related topics, she most frequently replied, "I don't know."

I began the conversation asking her some details about her experience growing up in Garabandal, which I had recently visited. We discussed the cow and sheep bells that still jingled

248

musically in the mountain pastures, and la barca, the wooden shoes that villagers wore with thick woolen stockings to keep their feet warm in the old days. But then I began to ask the controversial, sensational questions because I felt they were the most urgent: Will we soon be on the "last Pope"? Is the World-Wide Warning about to occur? Are the End Times about to commence?

I mentioned Conchita's controversial prophecy (covered in Chapter 5) of three more popes after John XXIII, and then the End Times. The original Spanish phrase was "el fin de los tiempos."

I asked Mari-Loli if *el fin de los tiempos* means "the end of these times," or "the end of our age" rather than the end of the world. She replied, "It can be either way."

I also asked Mari-Loli if she herself ever heard the Virgin Mary speaking about this particular prophecy—only 3 more popes after John XXIII and then the End Times begins—and she replied, "No."

540 *Rosary from Garabandal depicting a girl on the cross*

Nonetheless, Mari-Loli *was* quoted in the past as saying that she thought the pope would be persecuted at some point, even to the point of going into hiding. If the tribulation of communism occurs before the World-Wide Warning, as the girls reportedly said in the past, then it would seem possible that the pope's persecution would take place before the Warning as well.

I asked Mari-Loli if the persecution of the pope would indeed take place before the World-Wide Warning. Mari-Loli answered, "I don't know. I don't remember. My mind is not so good."

Conchita was recorded as saying: "When you see the Warning, you know we have opened up the end of time." The Warning is supposed to take place when things are at their "worst," since that is when it will most be needed. The Virgin Mary reportedly gave Mari-Loli the year of the Warning. Mari Loli has declared since 1975 that the Warning will be "soon." When questioned about this on a later date, she explained that time flies so quickly, everything is "soon." When asked once if she would be alive when the Warning occurred, she laughed and replied, "I hope so!" It was obvious that she considered it entirely plausible that she would be alive at the time of The Warning. But it also raises the question: Why *did* Mari-Loli repeatedly state that she knew the year of the Warning, and that it would be soon, when fifty years later, it still hasn't occurred? Is it possible that Mari-Loli—rather than being told an exact year—was told that the Warning would occur in the same year that a communist tribulation would overrun the world and overcome the Church? Is it possible, likewise, that Conchita, rather than being given an exact year, was told the Great Miracle would occur in the same year as a very specific great ecclesiastical event? Conchita's brother, Serafino, said that Conchita never told him the date of the Miracle, as had been reported. "(Conchita) told me a thing, a happening, which if it occurs will let me know the Miracle is coming."541

Could this be what the visionaries meant when they said they were given the year of these events—a moving target, so to speak, dependent on human free will and the unfolding of history on earth? If the Virgin Mary saved Pope John Paul II from assassination, and if his subsequent consecration of Russia saved the rest of us from 1980s nuclear war, who knows what other history-altering effects have occurred?

On the other hand, there is evidence that both girls were indeed given a specific year. Conchita did exclaim when first told about the Miracle, "*You say there's going to be a miracle? . . . And when? . . . So long away?*"[542] She said in a BBC documentary in 1980 and in other filmed interviews over the years that she knew *exactly* when the Miracle would occur but had been charged by "the Lady" not to speak of it until eight days beforehand[543] (which she obviously has not yet done.) And in 1991, Michael H. Brown asked, Mari-Loli, "Are you surprised it's taken so long for anything to happen?" She replied, "Well, with the Warning I know what year it's supposed to happen."[544] (Mari-Loli's children address this topic in the new final chapter of this book which follows.)

Mari-Loli has said in the past that she was never told *not* to reveal the Year of the Warning,[545] but when I asked Mari-Loli if she was going to reveal the Warning before it happened, she said, "No."

I specifically asked her if she would reveal the year of the Warning, and she kindly replied, "No. I don't like to talk about these things anymore. My memory is very bad. I said many things but now I don't remember what I said. I don't remember what happened. Other people have also said many things."

I asked Mari-Loli (this was in 2009) if Pope Benedict XVI would be pope when the Warning occurred, and she said, "I don't know." I then asked Mari-Loli if the Warning was going to occur soon. At this point she fell into a painful coughing spasm, and I never repeated the question.

In earlier interviews, Mari-Loli had said she wasn't sure the communism of the 20th century was the communist tribulation that the Virgin prophesied would suppress the Church. Instead, Mari-Loli had said that she believed the repression would be even more widespread than it was in the 20th century. Specifically, Mari-Loli told Needles Magazine in 1975 that the Virgin Mary had told her "Communism would dominate the world, that it would seem that the Church has disappeared because it will be very difficult for priests to say Mass."

I asked Mari-Loli in 2009 if she thought this communist tribulation of the Church was still to come or if she believed it had already been fulfilled in the 20th century persecutions. She answered, "I don't know. I know the world is very bad. What I see in the world right now, it doesn't look too good. Socialism is spreading everywhere, even this country (the U.S.)"

The Virgin Mary gave a shocking warning at Garabandal in the early 1960s that many cardinals, bishops, and priests were on the road to perdition and were taking many souls with them. Since then, terrible sexual abuse by some priests has been revealed, along with cover-ups by some bishops and cardinals, which has damaged the lives and faith of many.

I asked Mari-Loli if she thought this Garabandal warning from the Virgin was referring to the sexual abuse scandal. She replied, "I don't know, but it's very sad, and we need to pray for the Church very much."

I mentioned to Mari-Loli that for some people, the similarity in the messages between Garabandal and Medjugorje seems to be a confirmation of both apparitions.

I asked Mari-Loli if she thought that, as well. "Not for me because I haven't really read the Medjugorje messages, maybe a little here and there years ago. But it can be for other people." I then asked her if the Virgin might be appearing in Medjugorje because the Catholic Church didn't listen or believe at Garabandal. She replied, "I don't know."

Both Conchita and Jacinta in Garabandal have been quoted as saying that the Virgin told them that someday the Christian churches would re-unite, and villagers also said they heard the visionaries making this claim during an apparition.[546]

I asked Mari-Loli if it was true that the Virgin Mary spoke at Garabandal about the Christian churches re-uniting someday. She said, "I don't remember. People may have said they heard me say it. I don't remember."

The Virgin reportedly said that the visionaries' doubts and confusion paralleled the Church's,[547] and this confusion and darkness is predicted to finally lift after the Great Miracle. If the Great Miracle involves Catholic, Orthodox, and Protestant churches re-uniting, perhaps the confusion and darkness will also lift from the entire Body of Christ, which is greatly weakened by disunity and fragmentation.

I asked Mari-Loli if she thought it was possible that the re-unification of the Christian churches is the great ecclesiastical event that is predicted to occur at the same time as the Global Miracle. She replied, "It will be great if it happens. It will be something very important if it happens. We should pray for it."

At this point, family members arrived at Mari-Loli's house. She told me she needed to go, and she asked if we could finish the interview later. Mari-Loli's obvious reluctance to speak at length about Garabandal, as well as her clouded memories, confirmed all I had read about the Garabandal visionaries. In addition to Mari-Loli's reticence, she was also gravely ill, and frequently collapsed into coughing spasms that literally prevented her from speaking. On her deathbed, she was still being plagued by interviews and questions about Garabandal—this time coming from me. Author Judith Albright wrote that "Even as an adult (Mari-Loli) becomes confused and full of fear of sinning from either telling people about the apparitions or not telling them. The constant turmoil has been a heavy cross for her."[548]

Although I had many other questions I wanted to ask, I postponed calling Mari-Loli back because of her physical (and emotional) suffering. Yet when word came that she had died, I also regretted not getting the "final answer" from Mari-Loli that I really wanted. It was simply this: Was Garabandal true or not? At the end of her life, had Mari-Loli *really* believed it had occurred— or not? After all, she had said to me: "I don't like to talk about these things anymore. My memory is very bad. I said many things but now I don't remember what I said. I don't remember what happened. Other people have also said many things."

Before my interview with Mari-Loli, Maria Saraco had described the visionaries to me like this: "They remember what they told the people, certain things. They remember what they spoke of but they don't really remember it (the actual events)."

This was certainly what I experienced during the interview. After Mari-Loli died, I spoke with Maria Saraco again. She was in Garabandal during Mari-Loli's final days, and arrived back in the U.S. on the day Mari-Loli died.

"I talked to her on the phone the day before she died. She said, "I love you." I said, "Don't talk. I want you to save your strength."

I asked Maria Saraco if Mari-Loli still had doubts about Garabandal when she died. "I don't know. She had doubts when you tried to remind her of certain things that had happened at Garabandal. But her faith was wonderful. She went to Mass every day. I can't say whether she had doubts or didn't have doubts about believing in Garabandal. You had to know her. At one time she would say she didn't remember anything. But then another time she would start describing what St. Michael looked like."

Similar contradictions exist in the other visionaries' statements as well. This was the burning question which I still had to answer, and it looked like I had missed my only chance. What *had* Mari-Loli believed about the apparitions when she died?

Mari-Loli's Last Word

I started looking into Garabandal because I thought it was an odd mystery, these four girls and their ecstasies. I read everything

I could get my hands on, traveled to Garabandal, and even talked to an eyewitness and a visionary. In the end, I wound up in a very different place from where I had started. If Garabandal was true, it wasn't just about the Virgin Mary passing on another titillating, bizarre message of planetary doom. Instead, Jesus had placed his Mother prominently in Garabandal at exactly the time that some in the Church were trying to lower the Virgin's profile—and he had sent her to Garabandal to warn the priesthood and defend the Eucharist at a critical historical moment.

But that wasn't all. Both Fatima and Garabandal suggest that Jesus has given his mother a central role to play in human history, and the Church's response to Mary's role may be the difference between peace and tragedy. If the Church—both laity and hierarchy—had responded more quickly and wholeheartedly to Mary at Fatima, how much death and destruction might have been averted? If the Church—both laity and hierarchy—had paid more attention to Mary at Garabandal, how much sexual abuse and loss of faith might have been avoided? Because a layman and a bishop paid attention when Our Lady of Guadalupe appeared in Mexico, ten million indigenous people converted, resulting in reconciliation rather than bloodshed.

Pope Francis, when addressing the controversial topic of women priests, confirmed that Jesus' right-hand-man is the Virgin Mary, not any of his male apostles who jousted for the honor: "But think about it, Our Lady is more important than the Apostles. She is more important." Pope Francis went on to say that a "profound theology" of women in the Church needs to be developed which moves beyond a trite and tedious list of what women can and cannot do, and instead involves women "making risky choices, yet as women."[549]

A good start to this theology would involve embracing, rather than fearing, the risky choices made by the Virgin—not just 2,000 years ago—but today. Rather than being disdainful of or disturbed by the Virgin's contemporary appearances, what if laity and hierarchy alike just listened to her? In another recent interview, Pope Francis said, "The feminine genius is needed wherever we make important decisions."[550]

Our Lady of Guadalupe demonstrated a feminine genius in converting ten million Aztecs where the Church had thus far failed—a reality which belies the notion that private revelation is inconsequential. Presumably, the Virgin Mary does not show up in various locales because she's bored, but because God sends her out of profound love for humanity.

The feminine genius of the Virgin Mary was also on hand during those decisive years of 1961-1965, and she was speaking. But was she listened to? The claims of four girls from Garabandal were dismissed as nonsense by many. Two thousand years ago, outlandish female claims of a resurrected body were likewise dismissed as "nonsense" by the first apostles—yet to Peter's credit, he bucked peer pressure and set off running with all his might to that empty tomb anyway.[551]

Today, it's hard to understand what harm could have come all these years from paying more attention to the nonsense of Garabandal—by offering more prayers before the Holy Eucharist, especially for priests. What exactly is so dangerous about that?

In a 1984 filmed interview, Mari-Loli said she would never have started praying for priests without the apparitions since she thought in the 1960s that priests were already holy and there was no need to pray for them.[552] Mari-Loli's mother recalled an ecstasy in which Mari-Loli was distraught and sobbing. "Her face reflected such an expression of suffering. She said we had to make many sacrifices for priests...She said times of great doubt and confusion were to come, even to the priests."[553] Mari-Loli's mother actually scolded her daughter for those words because she, too, thought priests were too holy to need prayers.

In response to the urgent messages at Garabandal, "Garabandal centers" sprang up where Catholics held prayer vigils for priests.[554] These centers were at times the target of Church displeasure.[555] If the Garabandal apparitions had been encouraged to flourish rather than wilt under a shadow of suspicion all these decades, would those centers and prayers for priests have been greatly multiplied? What might the ripple effects have been?

I thought I finally understood why some persisted in their passion for Garabandal, and I wanted to believe in it. But Mari-Loli's words during our conversation bothered me. *I don't like to talk about these things anymore. My memory is very bad. I said many things but now I don't remember what I said. I don't remember what happened. Other people have also said many things.*

These sounded like words from someone tormented by a past mistake—someone who perhaps wished she could erase the entire episode known as Garabandal. Mari-Loli's words near the end of her life also eerily echoed Bernadette of Lourdes at the end of her life: "It is already far away...very far away...all these things: I do not remember them; I do not like to speak too much about them, in case, my God! I have been mistaken."[556]

I decided to make one last attempt to clear up for myself this question which had started to haunt me, the question which I had most wanted but failed to ask Mari-Loli: *What did she really believe about the Garabandal apparitions as she lay dying? Had she been tricked by the devil? Did the visionaries trick the rest of us? Had it all started as a joke, and ended up a nightmare? Or was it true?*

Consequently, I made some phone calls in search of interviews, and made plans to leave flowers at Mari-Loli's gravesite.

One individual I was able to interview about Garabandal was Bishop William McNaughton, who was one of the 2,300 bishops who participated in Vatican II, and who con-celebrated at Mari-Loli's funeral Mass. Bishop McNaughton, now retired, told me that he first learned about Garabandal in the 1970s in Korea where he worked as a Maryknoll priest. He was given a book containing the Garabandal messages. "I've always had a love for Our Lady of Garabandal." Another Maryknoll priest in Korea gave McNaughton a medal that was kissed by the Virgin in

Garabandal. Bishop McNaughton still prays over the sick using this Garabandal relic. "I have the sick kiss the relic and I tell them, "This is what Our Lady kissed." When he prays with the relic, he says, "I have a feeling Mary is present in a special way."

Around 1980, he went to visit Mari-Loli.

"I was profoundly impressed with the faith of Mari-Loli," he said. "She was a daily communicant (she received communion daily)." Over time, Bishop McNaughton also met the blind Joey Longamino, who was still waiting fifty years later to receive his sight. "Joey Longamino has the deepest faith in Our Lady of Garabandal."

Bishop McNaughton went to Conchita's home "in the 70s or 80s" to give a talk at a prayer meeting. "I said it was important to go to confession every month. Conchita corrected me and said, "It's better to go every week!"

As far as the doubts swirling around Garabandal, Bishop McNaughton said, "I think the devil was putting the doubt in the visionaries' minds. I think the apparitions really happened. The message is so simple. I say, "Look at the message. If it's consonant with the gospel, I believe it. I'm sure Mary is appearing in many places. After all, she's our mother."

Regarding the lack of official approval of the Garabandal apparitions, Bishop McNaughton said, "I think Our Lady is very humble and very, very patient." McNaughton openly admits, "I'm in a minority among bishops. Most don't accept it."

Bishop McNaughton said he thinks "Mary and Jesus are appearing constantly. We don't know if they're appearing more than in the past. How can we measure that? I don't know if it's the End Times. I know there will be a Warning, a Miracle and a Chastisement. We don't know how many people are paying attention to the messages of Our Lady. The more that do, it can push off or at least mitigate the Chastisement. I'm sure there's more than we think who are following the messages and offering up suffering."

After the interview, I bought some flowers and went in search of Mari-Loli's grave. I wandered into both a Jewish and Polish Catholic cemetery, but not the cemetery I was looking for. I drove in circles and wound up on a peaceful residential street that my GPS loudly insisted was a cemetery. Just when I was on the verge of giving up, I stumbled on the cemetery where she was buried. Once there, I wondered how I would possibly find Mari-Loli's gravestone. It was a large cemetery, and I had no clue where her grave might be. A man on a riding mower was cutting the summer grass.

I was trudging around in the hot sun listening to the whine of the mower when I turned and saw it, shimmering like a rose in a field of gray tombstones. I knew instantly that it was Mari-Loli's grave stone because of who graced it. Emblazoned on Mari-Loli's tombstone is the image of the Virgin Mary as she appeared in Garabandal: As Our Lady of Mt. Carmel holding the Infant Jesus.

On July 2, 1962, Mari-Loli had a vision of Mary and the infant Jesus, both wearing crowns. She was heard saying, "But why doesn't he talk? But he must be a year old! May I have him?" She then said, "Well, then, let me have the crown. Oh! how small it is. It doesn't fit me. Let me have yours."[557]

Fifty years later, Mari-Loli's tombstone not only bore this exact image of the crowned Virgin and Child Jesus, but also a pair of praying hands holding a rosary, a cross, and the words, *Hail Mary, Full of Grace, Pray for Us.*

⁵⁵⁸ *Bishop McNaughton with a medal from Garabandal*

Mari-Loli may have carried doubts, uncertainty, and anguish regarding the apparitions of Garabandal, and her role in them. Like the other visionaries, she may have second-guessed herself about whether she should or shouldn't speak of the events, about what she did or didn't accurately remember, about what did or did not actually occur. Yet despite the fact that her own visions and locutions of the Virgin Mary stopped, and her subsequent memories became clouded, Mari-Loli said years after the apparitions that she still felt the Virgin near her, helping her in all she did.⁵⁵⁹ And after her death she left a clear and permanent sign on her grave of her deep love for the very same Mother of God whom she claimed had appeared to her as a child.

The Garabandal visionaries have insisted that if you live the messages, you don't need to believe in the apparitions. It seems clear that Mari-Loli herself was not, at times, sure that the apparitions had occurred—yet her life was devoted to living the messages that were delivered during those apparitions.

Fifty years later and thousands of miles away from where she first claimed to see the Virgin Mary, Mari-Loli remained devoted to Our Lady of Mt. Carmel and to praying the rosary daily (she and her husband both wore the Mt. Carmel scapular and prayed the rosary together daily).[560] When she died, family members were praying the rosary at her bedside.[561] Mari-Loli told me in our conversation that she still prayed for priests, and a Eucharistic prayer vigil was held in Garabandal for Mari-Loli's intentions and for good and holy priests.[562] (Praying the rosary daily and praying for priests were two things the Virgin had specifically asked of Mari-Loli in the 1960s.[563]) The last Mass she attended was on Easter Sunday and afterward she still received daily communion,[564] so her devotion to the Eucharist remained intact, as the Virgin also requested in the Garabandal messages. Mari-Loli also had been praying the Divine Mercy Novena, which specifically asks for Divine Mercy on the whole world, and which culminated on Divine Mercy Sunday, April 19, the day before she died.[565]

Obviously, until the day Mari-Loli died, she was offering her prayers and suffering for the world, as Mary had specifically asked of the four seers, and as Mary had asked of everyone in the Garabandal messages. Visionaries Conchita and Jacinta—the two who also live in the U.S.—attended Mari-Loli's funeral. The music at her funeral Mass included numerous tributes to the Virgin Mary: "On This Day, O Beautiful Mother," "Ave Maria," "Immaculate Mary," and "Hail, Holy Queen."[566]

In the autumn of 1962, on the night of September 12th, some of the Garabandal apparitions were tape-recorded. Among them, 13-year-old Mari-Loli was heard speaking these words: *"Most Holy Virgin, let me not abandon you! Let me love you all my life! Oh! That I may never leave you. That I may love you always, always, until death."*[567]

One thing is obvious: Mari-Loli's prayer from that night in 1962 was resoundingly answered. She was born on one continent and died on another, yet what she carried across the waves and years with her was a great love and deep devotion to the Virgin Mary.

When I began to look into Garabandal, I wanted to solve the mystery of whether or not the apparitions were true, whether they had actually happened, whether we needed to worry about the warnings—or whether the visionaries were deceived by something sinister or had tragically deceived others. I was focused on the elusive and sensational aspects of Garabandal, so I squandered the opportunity I had with Mari-Loli and asked the wrong questions. I missed what mattered most: the compelling, lifelong relationship between Mari-Loli and the Virgin Mary.

In my dogged hunt for one final morsel of "proof," I thought Mari-Loli's last word on Garabandal might be to give us the Year of the Warning—but she took that information to her grave. Instead, Mari-Loli's grave *is* her last word on Garabandal. And it is not the last word of someone who took a bite of an unripe apple at the age of twelve and managed to carry out a fifty-year deception. It is not the last word of someone who died in unbelief. It *is* the last word of a young girl who deeply loved the Mother of Jesus and spent the rest of her life trying to fulfill her Mother's wishes.

Was it all just a pretty dream, as more than one of the visionaries have wondered? And if so, who sent the dream and cast the spell—an angel of God or an angel of darkness? Was it just a young girl's momentary flight of fancy one summer night that spun wildly out of control? Or was it a visitation from the Mother of Jesus filled with urgent concern for a church and a world that she deeply loves?

I don't know. I know that I heard a fascinating story which in many ways remains steeped in mystery. I know that I learned a deceptively simple message which may have cosmic consequence. And I know that with Mari-Loli's last words—*Hail Mary, Full of Grace, Pray for Us*—she exited this earth honoring the woman she claimed to meet fifty years earlier in her small Spanish village. The very same woman whose radiant image Mari-Loli chose to leave with us when she died: The woman of a thousand names, among them Our Lady of Garabandal.

568 *Visionary Mari-Loli's grave marker with both Mary and Jesus holding scapulars, just as they are in the plaque marking the Virgin Mary's appearance in Garabandal as Our Lady of Mount Carmel 50 years ago.*

569 *The plaque in Garabandal commemorating the Virgin's appearance.*

⁵⁷⁰ *Mari-Loli's last word in 2009*

"Most Holy Virgin, let me not abandon you! Let me love you all my life! Oh! That I may never leave you. That I may love you always, always, until death."—**Tape-recorded words of thirteen-year-old Mari-Loli in 1962**

Chapter 9

She Remembered. She Knew.

"She remembered a lot," Frank Lafleur insisted to me about his mother, visionary Mari-Loli, when he contacted me after reading my book.

For example, regarding the Warning, Frank recalled my speculation in the book that perhaps Mari-Loli hadn't been given a specific year, but rather a "moving target," a date which was tied to some other event and dependent on its occurrence. My own conjecture had been that maybe Mari-Loli was merely told that the Warning would occur in the same year that a communist tribulation would engulf the world and the Church.

Not so, said Frank.

"I know for a fact that she was given a date. She wouldn't tell us the date, either."

In fact, Frank told me that Mari-Loli's sister Sari had quizzed Mari-Loli on this very issue before she passed away in 2009.

"Sari was at my mother's bedside during the last 2 weeks of her life and they spoke about many things," Frank confirmed.

Sari asked, concerning the Warning, "Do you have a date in your mind?"

"Yes," replied Mari-Loli.

"Is it soon?"

Mari-Loli replied, "It's getting closer all the time."

But that wasn't the only occasion on which Mari-Loli spoke to her loved ones about the Garabandal apparitions before her death.

"You really need to talk to my sister, Maria," Frank suggested.

For Mari-Loli's daughter Maria Rosati, the first momentous revelation occurred while she and her sister were visiting, sitting in the den with their mother as her long struggle with lupus progressed.

"In one phase, she could go out with oxygen, then she couldn't go out at all. At one point, my son Anthony was 22 months, and I was pregnant, and I visited my parents a lot. I'd just made a visit, got home. Dad called and said, "You should come back. She's not doing well.""

Maria recalled sitting on the ottoman in front of her mother. "My mother gasped and looked back like she'd just seen something. Then she said, "Can you believe the Blessed Mother let me hold the baby Jesus and her crown?""

It was, as it would turn out, a question that Mari-Loli would raise again. The first reaction of Maria and her sister in the moment was, "Wow, she remembers."

"It was a special moment," Maria acknowledged. "We didn't really press her about it. Right after that moment, she had her normal, bashful look about the apparitions, and the moment passed."

Indeed, Maria confirmed her mother's reticence in speaking about the apparitions. "If you'd ask her a question about Garabandal, she'd answer, but she never brought it up herself. She was always hesitant when speaking about the apparitions. She'd say, "I don't remember." There was definitely doubt that had always been there."

Like her brother Frank, Maria remembers asking specifically for the date of the Warning.

"I'd tease her. I'd say, "You're not even going to tell me the date of the Warning? Come on!""

Meanwhile, Mari-Loli's lupus had progressed to such a painful stage that the family was about to call in hospice. She had recovered many times, Maria explained, but this latest turn seemed to indicate that death was near.

Maria found herself at her mother's bedside, when suddenly Mari-Loli raised the subject once again.

"She looked in my eyes, she put her hand on mine, and said, "Why do you think the Blessed Mother let me hold the baby Jesus and her crown?"

"I did not really answer her," Maria admitted. "I said, "I don't know, mom.""

At that moment, "she heard my brother come in. She said, "Oh, is that Francis? I have such good kids.""

Yet again, the moment passed. But Mari-Loli's poignant question, which clearly meant a great deal to her at the end of her life, would come to haunt Maria.

Maria recalled the first time she heard the story of Garabandal. "I was six or so and my dad sat us down and said, "I want to tell you a really special story about mommy. The Blessed Mother came to visit mommy." I wasn't shocked. I thought, "Of course she did.""

"In our house, there was a reverence toward the Garabandal apparitions. I'd always heard stories about the apparitions but hadn't sat down and read a lot of books about it. There were some books with pictures I'd look at sometimes as a kid. Garabandal was always in the background, it was our mom's thing, but I didn't pay a ton of attention. We'd go to Garabandal every summer, and sometimes we'd go to a lecture about it. It was always present."

Other apparitions also were sometimes mentioned in the family, but Garabandal was special because it had happened to their own mother. "Our life was centered around God and the Blessed Mother. It was just part of our life."

Even so, as an adult, Maria had fallen out of the habit of praying the rosary. "My parents prayed 15 decades every single day (plus daily mass and adoration.) From the outside, their lives were very boring. We prayed the rosary every day while growing up, but I was distracted and had trouble with it."

After her mother died, the rosary took on a new significance for Maria.

"I thought, I'm going to try to pray the rosary again. So I started trying. I pray the rosary now, and I invited my Episcopalian-raised husband to pray the rosary, too."

As Maria began to re-connect with the rosary, she also wrestled with her mother's final poignant question about Garabandal to her daughter: *Why do you think the Blessed Mother let me hold the baby Jesus and her crown?*

Maria eventually sought out the counsel of a priest.

"He said, "You have to answer that question for your mom. So I wrote a letter to my mom answering the question."

Maria's letter to her mother, her answer to her mother's question, is a beautiful and deeply personal meditation on the hands of a Mother who gives freely and generously to her children, but also a Mother who entrusts her children with the task of passing on those gifts to others. With Maria's permission, I have included some excerpts here. (Italics are mine.)

"Mom, you asked me a question in your final days that because of my seeking my own consolation I did not, or maybe I could not answer it. In amazement I realize nine years later, I have still not answered you...

"Your hand atop mine, eye to eye you asked me – "Why do you think the Blessed Mother would let me hold the Baby Jesus and her crown?

"Were you asking for you?

"Were you asking for me?

"Were you asking for the world?

"If you were asking for you, my answer is - I can think of no one more lovely than you. But I know that would not be a sufficient answer for you, as you are far too humble to see it.

...how your clothes must have been ripped and worn. How your hands may have been dirty, and certainly your nails were not manicured, dainty, or hand sanitized before you held the Sweet Baby Jesus.

"Why then?

"Could it be that as your mother the Blessed Mother, the Queen of Heaven and Earth, adorned in a crown of stars, *could give her children here on Earth everything?*

"Could it be that what heaven deems a pure choice would differ from acceptable hands in the world? Did the most Holy, Blessed Mother want to prepare you with love for the suffering and pain you were to experience? *She laughed with you. She played with you. She taught you how to pray. She taught you how to hold God...*

"If you asked for me, my answer is, I was raised by the hands of a mother who was chosen to hold the Baby Jesus and the Blessed Mother's crown. By the time I saw your hands one of the fingertips was missing, but they were still the most beautiful, hardworking, and loving hands I have ever seen. When *you laughed with me, played with me, taught me to pray, and how to hold my babies,* I could not and did not want any other hands beside me as *you did these things with Love;* the way the Blessed Mother showed you, the way that she taught you...

"If you asked for the World my answer is

"...Her hands were not manicured, were not beautiful as even one of her fingertips was missing. As her disease progressed she could barely make a fist from the pain from the arthritis. *But still I watched her hands.*

"Her final act of love for me, when it was almost too difficult to speak, she was barely able to move, yet she sat in her wheelchair for her final Mass beside me, her daughter – I could not stop from crying. I watched as her hands slowly moved to the pocket in her robe, where she found a tissue that she gave to console me. *Her hands were serving.*

"Mom, my answer for you, for me, and for the world,

"You were chosen to hold the Baby Jesus and the Blessed Mother's crown. And soon after you died, I know you looked into the Blessed Mother's eyes and she told you why – but as you lived here wondering, Could it be true and why, *you used your hands to serve – the way that she taught you...*for us...for the world..."

In her letter, Maria offers an intriguing insight into one of the common criticisms of Garabandal, that Mary would never show up repeatedly, day after day, and have mundane and seemingly useless conversations with four unimportant girls.

"And if the Blessed Mother was different with you girls in Garabandal, than in other times when she had appeared to others who had grown up for the religious life, then perhaps it was because she was preparing you girls to be mothers and that mothers learn to be mothers by being children to their mothers."

Maria pointed out that Garabandal is a good message for today, when "everything is out of your hands. You don't know what's going to happen next."

As far as the elusive question of when the World-Wide Warning will occur, Maria said, "My personal view doesn't matter any more than yours does. When I was young, I would think, "Mommy's sick, but the Miracle will come." I thought the Miracle would come and mom would be healed. But mom said, "No, that (her healing) is not going to happen."

Maria noted the growing significance of the Garabandal prophecy that the Warning will occur when "Communism comes again," especially in light of recent turmoil in US cities, some of which has included the toppled statues, expunged history and mob violence characteristic of Marxist revolution.

"A few years ago, I thought, "How can that possibly happen?" A lot of people thought the prophecy of communism returning was referring to Spain only."

"I think we're getting closer," Maria admitted. "How long? How bad will it get? I don't know. When you see everything that's going on, it seems a lot closer. I know I have to pray the rosary, go to adoration, just like Garabandal said. At the end of the day, if you pray the rosary, go to adoration and wear a scapular, that's what Garabandal asks for."

More than one of the visionaries was insistent that "if you believe but don't live the messages, it doesn't help. If you live the messages, it doesn't matter if you believe them." Maria's recollections of a family life that was centered around God and the Blessed Mother were confirmed by her brother Frank: "In our family, we went to mass and prayed the rosary every day. They talked to us about God. Even though Mom didn't talk a lot about what happened, we lived it (the messages)."

Both Frank and Maria agree that at the end of her life, Mari-Loli had certainly lived the messages. But more than that, "When we read your book, we thought, "We do know! She did believe!"

At the end of the day, Maria and Frank wanted me and others to know the answer to my question: *What did she really believe about the Garabandal apparitions as she lay dying? Had she been tricked by the devil? Did the visionaries trick the rest of us? Had it all started as a joke, and ended up a nightmare?*

Or did Mari-Loli believe that the apparitions of Garabandal were true?

"She absolutely believed it," Frank said. "She believed it all."

Based on her own conversations with her mother before she died, Maria wholeheartedly agrees. "She remembered. She knew."

For the foolishness of God is wiser than human wisdom, and the weakness of God is stronger than human strength...
Rather, God chose the foolish of the world to shame the wise, and God chose the weak of the world to shame the strong,
and God chose the lowly and despised of the world, those who count for nothing, to reduce to nothing those who are something,
so that no human being might boast before God.

First Corinthians Chapter 1[571]

Afterword

I have always loved a good mystery. I first heard about the mystery of Garabandal in the year 2000 in Bangkok, Thailand, where I was working with a Catholic organization in a Bangkok slum. One night, a Filipino sea merchant handed me a book of "messages." My reading material—at least in English—was in short supply, so I sat down that night and began to read. One of the recurring themes of the message was, "Garabandal is authentic." My response was: "What's Garabandal?" I didn't know it was a village in Spain. I didn't know it was the site of a purported appearance of the Virgin Mary in the early 1960s. In a Buddhist country, thanks to a Filipino sailor, I had stumbled on a mysterious message that lamented a forgotten Catholic apparition. Although my interest was piqued, I was busy at that time and my curiosity flickered and died. It wasn't until several years later, back in the U.S. as the 50th anniversary of the Garabandal apparitions approached, that I recalled the strange, insistent messages about Garabandal that I had stumbled across, and realized it was a mystery I wanted to unravel.

Here is some of what I read that night in Bangkok and in the days to come:

Garabandal is the sequel of other signs; Garabandal's apparitions are *authentic.*[572]

I wish to see My Holy See there and bless that place, rectifying all that has been distorted and wrongly proclaimed by My sacerdotal souls who wound Me, lift the doubts and efface the abuses given by those who defied the apparitions, would My Holy See do this for Me?[573]

I do not blame those who persecuted the apparitions; I only want them to realize and admit their errors and to come forward to Me for repentance; I will forgive them, pardoning their sin; daughter, many will persecute My

Message again denying that it is I, Jesus, for fear of admitting their fault, for <u>this is beyond their wisdom again</u>, child;

My Message was not properly diffused; many sacerdotals have denied My Apparitions, thus refusing Us a place in their heart; but I have not forgotten My beloved children; there were times where they themselves doubted, and falling into confusion, denied My Apparitions; this was given as a similitude; it is to show My children how and what a confusion reigns in the Church of today; I have promised that I will confirm My Apparitions of Garabandal; the hours are fleeing and My Messages were <u>not</u> diffused properly, neither has My Holiness been honoured;[574]

My Love will save you from My justice—justice which is bound to befall upon you if My creation will not listen again. I come out of My boundless Mercy to warn you; I desire My creation to repent and recognize Me. Fatima's Shrine weeps loudly for the abuses and rejections over Garabandal. My Soul is in deep sorrow again; the same sorrow I had in Fatima. How could they doubt now, when My Spirit is in them and they in Me? My Message at Fatima's was ignored and not until it was too late did they accept My Message. I love you all.[575]

…when I gave them My big Miracle at Fatima, I warned then My creation, but they paid little heed to My warning; they spent their time instead doubting, arguing, never diffusing My Mother's words properly, so that very few knew of the urgency of the Message; they have blood-stained their hands from their crime, dragging with them so many souls;

I shall remind them of their sins of the past, <u>I will remind them the urgency of Garabandal's Message</u>; …

<u>Garabandal is the sequel of Fatima</u>! do not repeat your errors!… - Peter! Peter be My Echo! feed My lambs Peter, do not deny Me again, beloved;[576]

(messages from *True Life in God   www.tlig.org*)

These strange messages perplexed me for several reasons, not the least of which was my complete ignorance about Fatima and Garabandal. At first, I didn't even understand who "Peter" was (other than the long-dead disciple). Raised a Protestant, I had simply never thought of the Pope as "Peter." As I learned more about Garabandal, I thought the apparitions sounded bizarre and unlikely. I assumed the girls had either deliberately instigated the hoax themselves for some reason, or had been unwitting victims of forces outside themselves, cultural or spiritual.

In fact, when I first converted to Catholicism, I harbored severe doubts about the rosary prayer itself—what was the point of it? Going one step further and entering into the peculiar world of Virgin Mary appearances felt even more alien to me. Many aspects of Garabandal left me queasy with doubt, not least the so-called "ecstatic marches." Why all the outlandish antics on the part of the visionaries? Why did they need to march around the village armed with rosaries under the direction of an invisible Virgin Mary?

With all my doubts, why did the Garabandal seed continue to grow until I couldn't ignore it any longer? In the *True Life in God* messages I read, it was the voice of Jesus himself that haunted me. If it actually was Jesus speaking so passionately about lost and forgotten Garabandal, didn't it behoove me, as a Christian, to listen? I had no reason whatsoever to care about Garabandal—unless God did. And if God actually cared about such a strange event, so much so that He couldn't stop bringing it up years after everyone had stopped listening, then I was consumed with curiosity as to *why*.

Indeed, as the years have passed, the Virgin Mary has won me over. Prior to becoming a Catholic—as a Protestant—I was always encouraged to seek a relationship with Jesus, but the Virgin Mary was relegated, for the most part, to a little extra attention at Christmas time. As a new Catholic, I was handed the gift of relationship with Mary. It wasn't remotely what I was looking for, but a completely surprising "side benefit." As I've grown to love Jesus more deeply over my years in the Catholic Church, I also have grown to deeply love Mary. She is a person, exceptionally close to God, and I have been gifted with a relationship to her thanks to the Catholic Church. I have over the years become a daily devotee of the rosary, that prayer bead mantra and meditation on the life, death, and resurrection of Jesus.

It was my love for Jesus and Mary that drew me to look more deeply into the neglected and controversial apparitions of Garabandal. I understand Protestant unease, and I know that "unease" is too mild a word to describe some Christians' feelings about devotion to the Virgin Mary because of their fear that it's idol worship which eclipses God. What I have learned over the years is that Mary always leads us faithfully to her Son. But what I've also learned from delving into the wild world of apparitions is that Jesus appears to have an extremely soft spot for his Mother—and that we might do well to pay more attention to this fact. Recent research reveals that during pregnancy, mothers and sons exchange DNA, an exchange which lasts for life—a finding which casts a whole new light on the profound reverence Catholicism has always had for the Mother of Jesus.

What I learned about Fatima and Garabandal during this journey helped me understand better my own experience with Christianity. I grew up in a church whose central focus was the Bible, and which emphasized strongly that the Lord's Supper was only a symbol. To make a long story short, I am a Roman Catholic today because of the powerful experience I have had with the Eucharist—receiving the Body and Blood of Jesus Christ.

My experience has been that the Catholic Eucharist is strengthening and transformative, that it is freely given mercy which brings me into greater intimacy with Jesus. I have experienced a power in the Catholic Eucharist that has brought me much closer to God's love. It was Jesus Himself who urged us in the Gospels to eat His body and drink His blood, and the Catholic Mass makes present His ultimate act of sacrificial love and feeds us daily with that love.

I became a Catholic because I was hungry for the love and mercy of God in the Eucharist, and I haven't looked back since.

Imagine my dismay when I began to learn that the two greatest treasures I have received from Catholicism—the burning love of Jesus for us in the Eucharist and his Mother's consoling love for us through the rosary and other devotions—are two treasures that have at times been threatened, not just from outside the Church, but from within the Catholic Church itself. That some Catholics have sought to diminish and even abolish these two treasures, ostensibly to build bridges with Protestants. This is one baptized Protestant who is eternally grateful for these treasures and who believes they are most precious gifts which need to be shared with the entire Body of Christ—not jettisoned.

I said at the end of the book that I didn't know the answer to the mystery of Garabandal. Like the visionaries, I vacillate in my belief, and I am easily infected by the doubt of others. But I did go to visit the village of Garabandal, where I felt the unmistakable presence of both Jesus and Mary, and experienced a deep attraction to their love. And while reading, researching, and writing this book, I found myself longing to live the messages of Garabandal so I could draw closer to the magnetic love of Jesus and his mother. So that's where I am leaving this—as a frequent believer in Garabandal and a sometimes-skeptic, who is trying to live the messages of Garabandal, whether the apparitions occurred or not.

About the Author

LR Walker is a convert to Catholicism who has worked as a journalist and taught English as a second language.

Selected Bibliography

Albright, Judith M., *Our Lady at Garabandal,* 1992, Faith Publishing Company

Brown, Michael H., *The Final Hour,* 1992, Queenship Publishing Company

Christian, William A., Jr. *Visionaries: The Spanish Republic and the Reign of Christ,* 1996, Berkeley: University of California Press

Conchita's Diary, http://www.stjosephpublications.com

Daley, Harry *Miracle at Garabandal,* www.stjosephpublications.com

Fr. Valentin's Journal, http://www.stjosephpublications.com

Gaillardetz, Richard R. and Clifford, Catherine E. *Keys to the Council: Unlocking the Teaching of Vatican II,* 2012, Order of Saint Benedict, Liturgical Press, Collegeville, Minnesota

García de Pesquera O.F.M., Eusebio *She Went in Haste to the Mountain,*1981, St. Joseph Publications (subsidiary of St. Joseph Foundation of Los Angeles) www.stjosephpublications.com

Garcia de la Riva, Jose Ramon *Memoirs of a Spanish Country Priest,* St. Joseph Publications (subsidiary of St. Joseph Foundation of Los Angeles), www.stjosephpublications.com

Joseph Cardinal Ratzinger with Vittorio Messori, *The Ratzinger Report,* 1985 Ignatius Press, San Francisco

Laffineur, Fr. M., *Star on the Mountain,* 1968, The Workers of Our Lady of Mt. Carmel, Inc. P.O. Box 606, Lindenhurst, NY 11757

Martins, Father Antonio Maria, S.J., *Documents on Fatima & the Memoirs of Sister Lucia,* Fatima Family Apostolate 2002 United States of America, Printed by Park Press, Inc. P.O. Box 475 Waite Park MN 56387 Original Edition in Portuguese beginning Chapter 2

McInerny, Ralph M., *What Went Wrong With Vatican II,* 1998, Sophia Institute Press

Muggeridge, Anne Roche, *The Desolate City: Revolution in the Catholic Church*, 1986, 1990, Harper & Row.

O'Malley, John W., *What Happened at Vatican II*, 2008, The Belknap Press of Harvard University Press

Pelletier, Joseph A., *Our Lady Comes to Garabandal* 1971 Assumption Publications, Worcester, Mass.

Perez, Ramon *Garabandal: The Village Speaks,* Translation 1981, The Workers of Our Lady of Mount Carmel, Inc. P.O. Box 606, Lindenhurst, NY 11757

Read, Piers Paul, *Alive,* 1974, Harper Perennial

Rolla, Gregory M., *Of Queen and Prophets-The Garabandal Events and "The End of the Times,"* 2011

Sanchez-Ventura Y Pascual, F., *The Apparitions of Garabandal,* 1965, St. Michael's Garabandal Center, www.garabandal.org

Serre, Jacques and Caux, Beatrice, *Garabandal: Apparitions of the Blessed Virgin Mary as "Our Lady of Mount Carmel,"* 2001, The Workers of Our Lady of Mount Carmel of Garabandal, Australia, www.garabandal.com

Sullivan, Randall, *The Miracle Detective,* 2004, Grove Press

Turner, Francois O.P., *Our Lady Teaches at Garabandal: O Children Listen to Me,* 1975, 1980 The Workers of Our Lady of Mt. Carmel, Inc. P.O. Box 606, Lindenhurst, NY 11757

Varghese, Roy Abraham, *God-Sent: A History of the Accredited Apparitions of Mary,* 2000, The Crossroad Publishing Company

Weible, Wayne, *Medjugorje: THE LAST APPARITION—How It Will Change the World,* 2013, New Hope Press

The Whole Truth About Fatima Vol. I-III by Brother Michel de la Sainte Trinité of the Little Brothers of the Sacred Heart and *Vol. IV* by Brother François de Marie des Anges of the Little Brothers of the Sacred Heart

End Notes

---

[1] Photo courtesy of Maria Saraco/St. Michael's Garabandal Center
http://www.garabandal.org/photos/8xtsy_62.shtmll
[2] Photo courtesy of http://www.stjosephpublications.com *She Went in Haste to the Mountain,* Book 1, p, 90, Eusebio García de Pesquera O.F.M.

Chapter 1

[3] *New American Bible, revised edition* © 2010, 1991, 1986, 1970 Confraternity of Christian Doctrine, Washington, D.C.
[4] *Conchita's Diary* 1, http://www.stjosephpublications.com
[5] https://www.youtube.com/watch?v=zeBo5LpF1vs; *backward march starts at 5:39*
[6] https://www.youtube.com/watch?v=zeBo5LpF1vs; *intertwined fall at 0:48;*
https://www.youtube.com/watch?v=T3wj7rRarIA; *levitation starts at 2:50*
[7] *Garabandal The Village Speaks*, p. 330, Ramon Perez, 1981, The Workers of Our Lady of Mt. Carmel, Inc. P.O. Box 606, Lindenhurst, NY 11757
[8] Photo by LR Walker
[9] *I Have Never Doubted, Interview with Miguel Gonzalez,* Garabandal Magazine, April-June 1986; http://www.garabandal.us/Workers of Our Lady of Mount Carmel
[10] *She Went in Haste to the Mountain,* Book 1 Ch. 5, p. 87, Eusebio García de Pesquera O.F.M., www.stjosephpublications.com; *Garabandal The Village Speaks*, p. 320, Ramon Perez, 1981, The Workers of Our Lady of Mt. Carmel, Inc. P.O. Box 606, Lindenhurst, NY 11757
[11] Photo courtesy of St. Joseph Publications
[12] *She Went in Haste to the Mountain,* Book 1, p, 23, Eusebio García de Pesquera O.F.M, http://www.stjosephpublications.com
[13] Photo courtesy of Maria Saraco/St. Michael's Garabandal Center
http://www.garabandal.org/photos/1pose_61.shtml
[14] *She Went in Haste to the Mountain,* Book 1, p, 24, Eusebio García de Pesquera O.F.M, http://www.stjosephpublications.com
[15] *Conchita's Diary* 1, http://www.stjosephpublications.com
[16] Ibid.
[17] *She Went in Haste to the Mountain,* Book 1, p, 25, Eusebio García de Pesquera O.F.M, http://www.stjosephpublications.com
[18] *The Final Hour,* p. 128, Michael H. Brown
[19] Photo courtesy of St. Joseph Publications
[20] *Garabandal The Village Speaks*, p. 175, Ramon Perez, 1981, The Workers of Our Lady of Mt. Carmel, Inc. P.O. Box 606, Lindenhurst, NY 11757
[21] Ibid., p. 183
[22] *Conchita's Diary,* http://www.stjosephpublications.com
[23] *The Apparitions of Garabandal,* p.37, F. Sanchez-Ventura Y Pascual, www.garabandal.org
[24] Photo courtesy of St. Joseph Publications
[25] *Conchita's Diary,* http://www.stjosephpublications.com
[26] Photo by LR Walker
[27] *Garabandal The Village Speaks*, p. 176, Ramon Perez, 1981, The Workers of Our Lady of Mt. Carmel, Inc. P.O. Box 606, Lindenhurst, NY 11757
[28] *She Went in Haste to the Mountain,* Book 2, Ch. 3, p. 80, Eusebio García de Pesquera O.F.M, http://www.stjosephpublications.com
[29] *Miracle at Garabandal,* Ch. 2, Harry Daley, www.stjosephpublications.com
[30] *Garabandal The Village Speaks* P. 275, Ramon Perez, 1981, The Workers of Our Lady of Mt. Carmel, Inc. P.O. Box 606, Lindenhurst, NY 11757

[31] Photo courtesy of St. Joseph Publications

[32] *Garabandal The Village Speaks* P. 323, Ramon Perez, 1981, The Workers of Our Lady of Mt. Carmel, Inc. P.O. Box 606, Lindenhurst, NY 11757

[33] Ibid., P. 176

[34] Ibid., P. 203

[35] Photo by LR Walker

[36] *Conchita's Diary,* www.stjosephpublications.com

[37] Photo courtesy of St. Joseph Publications

[38] *Fr. Valentin's Journal,* http://www.stjosephpublications.com

[39] Photo courtesy of St. Joseph Publications

[40] *She Went in Haste to the Mountain,* Book 1, p. 60, Eusebio García de Pesquera O.F.M, http://www.stjosephpublications.com

[41] Photo courtesy of St. Joseph Publications

[42] A scapular, based on a monk's garment, consists of two pieces of cloth connected by string. It is a blessed object worn to encourage one's devotion to God and is associated with a variety of promises and blessings in connection with Our Lady of Mt. Carmel.

[43] *She Went in Haste to the Mountain,* Book 1, p. 61, Eusebio García de Pesquera O.F.M, http://www.stjosephpublications.com

[44] Ibid.

[45] *Garabandal The Village Speaks,* p. 324, Ramon Perez, 1981, The Workers of Our Lady of Mt. Carmel, Inc. P.O. Box 606, Lindenhurst, NY 11757

[46] *The Final Hour,* p. 129, Michael H. Brown, 1992, Queenship Publishing

[47] *Star on the Mountain,* Ch. 36, p. 86, Fr. M. Laffineur, The Workers of Our Lady of Mt. Carmel, Inc. P.O. Box 606, Lindenhurst, NY 11757

[48] *Garabandal The Village Speaks,* p. 253, Ramon Perez, 1981, The Workers of Our Lady of Mt. Carmel, Inc. P.O. Box 606, Lindenhurst, NY 11757

[49] *She Went in Haste to the Mountain,* Book 1 Ch. 3, p. 66, Eusebio García de Pesquera O.F.M. www.stjosephpublications.com

[50] Luke 1:28

[51] Audio recording starts at 7:05 at https://www.youtube.com/watch?v=zeBo5LpF1vs

[52] Photo courtesy of St. Joseph Publications

[53] *Garabandal The Village Speaks,* p. 331, Ramon Perez, 1981, The Workers of Our Lady of Mt. Carmel, Inc. P.O. Box 606, Lindenhurst, NY 11757

[54] Photo by LR Walker

Chapter 2

[55] *The Apparitions of Garabandal,* p. 179, F. Sanchez-Ventura Y Pascual, www.garabandal.org

[56] Photo courtesy of Maria Saraco/St. Michael's Garabandal Center http://www.garabandal.org/photos/10xty_62.shtml

[57] *Conchita's Diary 3,* http://www.stjosephpublications.com

[58] *Garabandal The Village Speaks,* p. 257, 304, Ramon Perez, 1981, The Workers of Our Lady of Mt. Carmel, Inc. P.O. Box 606, Lindenhurst, NY 11757

[59] Ibid., p. 187, p. 316

[60] *Father Valentin's Journal, Part 1,* www.stjosephpublications.com

[61] *Garabandal The Village Speaks,* p. 111, 131, 148, 178, 179, Ramon Perez, 1981, The Workers of Our Lady of Mt. Carmel, Inc. P.O. Box 606, Lindenhurst, NY 11757

[62] Ibid., p. 167

[63] Ibid., p. 146, 171

[64] Ibid., 246

[65] Video recording of Jacinta ignoring a blinding light, starting at 5:10: https://www.youtube.com/watch?v=zeBo5LpF1vs

[66] *The Apparitions of Garabandal,* p.44-45, F. Sanchez-Ventura Y Pascual, www.garabandal.org

[67] Photo courtesy of St. Joseph Publications

[68] *Garabandal The Village Speaks*, p. 178-179, Ramon Perez, 1981, The Workers of Our Lady of Mt. Carmel, Inc. P.O. Box 606, Lindenhurst, NY 11757

[69] Ibid., p. 131

[70] *Garabandal The Village Speaks*, p. 238, 283, 298 Ramon Perez, 1981, The Workers of Our Lady of Mt. Carmel, Inc. P.O. Box 606, Lindenhurst, NY 11757

[71] Ibid., p. 149

[72] Photo courtesy of http://www.stjosephpublications.com/first_message_page.htm

[73] *Garabandal The Village Speaks*, p. 286, Ramon Perez, 1981, The Workers of Our Lady of Mt. Carmel, Inc. P.O. Box 606, Lindenhurst, NY 11757

[74] *Garabandal The Village Speaks*, p. 166-167, Ramon Perez, 1981, The Workers of Our Lady of Mt. Carmel, Inc. P.O. Box 606, Lindenhurst, NY 11757

[75] Photos courtesy of St. Joseph Publications

[76] *Garabandal The Village Speaks*, p. 147, Ramon Perez, 1981, The Workers of Our Lady of Mt. Carmel, Inc. P.O. Box 606, Lindenhurst, NY 11757

[77] Ibid., p. 213

[78] Ibid., p. 233

[79] Ibid., p. 140

[80] Photo courtesy of St. Joseph Publications

[81] *Garabandal The Village Speaks*, p. 275-276, Ramon Perez, 1981, The Workers of Our Lady of Mt. Carmel, Inc. P.O. Box 606, Lindenhurst, NY 11757

[82] Ibid., p. 148

[83] *Garabandal The Village Speaks*, p. 218, Ramon Perez, 1981, The Workers of Our Lady of Mt. Carmel, Inc. P.O. Box 606, Lindenhurst, NY 11757

[84] *Why I Believe in Garabandal,* by Dr. Ricardo Puncernau, Garabandal Magazine, Oct-Dec. 1980; http://www.garabandal.us/Workers of Our Lady of Mount Carmel

[85] Photo courtesy of Maria Saraco/St. Michael's Garabandal Center http://www.garabandal.org/photos/2walk_6.shtml

[86] *Interview with Julia Mazon,* Garabandal Magazine, 1978 ; http://www.garabandal.us/Workers of Our Lady of Mount Carmel

[87] *Garabandal The Village Speaks*, p. 235, Ramon Perez, 1981, The Workers of Our Lady of Mt. Carmel, Inc. P.O. Box 606, Lindenhurst, NY 11757

[88] Ibid., p. 213

[89] Photo courtesy of Maria Saraco/St. Michael's Garabandal Center http://www.garabandal.org/photos/2crss_62.shtml

[90] *Father Valentin's Journal, Part 1,* www.stjosephpublications.com; *Our Lady Teaches at Garabandal, O Children Listen to Me,* p. 22, Francois Turner, O.P., The Workers of Our Lady of Mt. Carmel, Inc. P.O. Box 606, Lindenhurst, NY 11757; *Garabandal The Village Speaks,* p. 189, Ramon Perez, 1981, The Workers of Our Lady of Mt. Carmel, Inc. P.O. Box 606, Lindenhurst, NY 11757

[91] Photo courtesy of St. Joseph Publications

[92] Photo courtesy of http://www.stjosephpublications.com *She Went in Haste to the Mountain,* Book 2, p, 51, Eusebio García de Pesquera O.F.M.

[93] *Warning,* www.stjosephpublications.com

[94] http://www.garabandal.org/News/Garabandal_Warning_Miracle_Interviews.shtml

[95] *2006 Interview with Mari Cruz,* www.garabandal.org

[96] *Miracle at Garabandal,* Ch. 3, Harry Daley, www.stjosephpublications.com

[97] *Warning,* www.stjosephpublications.com

[98] Ibid.

[99] http://www.garabandal.org/News/Garabandal_Warning_Miracle_Interviews.shtml

[100] http://www.garabandal.org/vigil/J_A_1988/Father_Morelos_1988.shtml
[101] http://www.catholicprophecy.info/warning3.html;
http://www.call2holiness.org/afterwarning/afterwarning.html
[102] Conchita's Journal (*Letter by Conchita written June 2, 1965, the Journal de Conchita, G. du Pilier (Paris: Nouvelles Editions Latines). P. 52, note (66).)*

Chapter 3

[103] Photo courtesy of St. Joseph Publications
[104] *Garabandal The Village Speaks*, p. 230, Ramon Perez, 1981, The Workers of Our Lady of Mt. Carmel, Inc. P.O. Box 606, Lindenhurst, NY 11757
[105] *Recollections of Chon de Luis* by Father Francois Turner;
http://www.garabandal.us/Workers of Our Lady of Mount Carmel; *Garabandal The Village Speaks*, p. 301, Ramon Perez, 1981, The Workers of Our Lady of Mt. Carmel, Inc. P.O. Box 606, Lindenhurst, NY 11757
[106] Photo courtesy of St. Joseph Publications
[107] *Star on the Mountain*, Ch. 55, p. 128, Fr. M. Laffineur, The Workers of Our Lady of Mt. Carmel, Inc. P.O. Box 606, Lindenhurst, NY 11757
[108] *She Went in Haste to the Mountain*, Book 2 Ch. 1, p. 21-23, Eusebio García de Pesquera O.F.M. www.stjosephpublications.com
[109] Photo courtesy of St. Joseph Publications
[110] *She Went in Haste to the Mountain*, Book 1, Ch. 9, p. 211 Eusebio García de Pesquera O.F.M., www.stjosephpublications.com
[111] *She Went in Haste to the Mountain*, Book 2, Ch. 6, p. 165 Eusebio García de Pesquera O.F.M., www.stjosephpublications.com
[112] *She Went in Haste to the Mountain*, Book 1, Ch. 10, p. 240 Eusebio García de Pesquera O.F.M. www.stjosephpublications.com
[113] http://stjosephpublications.com/testimonies_page.htm
[114] *Our Lady Teaches at Garabandal: O Children Listen to Me*, p. 76, Francois Turner, O.P., The Workers of Our Lady of Mt. Carmel, Inc. P.O. Box 606, Lindenhurst, NY 11757
[115] *She Went in Haste to the Mountain*, Book 2, Ch. 3, p. 96, Eusebio García de Pesquera O.F.M., www.stjosephpublications.com
[116] *Alive*, p.71, 383-391, Piers Paul Read, Harper Perennial, 2005.
[117] *The Apparitions of Garabandal*, p.69, F. Sanchez-Ventura Y Pascual, www.garabandal.org
[118] Don Gaudencio Cepeda Palacios from Torquemada, Don Jeronimo Diez Serrano from Cabezon de Liebana, Don Agustin Pinay Martinez from Santillana del Mar, Don Luis Toribio Millan and Don Jose Salcerda Calderon from Aguilar del Campo, Dona Maria del Rosario and Dona Maria Elisa Salceda. *The Apparitions of Garabandal*, p.70, F. Sanchez-Ventura Y Pascual
[119] *Our Lady Teaches at Garabandal: O Children Listen to Me*, p. 97, Francois Turner, O.P., The Workers of Our Lady of Mt. Carmel, Inc. P.O. Box 606, Lindenhurst, NY 11757
[120] *Fr. Valentin's Journal*, http://www.stjosephpublications.com ; *She Went in Haste to the Mountain*, Book 1, Ch. 6, p, 144, Eusebio García de Pesquera O.F.M, www.stjosephpublications.com
[121] *The Apparitions of Garabandal*, p.74, F. Sanchez-Ventura Y Pascual, www.garabandal.org
[122] *Father Valentin's Journal Part 1*, www.stjosephpublications.com; *Right from the Start*, Garabandal Magazine, Jan-March 1987; www.garabandal.us
[123] *She Went in Haste to the Mountain*, Book 3 Ch. 1, p. 21, Eusebio García de Pesquera O.F.M., www.stjosephpublications.com
[124] Ibid.

[125] Photo courtesy of www.stjosephpublications.com *She Went in Haste to the Mountain,* Book 2 p. 127, Eusebio García de Pesquera O.F.M.

[126] *She Went in Haste to the Mountain,* Book 3 Ch. 1, p. 28, Eusebio García de Pesquera O.F.M., www.stjosephpublications.com

[127] *Garabandal The Village Speaks,* p. 151, Ramon Perez, 1981, The Workers of Our Lady of Mt. Carmel, Inc. P.O. Box 606, Lindenhurst, NY 11757

[128] Ibid., p. 190

[129] Ibid., p. 152

[130] Ibid., p. 153

[131] Ibid., p. 169

[132] *She Went in Haste to the Mountain,* Book 3 Ch. 1, p. 31, Eusebio García de Pesquera O.F.M., www.stjosephpublications.com

[133] *Conchita's Diary,* www.stjosephpublications.com

[134] Photo courtesy of Maria Saraco/St. Michael's Garabandal Center http://www.garabandal.org/photos/1communion.shtml

[135] *The Apparitions of Garabandal,* p.130, F. Sanchez-Ventura Y Pascual, www.garabandal.org

[136] *A Conversation Between Two Witnesses,* Needles Magazine, spring 1969; http://www.garabandal.us/Workers of Our Lady of Mount Carmel

[137] Ibid.

[138] *Garabandal The Village Speaks,* p. 172, Ramon Perez, 1981, The Workers of Our Lady of Mt. Carmel, Inc. P.O. Box 606, Lindenhurst, NY 11757

[139] Photo courtesy of St. Joseph Publications

[140] Photo by LR Walker

[141] *Everything Will Come in Due Time: An Interview with Serafin Gonzalez,* Garabandal Magazine, July-September 1993; http://www.garabandal.us/Workers of Our Lady of Mount Carmel; *Garabandal The Village Speaks,* p. 147, 294, 309, Ramon Perez, 1981, The Workers of Our Lady of Mt. Carmel, Inc. P.O. Box 606, Lindenhurst, NY 11757

[142] *She Went in Haste to the Mountain,* Book 1 Ch. 3, p. 65, Eusebio García de Pesquera O.F.M., www.stjosephpublications.com

[143] *She Went in Haste to the Mountain,* Book 1 Ch. 9, p. 207, 209, Eusebio García de Pesquera O.F.M., www.stjosephpublications.com; *Garabandal The Village Speaks,* p. 136-137, Ramon Perez, 1981, The Workers of Our Lady of Mt. Carmel, Inc. P.O. Box 606, Lindenhurst, NY 11757

[144] Photo courtesy of http://www.stjosephpublications.com *She Went in Haste to the Mountain,* Book 1, p, 178, Eusebio García de Pesquera O.F.M.

[145] *The Village Speaks,* p. 263-264, Ramon Perez, 1981, The Workers of Our Lady of Mt. Carmel, Inc. P.O. Box 606, Lindenhurst, NY 11757

[146] *She Went in Haste to the Mountain,* Book 1, Ch. 9, p. 210-211, and Book 2, Ch. 3, p. 108, Eusebio García de Pesquera O.F.M., www.stjosephpublications.com; *Garabandal The Village Speaks,* p. 263-264, Ramon Perez, 1981, The Workers of Our Lady of Mt. Carmel, Inc. P.O. Box 606, Lindenhurst, NY 11757

[147] *She Went in Haste to the Mountain,* Book 1, Ch. 9, p. 210-211, Eusebio García de Pesquera O.F.M., www.stjosephpublications.com

[148] *Father Valentin's Journal Part 1,* www.stjosephpublications.com

[149] *She Went in Haste to the Mountain,* Book 2, Ch. 3, p. 86, Eusebio García de Pesquera O.F.M, http://www.stjosephpublications.com

[150] Ibid.

[151] *She Went in Haste to the Mountain,* Book 1, Ch. 6, p. 147, Eusebio García de Pesquera O.F.M., www.stjosephpublications.com; *Garabandal The Village Speaks,* p. 133, Ramon Perez, 1981, The Workers of Our Lady of Mt. Carmel, Inc. P.O. Box 606, Lindenhurst, NY 11757

152 Photo courtesy of Maria Saraco/St. Michael's Garabandal Center
http://www.garabandal.org/photos/loli4.shtml
153 *Garabandal The Village Speaks,* p. 192, Ramon Perez, 1981, The Workers of Our Lady
of Mt. Carmel, Inc. P.O. Box 606, Lindenhurst, NY 11757
154 *Miracle at Garabandal,* Appendix, Harry Daley;
http://www.youtube.com/watch?v=MnEdkgZCmeo
155 *She Went in Haste to the Mountain,* Book 1, Ch. 6, p. 139, Eusebio García de Pesquera
O.F.M., www.stjosephpublications.com
156 *The Apparitions of Garabandal,* p.74, F. Sanchez-Ventura Y Pascual,
www.garabandal.org
157 1984 Interview with Mari-Loli
http://www.youtube.com/watch?v=ayKUdVTMm04
158 *Our Lady Teaches at Garabandal: O Children Listen to Me,* p. 65, Francois Turner, O.P.,
The Workers of Our Lady of Mt. Carmel, Inc. P.O. Box 606, Lindenhurst, NY 11757
159 *Interview with Julia Mazon,* Garabandal Magazine, 1978 ;
http://www.garabandal.us/Workers of Our Lady of Mount Carmel; *Garabandal The
Village Speaks,* p. 314, Ramon Perez, 1981, The Workers of Our Lady of Mt. Carmel,
Inc. P.O. Box 606, Lindenhurst, NY 11757
160 *She Went in Haste to the Mountain,* Book 2 Ch. 3, p. 104, Eusebio García de Pesquera
O.F.M., www.stjosephpublications.com
161 Photo courtesy of http://www.stjosephpublications.com *She Went in Haste to the
Mountain,* Book 2, Ch. 1, p. 16, Eusebio García de Pesquera O.F.M.
162 *The Apparitions of Garabandal,* p.75, F. Sanchez-Ventura Y Pascual,
www.garabandal.org
163 *She Went in Haste to the Mountain,* Book 1 Ch. 8, p. 178-179, Eusebio García de
Pesquera O.F.M., www.stjosephpublications.com
164 Ibid., p. 181
165 *Star on the Mountain,* Ch. 26, p. 62, Fr. M. Laffineur, The Workers of Our Lady of
Mt. Carmel, Inc. P.O. Box 606, Lindenhurst, NY 11757
166 *Father Valentin's Journal Part 1,* www.stjosephpublications.com
167 *Our Lady Teaches at Garabandal: O Children Listen to Me,* p. 85, Francois Turner, O.P.,
The Workers of Our Lady of Mt. Carmel, Inc. P.O. Box 606, Lindenhurst, NY 11757
168 *Father Valentin's Journal Part 1,* www.stjosephpublications.com
169 *The Apparitions of Garabandal,* p.75, F. Sanchez-Ventura Y Pascual,
www.garabandal.org
170 *She Went in Haste to the Mountain,* Book 1 Ch. 8, p. 182, Eusebio García de Pesquera
O.F.M., www.stjosephpublications.com
171 *The Apparitions of Garabandal,* p.78, F. Sanchez-Ventura Y Pascual,
www.garabandal.org
172 1984 Interview with Mari-Loli
http://www.youtube.com/watch?v=ayKUdVTMm04
173 *Our Lady Comes to Garabandal,* Ch. 4, p. 76, Joseph A. Pelletier, A.A.; Assumption
Publications, Worcester, Mass., 1971
174 *Garabandal The Village Speaks,* p. 45, Ramon Perez, 1981, The Workers of Our Lady
of Mt. Carmel, Inc. P.O. Box 606, Lindenhurst, NY 11757
175 *She Went in Haste to the Mountain,* Book 1 Ch. 8, p. 188, Eusebio García de Pesquera
O.F.M., www.stjosephpublications.com
176 Photo courtesy of St. Joseph Publications
177 *Our Lady Comes to Garabandal,* Ch. 4, p. 78, Joseph A. Pelletier, A.A.; Assumption
Publications, Worcester, Mass., 1971
178 GARABANDAL JOURNAL March-April 2004
179 Photo courtesy of http://www.stjosephpublications.com/testimonies_page.htm
180 http://www.garabandal.org/story.shtml#miracle

[181] *Our Lady Comes to Garabandal*, Ch. 9, p. 151, Joseph A. Pelletier, A.A.; Assumption Publications, Worcester, Mass., 1971

[182] *New American Bible, revised edition* © 2010, 1991, 1986, 1970 Confraternity of Christian Doctrine, Washington, D.C.

[183] *New American Bible, revised edition* © 2010, 1991, 1986, 1970 Confraternity of Christian Doctrine, Washington, D.C.

[184] *Star on the Mountain*, Ch. 32, p. 72, Fr. M. Laffineur, The Workers of Our Lady of Mt. Carmel, Inc. P.O. Box 606, Lindenhurst, NY 11757

[185] http://www.garabandal.org/News/Garabandal_Warning_Miracle_Interviews.shtml

[186] *Garabandal The Village Speaks*, p. 46, Ramon Perez, 1981, The Workers of Our Lady of Mt. Carmel, Inc. P.O. Box 606, Lindenhurst, NY 11757

[187] *She Went in Haste to the Mountain*, Book 1 Ch. 8, p. 194, Eusebio García de Pesquera O.F.M., www.stjosephpublications.com

[188] Originally published in *Needles* magazine No. 3, 1972 (re-named *Garabandal*).From *Garabandal The Village Speaks*, p. 49, Ramon Perez, 1981, The Workers of Our Lady of Mt. Carmel, Inc. P.O. Box 606, Lindenhurst, NY 11757

[189] *Garabandal Magazine*, Special Issue 1996, p. 11

[190] Originally published in *Needles* magazine No. 3, 1972 (re-named *Garabandal*).From *Garabandal The Village Speaks*, p. 49, Ramon Perez, 1981, The Workers of Our Lady of Mt. Carmel, Inc. P.O. Box 606, Lindenhurst, NY 11757; also published in *Garabandal Magazine*, Special Issue 1996, p.2

[191] *Miracle at Garabandal*, Ch. 11, Harry Daley, www.stjosephpublications.com

[192] http://www.garabandal.us/the-message/

[193] *Star on the Mountain*, Ch. 61, p. 163, Fr. M. Laffineur, The Workers of Our Lady of Mt. Carmel, Inc. P.O. Box 606, Lindenhurst, NY 11757

[194] *Garabandal Magazine*, Special Issue 1996, p. 11

[195] *She Went in Haste to the Mountain*, Book 3, Ch. 6, p. 103, Eusebio García de Pesquera O.F.M.

[196] *She Went in Haste to the Mountain*, Book 3, Ch. 7, p. 134, Eusebio García de Pesquera O.F.M., www.stjosephpublications.com

Chapter 4

[197] *She Went in Haste to the Mountain*, Book 2, Ch. 7, p. 196, Eusebio García de Pesquera O.F.M., www.stjosephpublications.com

[198] *New American Bible, revised edition* © 2010, 1991, 1986, 1970 Confraternity of Christian Doctrine, Washington, D.C.

[199] Photo courtesy of Maria Saraco/St. Michael's Garabandal Center http://www.garabandal.org/photos/16xty_61.shtml

[200] *She Went in Haste to the Mountain*, Book 2, Ch. 7, p. 191, Eusebio García de Pesquera O.F.M., www.stjosephpublications.com

[201] *Garabandal The Village Speaks*, p. 132, Ramon Perez, 1981, The Workers of Our Lady of Mt. Carmel, Inc. P.O. Box 606, Lindenhurst, NY 11757

[202] *She Went in Haste to the Mountain*, Book 2, Ch. 7, p. 193, Eusebio García de Pesquera O.F.M., www.stjosephpublications.com

[203] *Garabandal: The Village Speaks*, p. 132, Ramon Perez, 1981, The Workers of Our Lady of Mt. Carmel, Inc. P.O. Box 606, Lindenhurst, NY 11757

[204] *She Went in Haste to the Mountain*, Book 2, Ch. 7, p. 195, Eusebio García de Pesquera O.F.M., www.stjosephpublications.com

[205] Ibid.

[206] *She Went in Haste to the Mountain*, Book 2, Ch. 7, p. 194, Eusebio García de Pesquera O.F.M., www.stjosephpublications.com

[207] Ibid., p. 195

208 Ibid., p. 199

209 Daniel 12; Matthew 24

210 http://www.garabandal.org/vigil/J_A_1988/Father_Morelos_1988.shtml

211 *Garabandal: The Village Speaks*, p. 206, Ramon Perez, 1981, The Workers of Our Lady of Mt. Carmel, Inc. P.O. Box 606, Lindenhurst, NY 11757

212 *The Call of Garabandal*, Apr-Jun 1984

213 *Garabandal—Der Zeigefinger Gottes (Garabandal—The Finger of God)*, Albrecht Weber; http://www.amazon.de/Garabandal-Zeigefinger-Gottes-Albrecht-Weber/dp/3923673116; http://www.weto-verlag.de/Buch%20-%20Garabanda,%20Der%20Zeigefinger%20Gottes.htm

214 Encyclical *Mater et Magistra*, May 15, 1961, n. 34, POPE JOHN XXIII, (1958-1963).

215 *Catechism of the Catholic Church*, n. 676

216 *Garabandal—Der Zeigefinger Gottes (Garabandal—The Finger of God)*, Albrecht Weber; http://www.amazon.de/Garabandal-Zeigefinger-Gottes-Albrecht-Weber/dp/3923673116; http://www.weto-verlag.de/Buch%20-%20Garabanda,%20Der%20Zeigefinger%20Gottes.htm

217 2 Peter 3:1-18; 1 Thessalonians 5:1-9; Matthew 24; . Luke 21:25-36; Acts 3:19-21; Joel 2 and 3; Malachi; Daniel 7 and 12; 2 Timothy 3:1-5, 4:3-4; Ezekiel 38 and 39; Revelation 6-22 ; Philippians 2: 9-11

218 Matthew 24; Daniel 12; Revelation 3:10; Revelation 7:14; Joel 2; Jeremiah 30:7; Isaiah 13: 6-13

219 Isaiah 2

220 Zechariah 14

221 *New American Bible, revised edition* © 2010, 1991, 1986, 1970 Confraternity of Christian Doctrine, Washington, D.C.

222 www.garabandal.org

223 *She Went in Haste to the Mountain*, Book 2, Ch. 7, p. 200-201, Eusebio García de Pesquera O.F.M., www.stjosephpublications.com

224 *1984 Interview with Mari-Loli:* http://www.youtube.com/watch?v=ZxbF1P60e0k

225 *Star on the Mountain*, Ch. 44, p. 109, Fr. M. Laffineur, The Workers of Our Lady of Mt. Carmel, Inc. P.O. Box 606, Lindenhurst, NY 11757

226 *God Speaks at Garabandal*, p. 124, Joseph A. Pelletier, 1970; http://www.garabandal.us/Workers of Our Lady of Mount Carmel.

227 *Conchita's Diary*, www.stjosephpublications.com

Chapter 5

228 Photo by LR Walker

229 *Documents on Fatima and the Memoirs of Sister Lucia*, Fatima Family Apostolate 2002, Park Press, Waite Park, MN, p. 166-167, Father Antonio Maria Martins, S.J.

230 Ibid., p. 191

231 A scapular, based on a monk's garment, consists of two small pieces of wool cloth connected by string that is worn over the neck, either under or over one's clothing. It is a blessed object worn by lay people to encourage one's devotion to God and is associated with a variety of promises and blessings.

232 Malachi 4; *New American Bible, revised edition* © 2010, 1991, 1986, 1970 Confraternity of Christian Doctrine, Washington, D.C.

233 Zephaniah 1

234 Malachi 4

235 http://www.vatican.va/roman_curia/congregations/cfaith/documents/rc_con_cfaith_doc_20000626_message-fatima_en.html

236 Ibid.

[237] Letter to Cardinal Franz Koenig dated January 29, 1996, in the *Archives of the Sanctuary of Our Lady of Fatima,* from *The Whole Truth About Fatima Vol. IV Ch.11* by Brother François de Marie des Anges of the Little Brothers of the Sacred Heart
[238] http://www.vatican.va/roman_curia/congregations/cfaith/documents/rc_con_cfaith_doc_20000626_message-fatima_en.html
[239] *The Whole Truth About Fatima Vol. II Ch.6* by Brother Michel de la Sainte Trinité of the Little Brothers of the Sacred Heart
[240] Floridi, p. 19-21 from *The Whole Truth About Fatima Vol. II Ch. 8* by Brother Michel de la Sainte Trinité of the Little Brothers of the Sacred Heart
[241] Written in his own hand, February 2, 1930, *Actes de S.S. Pie XI,* Vol. VI, p. 148-151 (Bonne Presse, 1934) from *The Whole Truth About Fatima Vol. II Ch. 7* by Brother Michel de la Sainte Trinité of the Little Brothers of the Sacred Heart
[242] *The Whole Truth About Fatima Vol. II Ch. 7* by Brother Michel de la Sainte Trinité of the Little Brothers of the Sacred Heart
[243] *An Exorcist Tells His Story,* p. 38-39, by Gabriele Amorth, 1999 Ignatius Press, San Francisco
[244] Ibid., *Ch. 9*
[245] D. Rops, *A Fight for God,* p. 330. Cf. Paul Lesourd, Pie XI, p. 45, Flammarion, 1939; Charles Ledré, *Un siècle sous la tiare, de Pie IX à Pie XII, les successeurs de Pierre face au monde moderne,* p. 148, Amiot-Dumont, 1955, from *The Whole Truth About Fatima* by Brother Michel de la Sainte Trinité of the Little Brothers of the Sacred Heart
[246] *The Whole Truth About Fatima Vol. II Ch. 9* by Brother Michel de la Sainte Trinité of the Little Brothers of the Sacred Heart
[247] *Documents on Fatima and the Memoirs of Sister Lucia,* Fatima Family Apostolate 2002, Park Press, Waite Park, MN, p. 366, Father Antonio Maria Martins, S.J.
[248] Claude Martin, *Franco, soldat et chef d'État,* p. 270, éd. Quatre fils Aymon, Paris 1959, from *The Whole Truth About Fatima* by Brother Michel de la Sainte Trinité of the Little Brothers of the Sacred Heart
[249] *Documents on Fatima and the Memoirs of Sister Lucia,* Fatima Family Apostolate 2002, Park Press, Waite Park, MN, p. 145, Father Antonio Maria Martins, S.J.
[250] Ibid., p. 395
[251] *Documents on Fatima and the Memoirs of Sister Lucia,* Fatima Family Apostolate 2002, Park Press, Waite Park, MN, p. 138, Father Antonio Maria Martins, S.J.
[252] Ibid., p. 145
[253] *The Whole Truth About Fatima Vol. III Ch.1* by Brother Michel de la Sainte Trinité of the Little Brothers of the Sacred Heart
[254] Ibid., *Vol. III Ch.4*
[255] http://www.ewtn.com/library/papaldoc/consecra.htm
[256] *Documents on Fatima and the Memoirs of Sister Lucia,* Fatima Family Apostolate 2002, Park Press, Waite Park, MN, p. 12, Father Antonio Maria Martins, S.J.
[257] http://www.garabandal.us/feast-of-the-immaculate-heart-of-mary/
[258] *Documents on Fatima and the Memoirs of Sister Lucia,* Fatima Family Apostolate 2002, Park Press, Waite Park, MN, p. 13, Father Antonio Maria Martins, S.J.
[259] http://www.newyorker.com/archive/2005/04/11/050411ta_talk_remnick; http://online.wsj.com/article/SB122479408458463941.html
[260] http://online.wsj.com/article/SB122479408458463941.html
[261] http://www.vatican.va/roman_curia/congregations/cfaith/documents/rc_con_cfaith_doc_20000626_message-fatima_en.html
[262] http://www.ewtn.com/library/papaldoc/consecra.htm

263

http://www.vatican.va/roman_curia/congregations/cfaith/documents/rc_con_cfaith_doc_20000626_message-fatima_en.html

[264] *Documents on Fatima and the Memoirs of Sister Lucia,* Fatima Family Apostolate 2002, Park Press, Waite Park, MN, p. 123, Father Antonio Maria Martins, S.J.

265

http://www.vatican.va/roman_curia/congregations/cfaith/documents/rc_con_cfaith_doc_20000626_message-fatima_en.html

[266] http://www.ewtn.com/library/papaldoc/consecra.htm

[267] *Documents on Fatima and the Memoirs of Sister Lucia,* Fatima Family Apostolate 2002, Park Press, Waite Park, MN, p. 42, Father Antonio Maria Martins, S.J.

268

http://www.vatican.va/roman_curia/congregations/cfaith/documents/rc_con_cfaith_doc_20000626_message-fatima_en.html

[269] *Documents on Fatima and the Memoirs of Sister Lucia,* Fatima Family Apostolate 2002, Park Press, Waite Park, MN, p. 123, Father Antonio Maria Martins, S.J.

[270] *The Whole Truth About Fatima Vol. IV Ch.10* by Brother François de Marie des Anges of the Little Brothers of the Sacred Heart

[271] *Documents on Fatima and the Memoirs of Sister Lucia,* Fatima Family Apostolate 2002, Park Press, Waite Park, MN, p. 41, Father Antonio Maria Martins, S.J.

[272] *The Whole Truth About Fatima Vol. IV Ch.11* by Brother François de Marie des Anges of the Little Brothers of the Sacred Heart

[273] *Documents on Fatima and the Memoirs of Sister Lucia,* Fatima Family Apostolate 2002, Park Press, Waite Park, MN, p. 40, Father Antonio Maria Martins, S.J.

[274] Ibid., p. 42

[275] http://www.ewtn.com/library/curia/cdflucia.htm

[276] *The Whole Truth About Fatima Vol. IV Ch.6* by Brother François de Marie des Anges of the Little Brothers of the Sacred Heart

277

http://www.catholicworldreport.com/Item/1798/why_did_vatican_ii_ignore_communism.aspx

[278] *The Desolate City: Revolution in the Catholic Church,* p. 70, Anne Roche Muggeridge, Harper & Row, 1986, 1990.

[279] *The Whole Truth About Fatima Vol. IV Ch.10* by Brother François de Marie des Anges of the Little Brothers of the Sacred Heart

[280] Ibid.

[281] http://www.ewtn.com/library/papaldoc/consecra.htm

[282] *Documents on Fatima and the Memoirs of Sister Lucia,* Fatima Family Apostolate 2002, Park Press, Waite Park, MN, p. 146, Father Antonio Maria Martins, S.J.

[283] Ibid., p. 394

[284] *Garabandal—Der Zeigefinger Gottes (Garabandal—The Finger of God),* Albrecht Weber; http://www.amazon.de/Garabandal-Zeigefinger-Gottes-Albrecht-Weber/dp/3923673116; http://www.weto-verlag.de/Buch%20-%20Garabanda,%20Der%20Zeigefinger%20Gottes.htm

[285] Daniel 12; Matthew 24

[286] *The Whole Truth About Fatima Vol. III Ch.2* by Brother Michel de la Sainte Trinité of the Little Brothers of the Sacred Heart

[287] *Documents on Fatima and the Memoirs of Sister Lucia,* Fatima Family Apostolate 2002, Park Press, Waite Park, MN, p. 139, Father Antonio Maria Martins, S.J.

[288] *The Whole Truth About Fatima Vol. III Ch.9* by Brother Michel de la Sainte Trinité of the Little Brothers of the Sacred Heart

289

http://www.vatican.va/roman_curia/congregations/cfaith/documents/rc_con_cfaith
_doc_20000626_message-fatima_en.html

290 http://asv.vatican.va/?lang=en

291

http://www.vatican.va/roman_curia/congregations/cfaith/documents/rc_con_cfaith
_doc_20000626_message-fatima_en.html

292 *The Whole Truth About Fatima Vol. III Part 2, Ch.2* by Brother Michel de la Sainte Trinité of the Little Brothers of the Sacred Heart

293 Ibid.

294 Reported John Paul II interview with Catholics at Fulda Germany, Nov. 1980, published in the German magazine, "Stimme des Glaubens." Found in English in Daniel J. Lynch, "The Call to Total Consecration to the Immaculate Heart of Mary" (St. Albans, Vermont: Missions of the Sorrowful and Immaculate Heart of Mary, Pub., 1991), pp 50-51

295 *The Whole Truth About Fatima Vol. III Part 3, Ch.3* by Brother Michel de la Sainte Trinité of the Little Brothers of the Sacred Heart

296 *The Whole Truth About Fatima Vol. IV Ch.10* by Brother François de Marie des Anges of the Little Brothers of the Sacred Heart

297 The Ratzinger Report, p. 110, Joseph Cardinal Ratzinger with Vittorio Messori, Ignatius Press San Francisco 1985

298

http://www.vatican.va/roman_curia/congregations/cfaith/documents/rc_con_cfaith
_doc_20000626_message-fatima_en.html

299 Ibid.

300

http://www.vatican.va/roman_curia/congregations/cfaith/documents/rc_con_cfaith
_doc_20000626_message-fatima_en.html

301 Luke 21:25, Matthew 24:22, Revelation 8:8-10

302 Daniel 11:31, Matthew 24:15, Mark 13:14

303 Matthew 24:9-14; Luke 18:8; 2 Thess. 2:3; 2 Timothy 4:3; Acts 20:29-30; Revelation 13:15

304 *Documents on Fatima and the Memoirs of Sister Lucia,* Fatima Family Apostolate 2002, Park Press, Waite Park, MN, p. 20, Father Antonio Maria Martins, S.J.

305 Daniel 12:7; Matthew 24:9, 10; Mark 13:9; Luke 21:12; Revelation 13:7

306 Daniel 9:27, Daniel 11:31, Daniel 12:11, Matthew 24:15

307 Ibid.

308 *Garabandal The Village Speaks,* p. 206, Ramon Perez, 1981, The Workers of Our Lady of Mt. Carmel, Inc. P.O. Box 606, Lindenhurst, NY 11757

309 Taken from: L'Osservatore Romano Weekly Edition in English 9 January 2002, page 7 https://www.ewtn.com/library/curia/cdflucia.htm

310

http://www.vatican.va/roman_curia/congregations/cfaith/documents/rc_con_cfaith
_doc_20000626_message-fatima_en.html

311 http://www.lucia.pt/news/biography-of-sister-lucia-in-polish:133;

http://www.lucia.pt/ficheiros/boletins_pdf/boletim18_en.pdf

312 http://www.oecumene.radiovaticana.org/en1/Articolo.asp?c=391999;

http://www.vatican.va/holy_father/benedict_xvi/speeches/2010/may/documents/hf
_ben-xvi_spe_20100511_portogallo-interview_en.html

313 *Documents on Fatima and the Memoirs of Sister Lucia,* Fatima Family Apostolate 2002, Park Press, Waite Park, MN, p. 32, Father Antonio Maria Martins, S.J.

314 *She Went In Haste to the Mountain* Book 3 Ch. 7 p. 137, Eusebio García de Pesquera O.F.M., www.stjosephpublications.com
315 *She Went In Haste to the Mountain,* Book 3 Ch. 7, p. 138 Eusebio García de Pesquera O.F.M., www.stjosephpublications.com
316 Ibid.
317 *Miracle at Garabandal,* Ch. 9, Harry Daley, www.stjosephpublications.com
318 http://www.garabandal.us/feast-of-the-immaculate-heart-of-mary/

Chapter 6

319 *New American Bible, revised edition* © 2010, 1991, 1986, 1970 Confraternity of Christian Doctrine, Washington, D.C.
320 *If Only We Had Listened* by Immaculée Ilibagiza
321 *New American Bible, revised edition* © 2010, 1991, 1986, 1970 Confraternity of Christian Doctrine, Washington, D.C.
322 *Medjugorje: THE LAST APPARITION--How It Will Change the World,* Wayne Weible, 2013, New Hope Press
323 http://www.medjugorje.eu/messages/ Castella, Andre, and Ljubic: (Medjugorje, Invitation for Prayer and Conversion), Hauteville, Paris, 1986. Reference to book of Ljubic Lj.(1984-85) (128).
324 http://www.vatican.va/archive/hist_councils/ii_vatican_council/documents/vat-ii_const_19641121_lumen-gentium_en.html
325 Message of July 24, 1982
326 http://www.medjugorje.eu/messages/ Latest News (1987) (Is the Virgin Mary Appearing at Medjugorje?) and supplemental updates by Fr. Rene Laurentin, December 1984 through July 1987. (2, 73)
327 Acts 10:35; Galatians 3:28; Romans 2:25-29; 1 Cor. 7:19
328 http://www.medjugorje.org/mirjana1.htm
329 *Medjugorje: THE LAST APPARITION--How It Will Change the World,* Wayne Weible, 2013, New Hope Press
330 http://www.medjugorje.eu/messages/ Friday, October 25th 1985
331 Luke 21: 7-11
332 Luke 21: 25-28
333 Luke 21: 7-11
334 Photo by LR Walker
335 http://www.medjugorje.eu/messages/ Apocalyptic Messages
336 http://www.medjugorje.eu/messages/ (T. Vlasic, Aug. 12, 1984. VB 1, 81)
337 Isaiah 9:6
338 Isaiah 53
339 John 2:19
340 *Medjugorje: THE LAST APPARITION--How It Will Change the World,* Wayne Weible, 2013, New Hope Press
341 Ibid.
342 http://www.medjugorje.ws/en/apparitions/docs-ten-medjugorje-secrets/
343 https://www.markmallett.com/blog/medjugorje-and-the-smoking-guns/
344 https://medjugorjelive.org/2020/03/18/the-end-of-mirjanas-apparitions/
345 *Medjugorje: THE LAST APPARITION--How It Will Change the World,* Wayne Weible, 2013, New Hope Press
346 *The Miracle Detective,* p. 208, Randall Sullivan, 2004, Grove Press

Chapter 7

347 Photo by LR Walker

[348] Photo courtesy of http://www.stjosephpublications.com *She Went in Haste to the Mountain,* Book 1, p, 39, Eusebio García de Pesquera O.F.M.

[349] *God Speaks at Garabandal,* p. 122, Joseph A. Pelletier; http://www.garabandal.us/Workers of Our Lady of Mount Carmel

[350] *Conchita's Diary,* www.stjosephpublications.com

[351] Ibid.

[352] *Garabandal The Village Speaks,* p. 222, Ramon Perez, 1981, The Workers of Our Lady of Mt. Carmel, Inc. P.O. Box 606, Lindenhurst, NY 11757

[353] Ibid., p. 211

[354] *She Went in Haste to the Mountain,* Book 3, Ch. 4, p. 73, Eusebio García de Pesquera O.F.M., www.stjosephpublications.com

[355] *She Went in Haste to the Mountain,* Book 3, Ch. 2, p. 51, Eusebio García de Pesquera O.F.M., www.stjosephpublications.com

[356] Ibid., p. 55

[357] *Our Lady Comes to Garabandal,* Ch. 13, p. 196, by Joseph A. Pelletier, Assumption Publications, Worcester, Mass., 1971; *Journal de Conchita,* p. 72, footnote (88).

[358] *She Went in Haste to the Mountain,* Book 3, Ch. 6, p. 108, Eusebio García de Pesquera O.F.M., www.stjosephpublications.com

[359] Ibid., p. 107

[360] *She Went in Haste to the Mountain,* Book 3, Ch. 4, p. 73, Eusebio García de Pesquera O.F.M., www.stjosephpublications.com

[361] *Memoirs of a Spanish Country Priest,* Ch. 7, Jose Ramon Garcia de la Riva, www.stjosephpublications.com

[362] Photo courtesy of St. Joseph Publications

[363] *Garabandal The Village Speaks,* p. 128, Ramon Perez, 1981, The Workers of Our Lady of Mt. Carmel, Inc. P.O. Box 606, Lindenhurst, NY 11757

[364] Ibid., p. 120, 121, 296, 313; *She Went in Haste to the Mountain,* Book 3, Ch. 6, p. 114, Eusebio García de Pesquera O.F.M.,

[365] *Memoirs of a Spanish Country Priest,* Ch. 8, Jose Ramon Garcia de la Riva, www.stjosephpublications.com

[366] Ibid., Ch. 9

[367] *Our Lady Teaches at Garabandal: O Children Listen to Me,* p. 145, Francois Turner, O.P., The Workers of Our Lady of Mt. Carmel, Inc. P.O. Box 606, Lindenhurst, NY 11757

[368] *She Went in Haste to the Mountain,* Book 2, Chapter 3, p. 80, 82, 86, 106, Eusebio García de Pesquera O.F.M, http://www.stjosephpublications.com

[369] *Garabandal The Village Speaks,* p. 191, Ramon Perez, 1981, The Workers of Our Lady of Mt. Carmel, Inc. P.O. Box 606, Lindenhurst, NY 11757

[370] Ibid., p. 197

[371] *Our Lady Teaches at Garabandal: O Children Listen to Me,* p. 97, Francois Turner, O.P., The Workers of Our Lady of Mt. Carmel, Inc. P.O. Box 606, Lindenhurst, NY 11757; *Garabandal The Village Speaks,* p. 267, Ramon Perez, 1981, The Workers of Our Lady of Mt. Carmel, Inc. P.O. Box 606, Lindenhurst, NY 11757

[372] Photo courtesy of St. Joseph Publications

[373] *She Went in Haste to the Mountain,* Book 3, Ch. 5, p. 112, Eusebio García de Pesquera O.F.M., www.stjosephpublications.com

[374] *She Went in Haste to the Mountain,* Book 3, Ch. 6, p. 119, Eusebio García de Pesquera O.F.M., www.stjosephpublications.com

[375] *She Went in Haste to the Mountain,* Book 3, Ch. 7, p. 124, Eusebio García de Pesquera O.F.M., www.stjosephpublications.com

[376] *Star on the Mountain,* Ch. 36, p. 85, Fr. M. Laffineur, The Workers of Our Lady of Mt. Carmel, Inc. P.O. Box 606, Lindenhurst, NY 11757

[377] *She Went in Haste to the Mountain,* Book 3, Ch. 7, p. 134, Eusebio García de Pesquera O.F.M., www.stjosephpublications.com
[378] Ibid., p. 136
[379] Ibid., p. 146
[380] *Garabandal The Village Speaks,* p. 325-326, Ramon Perez, 1981, The Workers of Our Lady of Mt. Carmel, Inc. P.O. Box 606, Lindenhurst, NY 11757
[381] *The Apparitions of Garabandal,* p.50, F. Sanchez-Ventura Y Pascual; www.garabandal.org
[382] *1984 Interview with Mari-Loli* http://www.youtube.com/watch?v=ZxbF1P60e0k
[383] *Garabandal The Village Speaks,* p. 329, Ramon Perez, 1981, The Workers of Our Lady of Mt. Carmel, Inc. P.O. Box 606, Lindenhurst, NY 11757
[384] Ibid., p. 329
[385] *She Went in Haste to the Mountain,* Book 2, Ch. 1, p. 30, Eusebio García de Pesquera O.F.M., www.stjosephpublications.com
[386] Photo courtesy of http://www.stjosephpublications.com/testimonies_page.htm
[387] Photo courtesy of St. Joseph Publications
[388] *She Went In Haste to the Mountain,* Book 2, Ch. 1, p. 34, Eusebio García de Pesquera O.F.M., www.stjosephpublications.com
[389] *She Went in Haste to the Mountain,* Book 2, Ch. 1, p. 42, Eusebio García de Pesquera O.F.M., www.stjosephpublications.com
[390] Ibid.
[391] *She Went in Haste to the Mountain,* Book 2, Ch. 1, p. 47, Eusebio García de Pesquera O.F.M., www.stjosephpublications.com
[392] Ibid., p. 43-44
[393] *She Went in Haste to the Mountain,* Book 3, Ch. 9, p. 153, Eusebio García de Pesquera O.F.M., www.stjosephpublications.com
[394] Photo courtesy of Maria Saraco/St. Michael's Garabandal Center http://www.garabandal.org/photos/11xty_63.shtml
[395] *She Went in Haste to the Mountain,* Book 3, Ch. 9, p. 156, Eusebio García de Pesquera O.F.M., www.stjosephpublications.com
[396] *She Went in Haste to the Mountain,* Book 3, Ch. 9, p. 161, Eusebio García de Pesquera O.F.M., www.stjosephpublications.com
[397] Ibid., p. 160
[398] *She Went in Haste to the Mountain,* Book 2, Ch. 6, p. 103, Eusebio García de Pesquera O.F.M., www.stjosephpublications.com
[399] *Star on the Mountain,* Ch. 36, p. 86, Fr. M. Laffineur, The Workers of Our Lady of Mt. Carmel, Inc. P.O. Box 606, Lindenhurst, NY 11757
[400] *Star on the Mountain,* Ch. 25, p. 60, Fr. M. Laffineur, The Workers of Our Lady of Mt. Carmel, Inc. P.O. Box 606, Lindenhurst, NY 11757
[401] *She Went in Haste to the Mountain,* Book 3, Ch. 9, p. 161, Eusebio García de Pesquera O.F.M., www.stjosephpublications.com
[402] *She Went in Haste to the Mountain,* Book 3, Ch. 9, p. 165, Eusebio García de Pesquera O.F.M., www.stjosephpublications.com
[403] Photo courtesy of St. Joseph Publications
[404] Ibid.
[405] *She Went in Haste to the Mountain,* Book 3, Ch. 9, p. 166, Eusebio García de Pesquera O.F.M., www.stjosephpublications.com
[406] *Father Valentin's Journal Part 1,* www.stjosephpublications.com
[407] *She Went in Haste to the Mountain,* Book 3, Ch. 9, p. 167, Eusebio García de Pesquera O.F.M., www.stjosephpublications.com
[408] Photo courtesy of http://www.stjosephpublications.com *She Went in Haste to the Mountain,* Book 2, p, 10, Eusebio García de Pesquera O.F.M.

[409] *She Went in Haste to the Mountain,* Book 3, Ch. 9, p. 171, Eusebio García de Pesquera O.F.M., www.stjosephpublications.com

[410] Photo courtesy of St. Joseph Publications

[411] *She Went in Haste to the Mountain,* Book 3, Ch. 5, p. 87, Eusebio García de Pesquera O.F.M., www.stjosephpublications.com

[412] Garabandal Journal November/Decemeber 2009

[413] Article by Mark Regis, *GARABANDAL JOURNAL Nov-Dec. 2002; Our Lady Teaches at Garabandal, O Children Listen to Me,* p. 56, Francois Turner, O.P., The Workers of Our Lady of Mt. Carmel, Inc. P.O. Box 606, Lindenhurst, NY 11757; *Garabandal: Apparitions of the Blessed Virgin Mary as "Our Lady of Mount Carmel,"* p. 31, by Jacques Serre and Beatrice Caux, 2001, The Workers of Our Lady of Mount Carmel of Garabandal, Australia, www.garabandal.com

[414] John 17: 21 *New American Bible, revised edition* © 2010, 1991, 1986, 1970 Confraternity of Christian Doctrine, Washington, D.C.

[415] *Documents on Fatima and the Memoirs of Sister Lucia,* Fatima Family Apostolate 2002, Park Press, Waite Park, MN, p. 138, 192, 197, 198; Father Antonio Maria Martins, S.J.

[416] *Miracle at Garabandal,* Ch. 14, Harry Daley, www.stjosephpublications.com

[417] http://www.vatican.va/holy_father/paul_vi/speeches/1964/index.htm; http://www.vatican.va/holy_father/john_paul_ii/audiences/1997/documents/hf_jp-ii_aud_17091997_en.html

[418] *What Happened at Vatican II,* p. 246, John W. O'Malley, The Belknap Press of Harvard University Press, 2008.

[419] *The Desolate City: Revolution in the Catholic Church,* p. 70, Anne Roche Muggeridge, Harper & Row, 1986, 1990.

[420] http://whispersintheloggia.blogspot.com/2013/10/the-great-untier-for-francis-theres.html

[421] *Mysterium Fidei ,* paragraphs 9-14; http://w2.vatican.va/content/paul-vi/en/encyclicals/documents/hf_p-vi_enc_03091965_mysterium.html

[422] *The Desolate City: Revolution in the Catholic Church,* Anne Roche Muggeridge, Harper & Row, 1986, 1990.

[423] Dogmatic Constitution on the Church (*Lumen Gentium*) Ch. II The People of God

[424] Dogmatic Constitution on the Church (*Lumen Gentium*) Paragraph 42

[425] *The Desolate City: Revolution in the Catholic Church,* p. 155, Anne Roche Muggeridge, Harper & Row, 1986, 1990.

[426] *Our Lady Teaches at Garabandal: O Children Listen to Me,* p. 137, Francois Turner, O.P., The Workers of Our Lady of Mt. Carmel, Inc. P.O. Box 606, Lindenhurst, NY 11757

[427] Video Interview with Conchita: http://www.youtube.com/watch?v=VDRO0UYWA6s&feature=youtu.be

[428] *The Whole Truth About Fatima Vol. III Ch.1* by Brother Michel de la Sainte Trinité of the Little Brothers of the Sacred Heart

[429] *Star on the Mountain,* Ch. 45, p. 111, Fr. M. Laffineur, The Workers of Our Lady of Mt. Carmel, Inc. P.O. Box 606, Lindenhurst, NY 11757

[430] Matt. 16:24, Matt. 10:38; Luke 14:27; 1 Peter 2:21

[431431] Phillipians 2:12

[432] 1 Peter 2:5

[433] Colossians 1:24 *New American Bible, revised edition* © 2010, 1991, 1986, 1970 Confraternity of Christian Doctrine, Washington, D.C.

[434] Garabandal Journal May-June 2004: Interview by Father Francis Benac, S.J., in June 1978

[435] http://www.americancatholic.org/news/clergysexabuse/johnjaycns.asp

[436] http://en.radiovaticana.va/news/2013/05/28/pope_to_lead_millions_in_global_hour

_of_adoration/en1-696274; http://www.catholicnewsagency.com/news/pontificate-of-pope-francis-consecrated-to-our-lady-of-fatima/

437 http://vaticaninsider.lastampa.it/en/the-vatican/detail/articolo/vaticano-vatican-maria-mary-fatima-27286/;
http://www.catholicherald.co.uk/news/2013/08/22/pope-francis-to-consecrate-the-world-to-immaculate-heart-of-mary/

438 *America Magazine,* Interview with Pope Francis, September 30, 2013, by Antonio Spadaro, S.J.; http://americamagazine.org/pope-interview

439 *The Letters and Diaries of John Henry Newman,* Vol. 27, editors C.S. Dessain and T. Gornal, Clarendon Press, Oxford, 1975.

440 *Garabandal The Village Speaks,* p. 328, Ramon Perez, 1981, The Workers of Our Lady of Mt. Carmel, Inc. P.O. Box 606, Lindenhurst, NY 11757

441 *She Went in Haste to the Mountain,* Book 3, Ch. 10, p. 177, Eusebio García de Pesquera O.F.M., www.stjosephpublications.com

442 *She Went in Haste to the Mountain,* Book 3, Ch. 7, p. 135, Eusebio García de Pesquera O.F.M., www.stjosephpublications.com

443 *Our Lady Comes to Garabandal,* p. 226, Joseph Pelletier, A.A.; Assumption Publications, Worcester, Mass., 1971

444 *She Went in Haste to the Mountain,* Book 3, Ch. 7, p. 135, Eusebio García de Pesquera O.F.M.,

445 Decree on the Ministry and Life of Priests *(Presbyterorum Ordinis)*

446 *New American Bible, revised edition* © 2010, 1991, 1986, 1970 Confraternity of Christian Doctrine, Washington, D.C.

447 *She Went in Haste to the Mountain,* Book 3, Ch. 5, p. 91, Eusebio García de Pesquera O.F.M., www.stjosephpublications.com

448 *Our Lady Comes to Garabandal* by Joseph A. Pelletier, Assumption Publications, Worcester, Mass., 1971

449 *The Whole Truth About Fatima Vol. III Ch.8* by Brother Michel de la Sainte Trinité of the Little Brothers of the Sacred Heart

450 *Star on the Mountain,* Ch. 24, p. 56, Fr. M. Laffineur, The Workers of Our Lady of Mt. Carmel, Inc. P.O. Box 606, Lindenhurst, NY 11757.

451 *The Whole Truth About Fatima Vol. III Ch.1* by Brother Michel de la Sainte Trinité of the Little Brothers of the Sacred Heart

452 *Visionaries: The Spanish Republic and the Reign of Christ* by William A. Christian, Jr. University of California Press, Berkeley and Los Angeles, California c1996

453 *Visionaries: The Spanish Republic and the Reign of Christ,* p. 398, by William A. Christian, Jr. University of California Press, Berkeley and Los Angeles, California c1996; *Of Queen and Prophets: The Garabandal Events and "The End of the Times,"* p. 282, by Gregory M. Rolla, 2011

454 *Garabandal The Village Speaks,* p. 255, Ramon Perez, 1981, The Workers of Our Lady of Mt. Carmel, Inc. P.O. Box 606, Lindenhurst, NY 11757

455 *She Went in Haste to the Mountain,* Book 3, Ch.10, p. 184, Eusebio García de Pesquera O.F.M., www.stjosephpublications.com

456 *She Went in Haste to the Mountain,* Book 2, Ch. 2, p. 65-66, Eusebio García de Pesquera O.F.M., www.stjosephpublications.com; *The Apparitions of Garabandal,* p.94, F. Sanchez-Ventura Y Pascual; www.garabandal.org; *Father Marichalar Speaks,* Needles Magazine, 1976, http://www.garabandal.us/Workers of Our Lady of Mount Carmel; *Garabandal The Village Speaks,* p. 257-258, Ramon Perez, 1981, The Workers of Our Lady of Mt. Carmel, Inc. P.O. Box 606, Lindenhurst, NY 11757

457 *Father Ramon Andreu's Notebooks Part 3 Dec. 16, 1961 and Dec. 30, 1961,* www.stjosephpublications.com; *Garabandal The Village Speaks,* p. 71, 75, 77, Ramon Perez, 1981, The Workers of Our Lady of Mt. Carmel, Inc. P.O. Box 606, Lindenhurst, NY 11757

[458] *Everything Will Come in Due Time: An Interview with Serafin Gonzalez,* Garabandal Magazine, July-September 1993; http://www.garabandal.us/Workers of Our Lady of Mount Carmel

[459] *Garabandal The Village Speaks*, p. 331, Ramon Perez, 1981, The Workers of Our Lady of Mt. Carmel, Inc. P.O. Box 606, Lindenhurst, NY 11757

[460] *Garabandal The Village Speaks*, p. 77, Ramon Perez, 1981, The Workers of Our Lady of Mt. Carmel, Inc. P.O. Box 606, Lindenhurst, NY 11757; *Star on the Mountain,* Ch. 57, p. 132, Fr. M. Laffineur, The Workers of Our Lady of Mt. Carmel, Inc. P.O. Box 606, Lindenhurst, NY 11757

[461] *Star on the Mountain,* Ch. 57, p. 134-5, Fr. M. Laffineur, The Workers of Our Lady of Mt. Carmel, Inc. P.O. Box 606, Lindenhurst, NY 11757

[462] Ibid., p. 136

[463] http://www.youtube.com/watch?v=_fENtReLWHY *Garabandal After the Visions* 1980 BBC

[464] *Father Marichalar Speaks,* Needles Magazine, 1976; http://www.garabandal.us/Workers of Our Lady of Mount Carmel.

[465] http://www.youtube.com/watch?v=_fENtReLWHY *Garabandal After the Visions* 1980 BBC

[466] *Garabandal : The Village Speaks*, p. 119, Ramon Perez, 1981, The Workers of Our Lady of Mt. Carmel, Inc. P.O. Box 606, Lindenhurst, NY 11757

[467] *Star on the Mountain,* Ch. 41, p. 102, Fr. M. Laffineur, The Workers of Our Lady of Mt. Carmel, Inc. P.O. Box 606, Lindenhurst, NY 11757

[468] Ibid., Ch. 36, p. 87

[469] *Conchita's Diary,* www.stjosephpublications.com

[470] *Our Lady Comes to Garabandal*, p. 91-92, Joseph Pelletier, A.A.; Assumption Publications, Worcester, Mass., 1971

[471] *Garabandal: The Village Speaks*, p. 155, Ramon Perez, 1981, The Workers of Our Lady of Mt. Carmel, Inc. P.O. Box 606, Lindenhurst, NY 11757Ibid., p. 155

[472] Ibid., p. 156

[473] *She Went in Haste to the Mountain,* Book 2, Ch. 3, p. 106, Eusebio García de Pesquera O.F.M., www.stjosephpublications.com

[474] *Star on the Mountain,* Ch. 57, p. 139, Fr. M. Laffineur, The Workers of Our Lady of Mt. Carmel, Inc. P.O. Box 606, Lindenhurst, NY 11757

[475] *She Went in Haste to the Mountain,* Book 2, Ch. 3, p. 100, Eusebio García de Pesquera O.F.M., www.stjosephpublications.com

[476] *Of Queen and Prophets: The Garabandal Events and "The End of the Times,"* p. 279, by Gregory M. Rolla, 2011

[477] http://www.catholic-hierarchy.org/bishop/bpuch.html

[478] *Visionaries: The Spanish Republic and the Reign of Christ,* p. 334, by William A. Christian, Jr. University of California Press, Berkeley and Los Angeles, California c1996

[479] *She Went in Haste to the Mountain,* Book 2, P. 106, Eusebio García de Pesquera O.F.M., www.stjosephpublications.com

[480] Transcription: http://www.garabandal.org/vigil; Video interview A1: http://www.garabandal.org/index.shtml

[481] Canon 1399 forbade, by right of publication, certain books such as those that deal with revelations, visions, prophecies and miracles. This canon was repealed on March 29, 1967. This means that as far as these publications are concerned, prohibition is lifted as to their being bound by ecclesiastical law and henceforth, Catholics are permitted, without need of imprimatur, Nihil Obstat, or any other permission, to publish accounts of revelations, visions, prophecies and miracles. Of course, these publications must not put in danger the faith or morals. This is the general rule, which every Catholic must follow in all his actions, even journalists, especially journalists.

There is henceforth no longer any prohibition concerning the narrative of seers, be they recognized or not by ecclesiastical authority. All the more reason is it permitted for Catholics to frequent places of apparitions, even those not recognized by ordinaries of their dioceses or by the Holy Father, granted that the Catholic visitors who frequent these places must respect the faith and morals. However, they are not subject to any ecclesiastical discipline, not even for their public prayers. Permission is required only for the celebration of Holy Mass or any other religious service.

Canon 2318 carried penalties against those who violated the laws of censure and prohibition. This canon has been abrogated (revoked) since 1966. None can incur ecclesiastical censure for frequenting places of apparitions, even those not recognized by the Ordinaries of their Dioceses or by the Holy Father. Also, "those who would have incurred the censured treatment in Canon 2318 will be likewise absolved by the very facts of the abrogation [revocation] of this Canon."   — Alfredo Cardinal Ottaviani.

A decree of the "Sacred Congregation for the Doctrine and the Faith" was published in the Official Acts of the Holy See" (A.A.S.) 58/16, dated December 29, 1966. Articles 1399 and 2318 of Canon Law are abrogated by this decree. This decree of abrogation was approved on October 14, 1966 by His Holiness, the Sovereign Pontiff Paul VI, who ordered its publication at the same time.

[482] http://www.garabandal.org/News/Bishops_Letter.shtml

[483] Letter from Father Francis A. Benac, S.J.; Garabandal Journal November-December 2005

[484] *Star on the Mountain,* Ch. 33, p. 78, Fr. M. Laffineur, The Workers of Our Lady of Mt. Carmel, Inc. P.O. Box 606, Lindenhurst, NY 11757

[485] *Our Lady Teaches at Garabandal: O Children Listen to Me,* p. 57, Francois Turner, O.P., The Workers of Our Lady of Mt. Carmel, Inc. P.O. Box 606, Lindenhurst, NY 11757

Chapter 8

[486] Photo courtesy of St. Joseph Publications

[487] *She Went in Haste to the Mountain,* Book 3, Ch. 11, p. 195, Eusebio García de Pesquera O.F.M., www.stjosephpublications.com; *Star on the Mountain,* Ch. 36, p. 84, Fr. M. Laffineur, The Workers of Our Lady of Mt. Carmel, Inc. P.O. Box 606, Lindenhurst, NY 11757

[488] *Star on the Mountain,* Ch. 30, p. 70, Fr. M. Laffineur, The Workers of Our Lady of Mt. Carmel, Inc. P.O. Box 606, Lindenhurst, NY 11757

[489] *She Went in Haste to the Mountain,* Book 3, Ch. 11, p. 187, Eusebio García de Pesquera O.F.M., www.stjosephpublications.com

[490] Ibid., p. 202-203

[491] Ibid., p. 203

[492] *Star on the Mountain,* Ch. 42, p. 107, Fr. M. Laffineur, The Workers of Our Lady of Mt. Carmel, Inc. P.O. Box 606, Lindenhurst, NY 11757

[493] *She Went in Haste to the Mountain,* Book 3, Ch. 11, p. 195, Eusebio García de Pesquera O.F.M., www.stjosephpublications.com

[494] *She Went in Haste to the Mountain,* Book 2, Ch. 3, p. 110, Eusebio García de Pesquera O.F.M., www.stjosephpublications.com

[495] Ibid., p. 96

[496] Photo courtesy of Maria Saraco/St. Michael's Garabandal Center http://www.garabandal.org/photos/con_loli_pines.shtml

[497] *She Went in Haste to the Mountain,* Book 2, Ch. 3, p. 96, Eusebio García de Pesquera O.F.M., www.stjosephpublications.com

[498] Ibid., p. 102

[499] Ibid., p. 98

[500] Ibid.

501 *Star on the Mountain,* Ch. 56, p. 129, Fr. M. Laffineur, The Workers of Our Lady of Mt. Carmel, Inc. P.O. Box 606, Lindenhurst, NY 11757

502 *She Went in Haste to the Mountain,* Book 2, Ch. 3, p. 94, Eusebio García de Pesquera O.F.M., www.stjosephpublications.com

503 *Star on the Mountain,* Ch. 57, p. 137, Fr. M. Laffineur, The Workers of Our Lady of Mt. Carmel, Inc. P.O. Box 606, Lindenhurst, NY 11757

504 *She Went in Haste to the Mountain,* Book 2, Ch. 3, p. 98, Eusebio García de Pesquera O.F.M., www.stjosephpublications.com

505 *Miracle at Garabandal,* Ch. 10, Harry Daley; http://www.youtube.com/watch?v=MnEdkgZCmeo

506 *Conchita's Diary,* www.stjosephpublications.com

507 *She Went in Haste to the Mountain,* Book 3, Ch. 5, p.91, Eusebio García de Pesquera O.F.M., www.stjosephpublications.com; http://www.vatican.va/holy_father/paul_vi/homilies/1972/documents/hf_p-vi_hom_19720629_it.html; http://catholicstand.com/109/

508 *Miracle at Garabandal,* Appendix, Harry Daley, http://stjosephpublications.com/book_manuscripts_pages/page_templates/book5_page.htm

509 Interview on Sept. 1, 1877, with Bishop Bourret, Bishop of Rodez. *Garabandal The Village Speaks,* p. 79, Ramon Perez, 1981, The Workers of Our Lady of Mt. Carmel, Inc. P.O. Box 606, Lindenhurst, NY 11757

510 *Miracle at Garabandal,* Ch. 14, Harry Daley, http://stjosephpublications.com/book_manuscripts_pages/page_templates/book5_page.htm

511 Ibid., Ch. 9

512 Ibid., Ch. 10

513 *Why I Believe in Garabandal,* by Dr. Ricardo Puncernau, Garabandal Magazine, July-August 1980; http://www.garabandal.us/category/new-york-center-archive/eyewitness-testimony/

514 *Star on the Mountain,* Ch. 57, p. 140, Fr. M. Laffineur, The Workers of Our Lady of Mt. Carmel, Inc. P.O. Box 606, Lindenhurst, NY 11757

515 *Garabandal After the Visions* BBC 1980 http://www.youtube.com/watch?v=_fENtReLWHY

516 *She Went in Haste to the Mountain,* Book 2, Ch. 3, 92, Eusebio García de Pesquera O.F.M.

517 Ibid., p. 102

518 Photo courtesy of St. Joseph Publications

519 *Garabandal After the Visions* BBC 1980 http://www.youtube.com/watch?v=_fENtReLWHY

520 Ibid.

521 *She Went in Haste to the Mountain,* Book 3, Ch. 7, 126, Eusebio García de Pesquera O.F.M.

522 http://elpais.com/diario/1984/06/17/espana/456271202_850215.html

523 *Our Lady Comes to Garabandal,* Ch. 13, p. 196, by Joseph A. Pelletier, Assumption Publications, Worcester, Mass., 1971; *Journal de Conchita,* p. 72, footnote (88).

524 *She Went in Haste to the Mountain,* Book 3, Ch. 10, 181, Eusebio García de Pesquera O.F.M., www.stjosephpublications.com

525 *Garabandal The Village Speaks,* p. 292, Ramon Perez, 1981, The Workers of Our Lady of Mt. Carmel, Inc. P.O. Box 606, Lindenhurst, NY 11757

526 http://www.garabandal.org/News/Mari_Cruz_interview.shtml

527 *Garabandal The Village Speaks,* p. 292, Ramon Perez, 1981, The Workers of Our Lady of Mt. Carmel, Inc. P.O. Box 606, Lindenhurst, NY 11757

[528] Photo courtesy of *St. Joseph Publications*, www.stjosephpublications.com

[529] *She Went in Haste to the Mountain,* Book 2, Ch. 3, p. 96, Eusebio García de Pesquera O.F.M., www.stjosephpublications.com

[530] *Garabandal After the Visions* BBC 1980 http://www.youtube.com/watch?v=_fENtReLWHY

[531] Photo courtesy of St. Joseph Publications

[532] *Interview with Jacinta* https://www.youtube.com/watch?v=T3wj7rRarIA; *Interview with Mari-Loli* http://www.youtube.com/watch?v=ayKUdVTMm04

[533] *Miracle at Garabandal* Ch. 3 Harry Daley, www.stjosephpublications.com

[534] *Our Lady Teaches at Garabandal: O Children Listen to Me,* p. 66, Francois Turner, O.P., The Workers of Our Lady of Mt. Carmel, Inc. P.O. Box 606, Lindenhurst, NY 11757

[535] http://www.garabandal.us/the-workers-of-our-lady-of-mount-carmel/5/

[536] *Garabandal: Apparitions of the Blessed Virgin Mary as "Our Lady of Mount Carmel,"* p. 218, by Jacques Serre and Beatrice Caux, 2001, The Workers of Our Lady of Mount Carmel of Garabandal, Australia, www.garabandal.com

[537] *1983 Interview with Jacinta:* https://www.youtube.com/watch?v=Ms9e_qMTMNk

[538] *Our Lady Comes to Garabandal,* Ch. 12, p. 188, Joseph A. Pelletier, A.A.; Assumption Publications, Worcester, Mass., 1971

[539] *Our Lady at Garabandal,* p. 85, Judith M. Albright

[540] Photo by LR Walker

[541] *She Went in Haste to the Mountain,* Book 3, Ch. 7, p. 144-145, Eusebio García de Pesquera O.F.M., www.stjosephpublications.com

[542] *She Went in Haste to the Mountain,* Book 3, Ch. 4, p. 73, Eusebio García de Pesquera O.F.M., www.stjosephpublications.com

[543] *Garabandal After the Visions* BBC 1980 http://www.youtube.com/watch?v=_fENtReLWHY

[544] http://www.spiritdaily.org/marilolideath.htm

[545] *1984 Interview with Mari-Loli:* http://www.youtube.com/watch?v=ZxbF1P60e0k

[546] *Garabandal The Village Speaks,* p. 206, Ramon Perez, 1981, The Workers of Our Lady of Mt. Carmel, Inc. P.O. Box 606, Lindenhurst, NY 11757; *Star on the Mountain,* Ch. 57, p. 132, Fr. M. Laffineur, The Workers of Our Lady of Mt. Carmel, Inc. P.O. Box 606, Lindenhurst, NY 11757;Article by Mark Regis, *GARABANDAL JOURNAL Nov-Dec. 2002; Our Lady Teaches at Garabandal, O Children Listen to Me,* p. 56, Francois Turner, O.P., The Workers of Our Lady of Mt. Carmel, Inc. P.O. Box 606, Lindenhurst, NY 11757

[547] *God Speaks at Garabandal,* p. 122, Joseph A. Pelletier; http//www.garabandal.us/Workers of Our Lady of Mount Carmel

[548] *Our Lady at Garabandal,* p. 86, Judith M. Albright

[549] *Catholic Voices Comment;* http://cvcomment.org/2013/08/12/francis-on-women-and-the-church-what-did-he-mean/

[550] *America Magazine,* Interview with Pope Francis, September 30, 2013, by Antonio Spadaro, S.J.; http://americamagazine.org/pope-interview

[551] Luke 24

[552] *1984 Interview with Mari-Loli:* http://www.youtube.com/watch?v=ayKUdVTMm04

[553] *Interview with Julia Mazon,* Garabandal Magazine, 1978; http://www.garabandal.us/category/new-york-center-archive/eyewitness-testimony/page/2/

[554] *God Speaks at Garabandal,* p. 98, Joseph A. Pelletier, 1970, http://www.garabandal.us/Workers of Our Lady of Mount Carmel; *1984 Interview with Mari-Loli:* http://www.youtube.com/watch?v=ayKUdVTMm04

[555] In a 1970 letter from Francis Cardinal Seper, Prefect of the Sacred Congregation for the Doctrine of the Faith: "...this Sacred Congregation wishes to assert that the Holy See has never approved, even indirectly, the Garabandal movement, that it has never

encouraged or blessed Garabandal promoters or centres."...In a 1968 note issued by
Bishop D. Jose Maria Cirarda Lachiondo: "It is very regrettable the obstinacy with
which some are bent on promoting large-scale advertising campaigns within and
outside Spain, to erect "Garabandal Centres, in conferences of the same name, to
organize visits to the place of events...". Also see conversation with Joey Lomangino
who established centers in the U.S., *Miracle at Garabandal,* Ch. 11, by Harry Daly.
http://stjosephpublications.com/book_manuscripts_pages/page_templates/book5_pa
ge.htm

[556] Interview on Sept. 1, 1877, with Bishop Bourret, Bishop of Rodez. *Garabandal The Village Speaks,* p. 79, Ramon Perez, 1981, The Workers of Our Lady of Mt. Carmel, Inc. P.O. Box 606, Lindenhurst, NY 11757

[557] *Garabandal The Village Speaks*, p. 248, Ramon Perez, 1981, The Workers of Our Lady of Mt. Carmel, Inc. P.O. Box 606, Lindenhurst, NY 11757

[558] Photo by LR Walker

[559] *Needles Magazine,* 1975

[560] *Our Lady at Garabandal,* p. 86, Judith M. Albright; *Our Lady Teaches at Garabandal, O Children Listen to Me,* p. 94, Francois Turner, O.P., The Workers of Our Lady of Mt. Carmel, Inc. P.O. Box 606, Lindenhurst, NY 11757

[561] St. Michael's Garabandal Center http://www.garabandal.org/

[562] Ibid.

[563] *Star on the Mountain,* Ch. 52, p. 124, Fr. M. Laffineur, The Workers of Our Lady of Mt. Carmel, Inc. P.O. Box 606, Lindenhurst, NY 11757 ; *Our Lady Comes to Garabandal,* p. 197, Joseph A. Pelletier, A.A., Assumption Publications, Worcester, Mass., 1971; *Our Lady at Garabandal,* p. 85, Judith M. Albright;

[564] St. Michael's Garabandal Center http://www.garabandal.org/

[565] Ibid.

[566] Information courtesy of Bishop William McNaughton

[567] *She Went in Haste to the Mountain,* Book 3, Ch. 4, p. 80, Eusebio García de Pesquera O.F.M., www.stjosephpublications.com

[568] Photos by LR Walker

[569] Photos by LR Walker

[570] Photos by LR Walker

[571] *New American Bible, revised edition* © 2010, 1991, 1986, 1970 Confraternity of Christian Doctrine, Washington, D.C.

Afterword

All messages in the Afterword from *True Life In God*
http://www.tlig.org/

[572] 9-4-87: http://www.tlig.org/en/messages/145/

[573] 9-20-87: http://www.tlig.org/en/messages/154/

[574] 12-4-87: http://www.tlig.org/en/messages/205/

[575] 1-18-88: http://www.tlig.org/en/messages/228/

[576] 12-1-87: http://www.tlig.org/en/messages/203/

Made in the USA
Middletown, DE
19 March 2023

27059401R00166